Supply Chain Forecasting Software

Shaun Snapp

Copyrighted Material

Supply Chain Forecasting Software

Copyright © 2012 by SCM Focus Press

ALL RIGHTS RESERVED

No part of this publication may be reproduced, stored in a retrieval system or transmitted, in any form or by any means—electronic, mechanical, photocopying, recording or otherwise—without prior written permission, except for the inclusion of brief quotations in a review.

For information about this title or to order other books and/or electronic media, contact the publisher:
SCM Focus Press
PO Box 29502 #9059
Las Vegas, NV 89126-9502
http://www.scmfocus.com/scmfocuspress
(408) 657-0249

ISBN: 978-0-9837155-2-8

Printed in the United States of America

Cover and Interior design by: 1106 Design

Contents

CHAPTER 1:	Introduction	1
CHAPTER 2:	Where Forecasting Fits Within the Supply Chain Planning Footprint	9
CHAPTER 3:	Statistical Forecasting Explained	17
CHAPTER 4:	Why Attributes-based Forecasting is the Future of Statistical Forecasting	55
CHAPTER 5:	The Statistical Forecasting Data Layer	77
CHAPTER 6:	Removing Demand History and Outliers	93
CHAPTER 7:	Consensus-based Forecasting Explained	103
CHAPTER 8:	Collaborative Forecasting Explained	139
CHAPTER 9:	Bias Removal	149
CHAPTER 10:	Effective Forecast Error Management	163
CHAPTER 11:	Lifecycle Planning	177
CHAPTER 12:	Forecastable Versus Unforecastable Products	187
CHAPTER 13:	Why Companies Select the Wrong Forecasting Software	209
CHAPTER 14:	Conclusion	219
Appendix A:		227
Appendix B:	Forecast Locking	231
Appendix C:	The Lewandowski Algorithm	233

Vendor Acknowledgements and Profiles 237
Author Profile 241
Abbreviations 245
Definitions 247
Links in the Book 251
References 257
Index 263

CHAPTER 1

Introduction

Background and Motivation

The book you are holding is a different type of forecasting book from others in this category. In fact, one motivation for writing *Supply Chain Forecasting Software* is that most books on forecasting do not address the need for practical demand planning software education that I have witnessed at companies where I have consulted. Demand planning books tend to fall into three categories:

- They cover forecasting from the mathematical angle
- They discuss forecasting from the business perspective
- They are dedicated to just one application, such as SAP

I like some forecasting books quite a bit, and I quote from several of them in this book. However, no book that I am familiar with makes a significant contribution to helping the reader view forecasting software in an overall light, and to helping improve decision-making in the area of forecasting software. *Supply Chain Forecasting Software* does. Individuals can improve their company's situation by implementing just one of the approaches recommended in this book, which takes a practical approach to topics that are often covered in a theoretical light.

Forecasting is an area of study with many options. Unless one has taken the time to read books and academic literature and then compare the different options during actual software implementations, it is difficult to know which options are the best ones to take and which options improve forecast accuracy. Separating theoretical areas of improvement from practical areas is a similar process to the one I go through when I test software and determine what sections of an application's release notes are the most useful for my clients to activate.

The Importance of Software Screenshots and Vendor Diversity

Unlike most books about software, this book showcases more than one vendor. Focusing an entire book on a single software application is beneficial for those that want to use solely the application in question. However, only the biggest vendors like Oracle and SAP tend to get books that showcase their applications, leaving out a lot of educational and interesting functionality that is distributed across other vendors. I prefer to use examples of software from multiple vendors to demonstrate concepts, meaning that I sometimes draw examples from multiple vendor applications. Using more than one vendor provides a much greater flexibility in this regard. However, it's also important for the reader to understand that I am completely independent from all the software companies whose products I cover. The specific application screen shots used in this book were selected because I found them to be good examples of functionality in an area, and they helped me demonstrate a concept.

I consult in some popular and well-known applications, and I've found that companies have often been given the wrong impression of an application's capabilities. As part of my consulting work, I am required to present the results of testing and research about various applications. The research may show that a well-known application is not able to perform some functionality well enough to be used by a company, and point to a lesser-known application where this functionality is easily performed. Because I am routinely in this situation, I am asked to provide evidence of various statements of the testing results within applications, and screen shots provide this necessary evidence.

Furthermore, some time ago it became a habit for me to include extensive screen shots in most of my project documentation. A screen shot does not, of course, guarantee that a particular functionality works, but it is the best that can be done in a document format. Everything in this book exists in one application or another, and nothing described in the book is hypothetical.

How Writing Bias is Controlled at SCM Focus and SCM Focus Press

Bias is a serious problem in the enterprise software field. Large vendors receive uncritical coverage of their products, and large consulting companies recommend the large vendors with the resources to hire and pay consultants rather than the vendors with the best software for the client's needs.

Just as in my consulting practice, I do not financially benefit from a company's decision to buy an application that I showcase. SCM Focus has the most stringent rules related to controlling bias and restricting commercial influence of any information provider in the space. These "writing rules" are expressed in the link below:

   http://www.scmfocus.com/writing-rules/

If other information providers in this space followed these rules, I would be able to learn about software without being required to perform my own research and testing project on every topic.

Information about enterprise supply chain planning software can be found on the Internet, but it is primarily promotional or written at such a high level that none of the important details or limitations of the application are exposed; this is true of books as well. When only one enterprise software application is covered in a book, the application works perfectly; the application operates as expected, and there are no problems during the implementation to bring the application live. This is all quite amazing and quite different from my experience of implementing enterprise software. However, it is very difficult to make a living by providing objective information about enterprise supply chain software, especially as it means being critical at some time. I once remarked to a friend that SCM Focus had very little competition in providing unvarnished information on this software category, and he said, "Of course, there is no money in it."

Making the Perfect Book for Those Hungry for Precise Information on Demand Planning Software

With this book, I want to help people get exactly the information they need without having to read a lengthy volume. The approach to the book is essentially the same as my previous two books: *Inventory Optimization and Multi Echelon Planning Software* and *Supply Planning with MRP, DRP and APS Software*. With that in mind, here are some of the principles I knew this book needed to follow:

- **Be direct and concise.** There is very little theory in this book and the reader is only subjected to very simple math when appropriate. There are a number of books that deal with forecasting mathematics. I did not want to cover the same ground that has already been extensively covered in other sources.

- **Clearly define the different categories of demand planning and explain how each works.** Just understanding the categories of demand planning can put a company on the right track in terms of knowing how to design their demand planning solution. The tendency of many companies is to try to meet most of their forecasting needs through one application—not the best approach as no one application does every type of forecasting well.

- **Base content on project experience.** Most demand planning books focus on things like forecasting methods and forecast error measurements. While covering these topics adequately, this book also focuses on controversial subjects rarely brought up in other forecasting books, and that require implementation experience to differentiate the best approach from among several possibilities.

- **Share various viewpoints on how concepts are implemented by different demand planning applications.** Discussing different viewpoints solidifies the understanding of functionality. By showing how different vendors take different approaches, the reader is provided with a broad understanding of demand planning software.

- **Saturate the book with graphics.** Roughly two-thirds of a human's sensory input is visual, and books that do not use graphics—especially educational and training books such as this one—can fall short of their purpose. Graphics have also been used consistently and extensively on the SCM Focus website.

- **The use of case studies.** The book uses actual projects and real situations (without naming the client) to describe how the discussed topic was tested and what the findings were. The case studies, which follow some of the chapters, are not traditional: they do not describe the overall project, but rather are short explanations targeted at a topic in the chapter.

Why Are There So Few Books on Enterprise Demand Planning Software?

While doing the research for this book, I noticed that few books distinctly on this topic are listed on Amazon.com. The search for the term "demand planning software" resulted in no hits. The term "forecasting software" resulted in a number of hits—mostly books related to forecasting in Excel (the books are on using Excel as the forecasting system and not on enterprise software). However, there are a number of books on forecasting software (such as *SAS for Forecasting Time Series*) that focus exclusively on one application, and there are a number of books on demand planning and forecasting without any software focus. This lack of coverage in a critical area prompted me to make the investment to write this book. I felt a book on enterprise demand planning software for the supply chain—particularly a book in plain English—was missing from the marketplace.

Why So Few Books on Enterprise Consensus-based Forecasting?
I also noticed that there are few books distinctly on Enterprise Consensus-based Forecasting listed on Amazon.com. The search for the term "consensus-based forecasting" resulted in no results. I found it interesting that an area in which so many people are placing their hopes for forecast improvement has no book specifically dedicated to it. Consensus-based forecasting is discussed in a number of books on forecasting; however, the treatment is more as an overview. No book that I found spent more than a few pages on the topic or explained how to actually do consensus-based forecasting, nor was its history, the research into it, what has worked and what hasn't and so on explored.[1]

Therefore, given the shortage of material about enterprise demand planning software, it is very clear why there is so much misunderstanding about how to successfully implement enterprise demand planning software projects.

The SCM Focus Site
The SCM website dedicated specifically to demand planning is http://www.scmfocus.com/demandplanning. This book contains many links to articles on the site, which provide more detail on specific subjects. This is an effective way of providing more detail to those that are interested without cluttering up the book with sometimes tangential or supportive material. The SCM Focus website is a good resource to which articles are continually added. The "Links in the Book" section at the end of this book lists the links by chapter.

Who Is This Book For?
This book is an effective primer for anyone who is about to perform a demand planning software selection or who is beginning a demand planning project at their company. The book is also useful for anyone who wants to better understand forecasting software or who wants to find out about some leading edge approaches

---

[1] A book that is not distinctly about consensus-based forecasting but can be most effectively applied to this area is *Demand-Driven Forecasting: A Structured Approach to Forecasting,* by Charles Chase. This book explains a number of concepts that are central to consensus-based forecasting, including the necessity to remove bias from the forecast.

and functionalities that have yet to see broad application, but which can improve forecast accuracy.

If you have any questions or comments on the book, please email me at shaunsnapp@scmfocus.com.

Abbreviations
At the end of this book is a listing of all abbreviations used herein.

CHAPTER 2

Where Forecasting Fits Within the Supply Chain Planning Footprint

Background

Demand planning is the starting point and first process to be performed in supply chain planning as everything starts with what is the expected demand. The reason for forecasting is simply that the lead times for production and procurement are longer than the customer demand lead time. Not all companies need to forecast the demand of their products. For example, defense contractors frequently know years in advance what they will be building because they have firm government contracts that contain quantities and dates. However, even these companies are still required to create forecasts for the service parts that support the products they sell.

There is a great deal of discussion about build-to-order (where no forecast is required); the concept is extremely appealing to many companies as it certainly reduces the complexity of the supply chain planning process. Some environments that traditionally "built-to-stock" are moving toward "build-to-order." An example is book publishing, where books can now be printed in batches of one—at a higher price and a lower quality of course. However, it is not possible for the vast majority of companies to move to a build-to-order environment. Except for extremely specialized manufacturing (such as print-on-demand publishing), it's difficult to come up with examples of products that cost the same amount to produce whether making one or a hundred or a thousand. Similar limitations apply to procurement, as procuring in larger batches is less expensive than procuring in smaller batches. Unless a customer is willing to provide their order in advance, the creation of a physical thing requires a lead time. As such, there are, in fact, very few build-to-order environments. Most environments that people call "build-to-order" are actually "assemble-to-order." However, assemble to order still requires a forecast at the subcomponent level. This is why companies must forecast.

Demand Planning Software Within Supply Chain Software

The different types of software that comprise demand planning will be described in this book. But first it is important to understand where demand planning fits among the different supply chain applications, as shown in the graphic below:

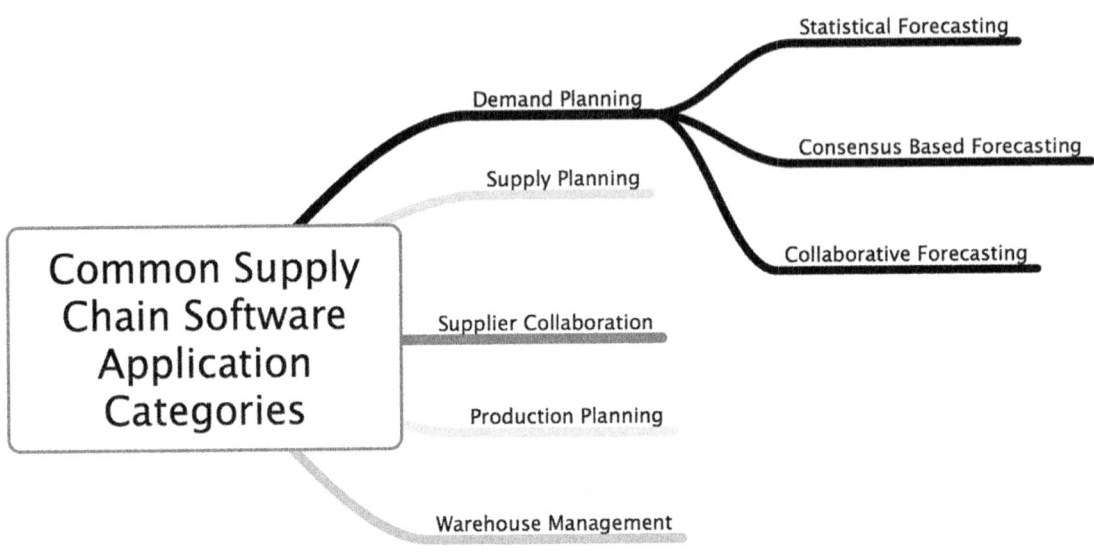

Demand planning one of the major categories of supply chain software. When companies implement an external supply chain planning module to be connected to their ERP system, they most often start with demand planning.

Within the demand planning software category there are three major subcategories. While many supply chain professionals don't know it, each forecasting subcategory has its own specialized software, and this is critical to understand. Companies frequently choose a forecasting application that they think is designed for one category of demand planning, when in fact it was designed for another category. This problem is described in Chapter 13: "Why Companies Select the Wrong Forecasting Software."

The Demand Planning Application Categories

As with other categories of supply chain planning software, over time the demand planning categories have become more defined and more specialized vendors have matured to address different processes. These demand planning categories are listed in the graphic below:

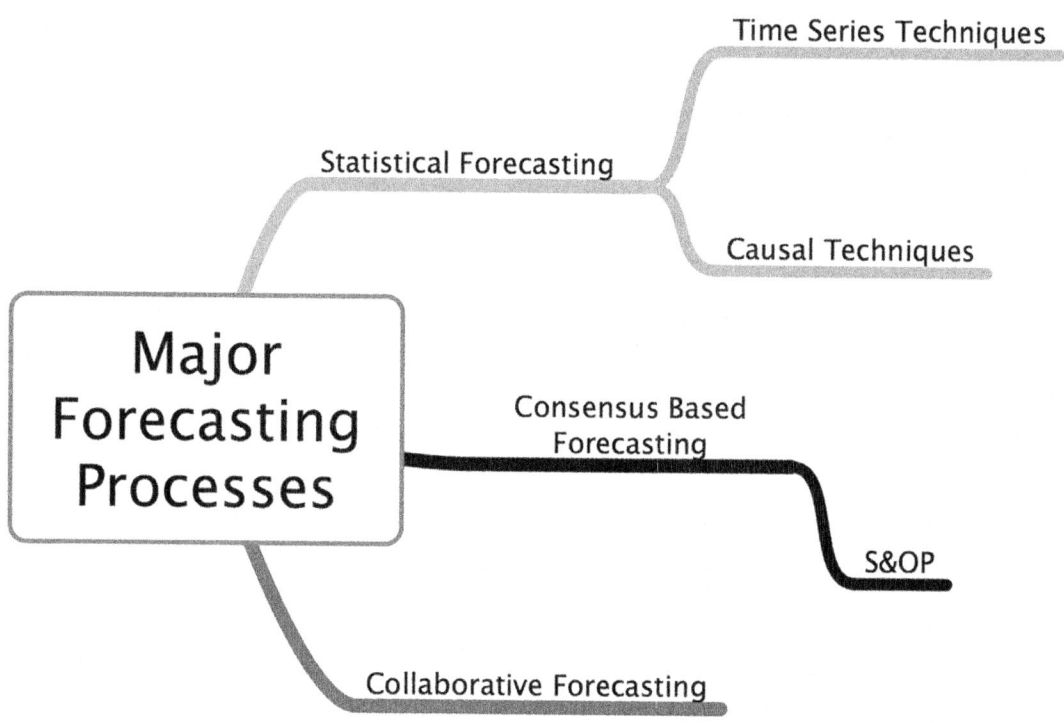

I anticipate that this graphic will be controversial with respect to the location of sales and operations planning (S&OP). Some people think that consensus-based forecasting (CBF) is a subcategory of S&OP. While there is no perfect answer to this question, placing CBF as a subcategory of S&OP is not the most accurate way to depict the relationship between S&OP and CBF.

CBF is used for more than just S&OP. Consensus forecasting systems gather input from multiple human sources within one company in order to drive to a forecast based upon a consensus. S&OP is a high-level forecasting process that deals in dollars and is a consensus forecasting method that involves individuals in sales, operations and finance. However, S&OP is only one type of consensus forecasting performed in a company; companies use consensus processes to develop forecasts at all different levels of the product hierarchy, which have nothing to do with the S&OP forecast.

For these reasons, I have S&OP listed as a subcategory of CBF. However, the categorization discussion does not end there, because S&OP is not only a forecasting process, but is also a capacity planning process, as well as a constraint evaluation process. The S&OP process is (or is supposed to be) the most integrative of planning processes, so it cuts across the supply chain domains of demand planning, supply planning and production planning.

Collaborative forecasting is the final type of forecasting covered in this book. Collaborative forecasting is quite similar to consensus-based forecasting in several respects but involves obtaining inputs from outside of the company. The concept behind collaborative forecasting is that customers and suppliers can help drive improved forecast accuracy by providing their input and data to the company in question.

The Forecast Category, Method and Model Employed

Below the demand planning category, as shown in the previous graphic, is the method (sometimes called methodology) that is used. Statistical forecasting is a demand planning category; however, it employs methods, such as time series methods. Exponential smoothing is one of the time series methods. When the exact parameters are assigned, this becomes a forecasting model. Therefore, the hierarchy is as follows:

- Forecast Category

- Forecast Method
- Forecast Model

However, this hierarchy does not apply the same way to consensus-based forecasting or to collaborative forecasting. For instance, the Delphi Technique is one CBF method. But we don't typically discuss CBF "models." Collaborative forecasting does not include many methods. CPFR (Collaborative Planning Forecasting and Replenishment) is the best-known method within the collaborative forecasting category. I am not aware of any collaborative forecasting models, because collaborative forecasting is about sharing forecasts that have already been created using some type of statistical model or judgment technique or both.

Time Series Forecasting Category
- Simple Arithmetic (last period + two periods ago, etc..) Methods
- Exponential Smoothing (earlier, middle or later periods given different weights) Methods

The graphic above shows the methods that are part of the statistical forecasting category.

Some applications can calculate and show what percentage of the product database uses each method. These methods can be assigned to the product or product location using best-fit functionality. Best-fit functionality is a software procedure that runs different forecasting models using past history and compares their forecast results to actuals. It then ranks the different models based upon their distance from the actuals or their forecast error. The forecasting model with the lowest overall error (a combination of all the individual errors for every period) is then selected, and that is the "best fit." Best-fit functionality can be automated within the application (and run as soon as the application is loaded with data), or can be run as a procedure. Best-fit procedures can only say what the best forecast model would have been in the past, and cannot be said definitively to be the best model to use in the future. Quite often, more complex methods can be made to better fit the history than simpler methods. We will see best-fit forecasting again in Chapter 3: "Statistical Forecasting Explained."

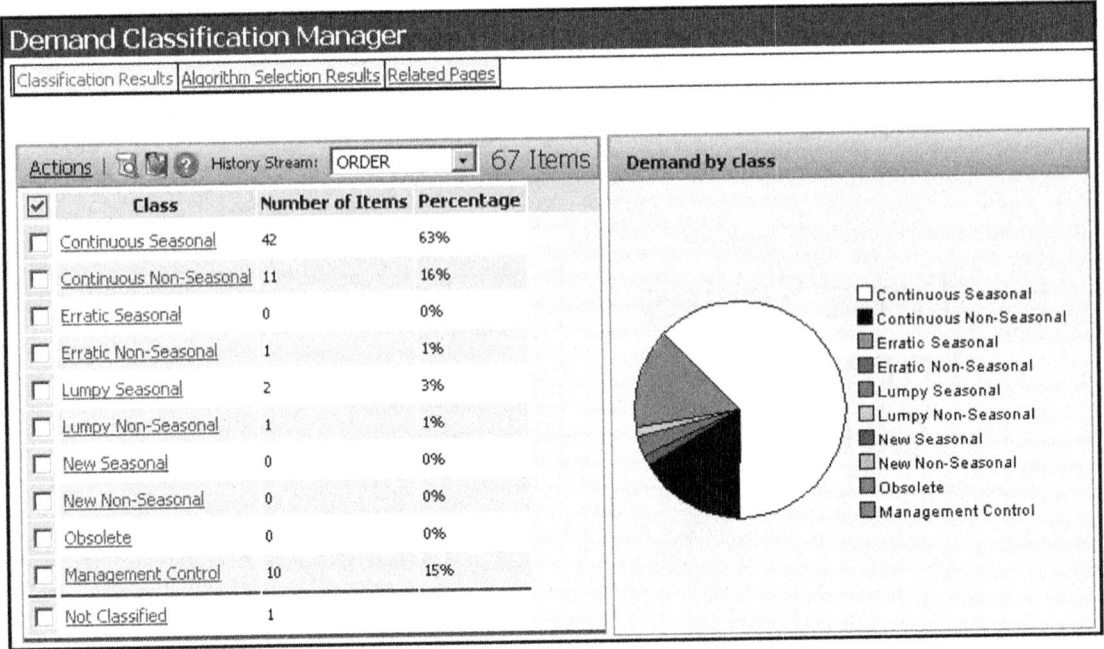

In JDA's DM Classification Manager, it is clear that with this data, the majority of the product database goes out on the continuous non-seasonal method. What is shown in the graphic above are not models because within each method are multiple models which contain specific configuration details. For instance, a moving average is a method; however, a three-period moving average is a specific model.

Connecting the Demand Planning System to Supply Planning

The focus of this book is predominately on demand planning applications, which are separate from ERP systems. ERP systems offer basic demand planning, and while most companies find the ERP demand planning inadequate for their needs, some use only ERP-based demand planning. Because of this fact, there are two system connections between the demand planning system and the supply planning system.

1. The ERP demand planning module connects to the (usually MRP/DRP) supply planning module within the ERP system.

2. The demand planning APS forecast is sent to the supply planning APS. The forecast finds its way to the ERP system indirectly through the release of the supply plan to the ERP system (although there are several different options here as well).[2]

It is now quite common to have an external APS for both demand and supply planning, although this is more common for larger than smaller companies. Demand planning tends to be the first application that is moved to an APS system, and demand planning is the most commonly purchased and installed application/module in the supply chain planning space. It also tends to have the highest executive profile.

Conclusion

Demand planning is one of the major categories of supply chain software. It is composed of three different categories of demand planning, each of which has specifically designed software. Statistical forecasting was the first forecasting process to be placed into software and sold to the enterprise market, and it serves as the baseline or main point of reference for many supply chain professionals as to what forecasting software should "look like." However, using the design of statistical forecasting applications to generalize toward other categories of demand planning software is not good practice. Therefore, the most common misapplication of a category of demand planning software is typically when a statistical

---

[2] Another possibility is to connect the non-ERP demand planning system (often referred to as advanced planning and scheduling [APS]) to the ERP supply planning module. However, this is very rarely done.

forecasting application is used for consensus or collaborative forecasting. This bears emphasis: there is not simply "one type" of demand planning process in supply chain management. Each forecasting process may not absolutely require a custom application, but in practice is often optimized by a different software design, and there is no single forecasting application that handles all of the forecasting processes equally well. This book will describe all the processes and explain the different forecasting application categories.

CHAPTER 3

Statistical Forecasting Explained

The Initial Attempts at Demand Planning Software Implementation

Statistical methods were the first forecasting methods to be placed into software and sold to the enterprise market. With the benefit of hindsight, it is comical to read the historical projections of what placing statistical methods into applications would do for companies. When statistical forecasting was first introduced to the supply chain market, it was commonly expected that the "case would be closed" and forecasting problems would be solved as soon as demand history was placed into a computer and the software was able to run advanced statistical techniques against the historical data. As alluded to in Chapter 12: "Forecastable Versus Unforecastable Products," these projections were partially hyperbole on the part of vendor and consulting companies, and partly a genuine over-estimation of the potential for much more complex and sophisticated forecasting methods to improve the forecast. J. Scott Armstrong, a forecasting expert who lived through the computerization of forecasting methods, admits to being surprised that more complex forecasting models so infrequently improved more simple forecasting models.

> *In general, the findings on sophisticated methods are puzzling, and it is unlikely that they could have been anticipated in 1960. Many of the sophisticated methods made good sense. For example, it seemed reasonable to expect that models in which the parameters are automatically revised as new information comes in should be more accurate.*

Statistical forecasting turned out to be much more complicated to implement and to maintain. Software was sold, but training was often weak, and a large amount of dense terminology reduced the ability of the people implementing and using the software to gain an intuitive understanding of how these systems operated. This is a point brought up by J. Scott Armstrong:

> *Sophisticated approaches frequently lead to more complex forecasting models which are difficult to understand. Forecasters tell me that few of the people in their organizations understand these sophisticated methods.*

It took many years for vendors to offer automations that reduced unnecessary demand planner maintenance, such as the optimization of alpha, beta and gamma parameters. Finally, few forecasting interfaces were sufficiently user friendly enough to really enable the user to take advantage of and access the power of the mathematics that was within the software. Poor user interface design has been particularly perplexing because demand planning should be a natural application for developing exceptional interfaces. Some of the most interesting and simple graphics show the changes to an element, or series of elements over time. I discuss this at more length in the link below:

> http://www.scmfocus.com/demandplanning/2010/02/why-are-forecasting-interfaces-so-hard-to-design/

The end result is that demand planning applications have one of the greatest differentials between the functionality built into the software and how that software is used. Even as I write this book, most companies still use only a few models to create their forecasts. When I read the software manuals of many applications,

I realize that they have very little to do with how the software is implemented in reality.

In this book, I showcase some of the best user interfaces in the demand planning space that I have seen in order to demonstrate that it is unnecessary to accept weak interfaces. There are some good alternatives out there, which can help planners work very well with their data and create better forecasts.

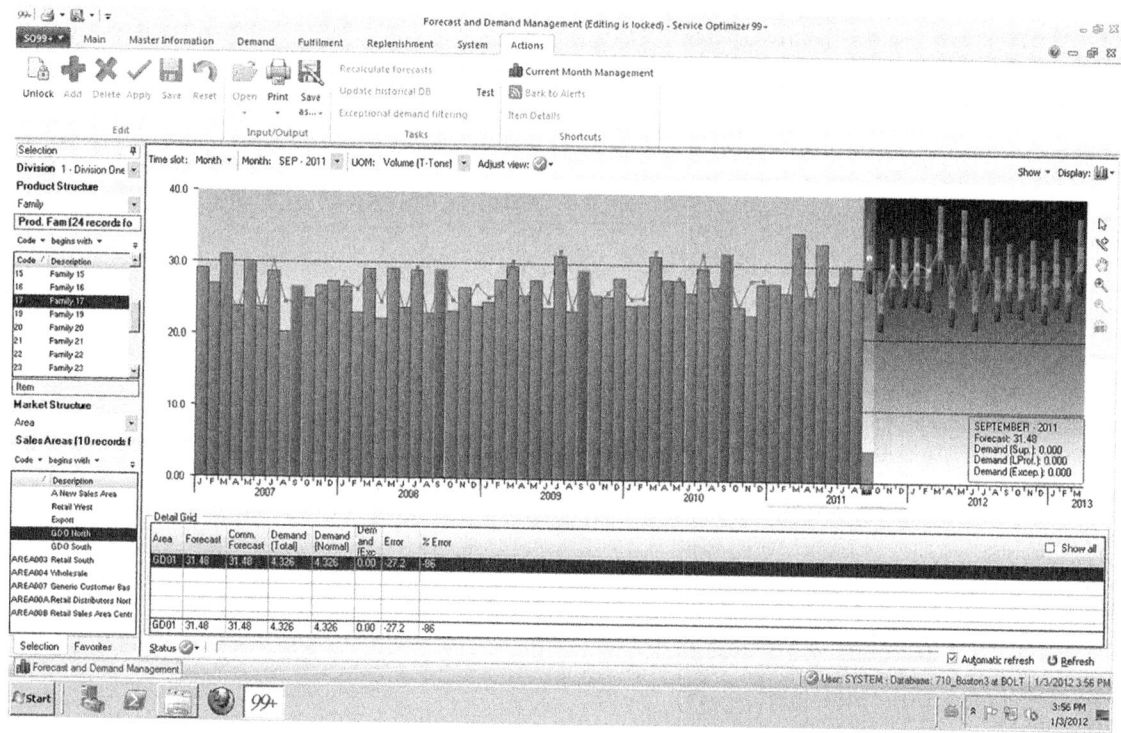

ToolsGroup has a very effective user interface, and there are many things that I like about it. The menu is very clear and the demand tab has what you need to get work done. The forecasting and demand planning drop downs offer more options. The flexible selection criteria to the right can get you to where you need to go, with the product structure and the market structure selection being the most powerful. Along the top I can drill down to different levels of date detail, and the time slot is really the bucket in which the green bars will be shown. Over to the far right, there is a selection for graphic display.

Supply Chain Forecasting Software

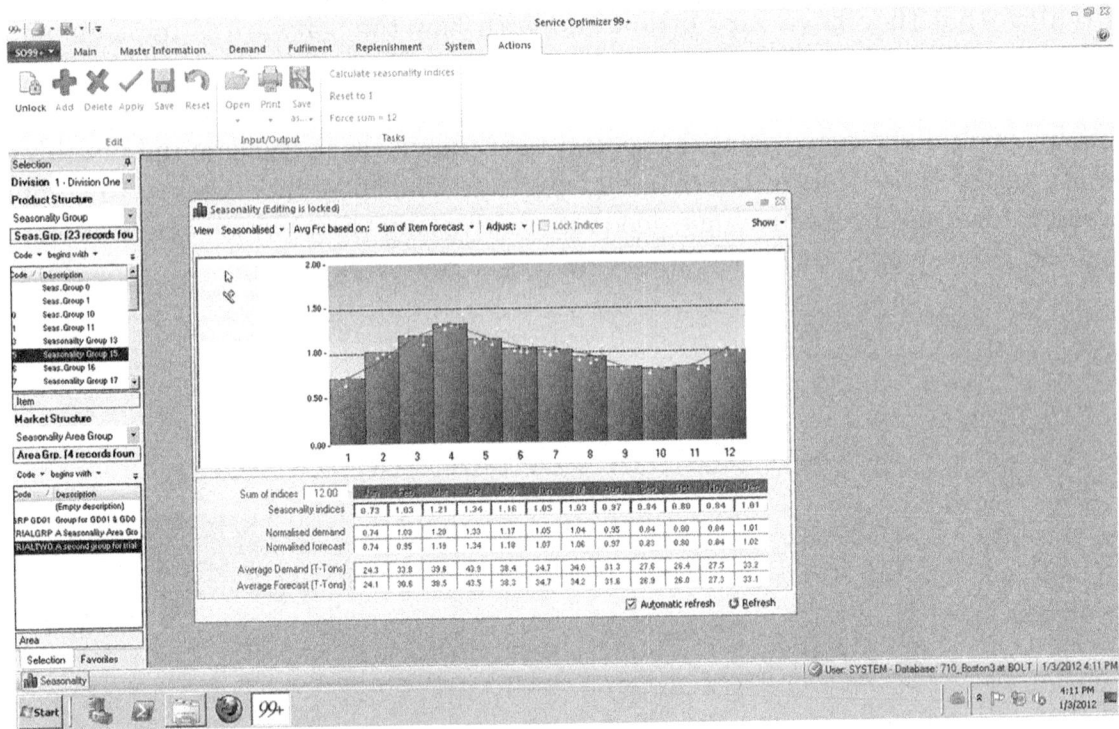

This view shows the Seasonality index in addition to the normalized demand. The navigation to the left makes it easy to get to the area where the planner wants to focus.

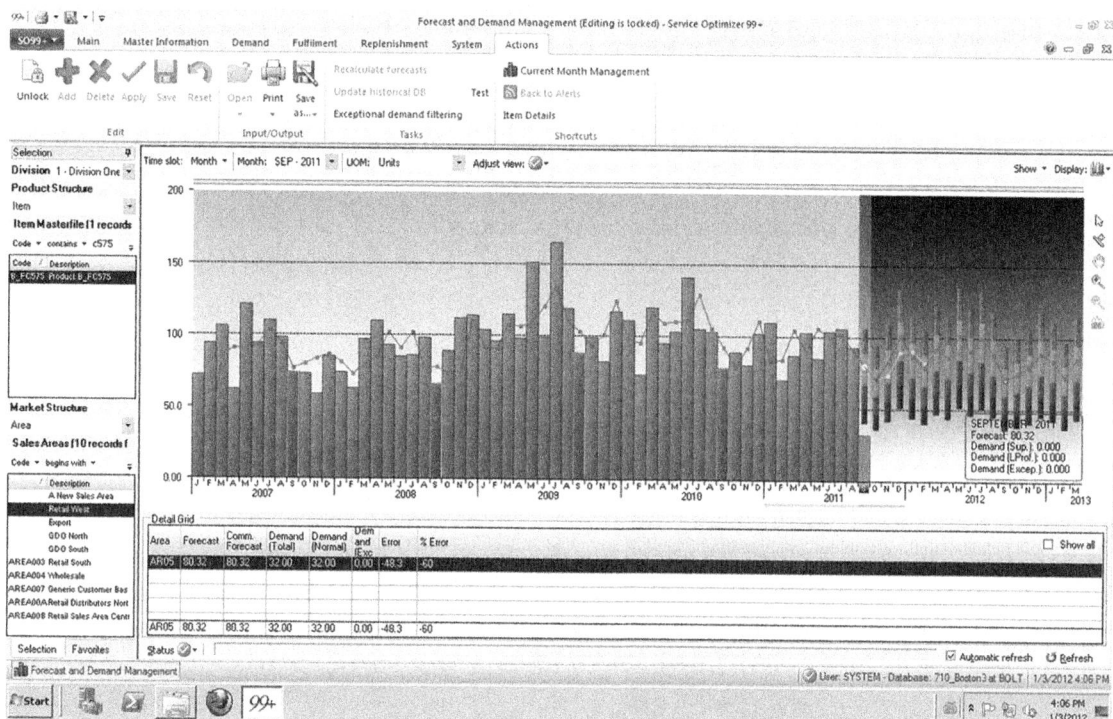

The legend along the top of the screen shot above shows what each of the bars represent. The green bars are history and the blue bars are the forecast. Notice that the forecast has a series of different colored bars that represent the variability of the demand. With SO99, forecasts are not seen as a single value, but as a range of values, all of which are probabilistic. This application is one of the few that illustrate the fact that forecasts are probabilistic by displaying forecast variability right in the user interface.

What Makes Statistical Forecasting "Statistical"?

While "statistical forecasting" is a frequently-used term, not many people actually know how or why the loose affiliation of methods under the statistical category came to be known as "statistical." Why mathematical forecasting is called "statistical forecasting" in the first place is confusing and rarely discussed, but understanding the reason behind the name yields an important insight as to how statistical forecasting works.

Let's start by understanding the term "statistics." Below are some instructive quotations that describe this term:

> *The practice or science of collecting and analyzing numerical data in large quantities, especially for the purpose of inferring proportions in a whole from those in a representative sample.*
> — Apple Dictionary

> *A common goal for a statistical research project is to investigate causality, and in particular to draw a conclusion on the effect of changes in the values of predictors or independent variables on dependent variables or response.*
> — Wikipedia

> *Statisticians improve the quality of data with the design of experiments and survey sampling. Statistics also provides tools for prediction and forecasting using data and statistical models.*
> — Wikipedia

Upon reading the actual definitions it can be difficult to see—without doing some thinking on the topic—how the majority of methods that are contained within statistical forecasting are actually "statistical." For instance, many statistical methods do not employ any statistics at all in their formulas. A simple moving average is an arithmetic function, and does not involve statistics. This lack of apparent statistics does not only apply to the simple statistical forecasting methods. Causal or regression forecasting methods do not seem to be "statistical" either (for instance, $Y = MX + B$, where B is the constant and Y is the dependent variable and X is the independent variable. M is then the degree to which Y increases with an increase in X).

However, all of these methods are in fact statistical, and here is why: statistics is the practice or science of making positive statements about entire populations based upon sampling, or the observation and measurement of portions of fractions of the population. The objective of statistics is to gather and measure a subset of data points that is representative of the population so that the entire population does not need to be analyzed (which would in most cases be too expensive and time consuming to accomplish). Rather than analyzing the entire population (i.e., the entire demand history) to make a prediction about future demand, statistical methods are used to select or emphasize different data points from the population and exclude or de-emphasize others, and use these data points to improve the forecast. *Therefore, sampling is what makes a method statistical.* Using a straight average based upon the entire demand history of a product would not be statistical. However, the same mathematical method (the average) becomes statistical by removing some periods from the average (i.e., the emphasized or de-emphasized periods) based upon some quantitative analysis. Therefore, it is not the complexity of the math that makes a statistical model statistical, but whether the method *samples* the demand history.

The exclusion—or the emphasis or de-emphasis—of historical data points can be performed with the mathematics of the method or can be accomplished by adjusting the historical data before the method is applied. (This is a topic I will discuss in more detail further on in this chapter.) In this case, statistical methods or data point selection are used not because it is too expensive or time consuming to observe the entire population (the entire population of data points is within the demand history file), but because some periods or data points are more representative of the future sales of a product than others. This is an important point to understand because the majority of statistical sampling that people are generally exposed to (such as the sampling used to develop polls) is based upon the fact that *obtaining information about the entire population is infeasible.* However, the statistical sampling that underpins statistical forecasting is not based upon the infeasibility of collecting information about the entire population. In most cases, *all the demand history* is available; however, statistical methods *choose* not to use all periods in order to use only those that the model predicts will improve the forecast.

	Jan	Feb	Mar	Apr	May	June	January Forecast
	P-6	P-5	P-4	P-3	P-2	P-1	P = Forecasted Period
Demand History	0	0	0	4	2	6	
3 Period Simple Moving Average							4.00
6 Period Simple Moving Average							2.00

A simple moving average defined by (P-1P + P-2P + P-3P)/3, where P is the future period to be forecasted, would produce a forecast of 4. This method produces a different forecast than if all six periods were used, in which case the forecast would be 2. The selection of just a three-month moving average is statistical because it makes the judgment that the last three periods are a better predictor than all six periods; perhaps the product is going into its high season, or is a new product that is trending upward.

Similarly, as soon as a best-fit procedure is used to select the best mathematical forecasting method, or a planner performs analysis to manually select a mathematical forecasting method, a statistical method has been employed. This can be easily contrasted with non-statistical methods. For instance, if a person with domain expertise in a certain product produces a forecast based upon what they think the market's interest will be, then they are not necessarily basing their forecast on history. Perhaps the forecast is based upon a new trend they have observed. However, if they overlay the history of a related product, and if they in some way sample the history in order to produce the forecast, they have also engaged in statistical forecasting.

Statistical Forecasting and Inferential Statistics

At this point, it is important to differentiate between two different types of statistics. One type is called "descriptive statistics," which simply uses numerical values to describe the collection of data. A list of batting averages is classified as a descriptive statistic. Descriptive statistics provide details about an activity or object that allow it to be better understood. "Inferential statistics" are often used to sample data and predict the future. For instance, if we wanted to predict the batting average next year of a baseball player with ten years of playing experience, using his historical batting averages would be inferential statistics. When a poll is taken to see which political candidate is likely to win an election, pollsters may not look back historically, but instead will sample a small fraction of the overall voting population based upon finding a representative sample and is also inferential statistics. Inferential statistics are described in the quote below:

> *There are two forms of statistics, descriptive and inferential. This can be seen as the understanding (descriptive) and predictive (inferential) steps to statistics.*
>
> *Inferential statistics use patterns in the sample data to draw inferences about the population represented, accounting for randomness. These inferences may take the form of: answering yes/no questions about the data (hypothesis testing), estimating numerical characteristics of the data (estimation), describing associations within the data (correlation) and modeling relationships within the data (for example, using regression analysis). Inference can extend to forecasting, prediction and estimation of unobserved values either in or associated with the population being studied; it can include extrapolation and interpolation of time series or spatial data, and can also include data mining.*
>
> — Wikipedia

The Relationship between Probability Theory and Statistics

Statistical forecasting has another intersection with statistics and this connection is related to probability theory.

> *Statistics is closely related to probability theory, with which it is often grouped; the difference is roughly that in probability theory, one starts from the given parameters of a total population to deduce probabilities pertaining to samples, but statistical inference moves in the opposite direction, inductive inference from samples to the parameters of a larger or total population.*
>
> — Wikipedia

However, this intersection goes beyond statistical forecasting and connects to all forms of forecasting. As all forecasts deal with the future, every forecast is necessarily probabilistic. In fact, while forecasts are often expected and given as a specific value, forecasts are most accurately interpreted as a mean value, around which higher or lower quantities with lower probabilities than the mean value are likely. In the technical literature this is referred to as the "prediction interval." Let's review a screenshot we have already seen to demonstrate this point directly in an application interface:

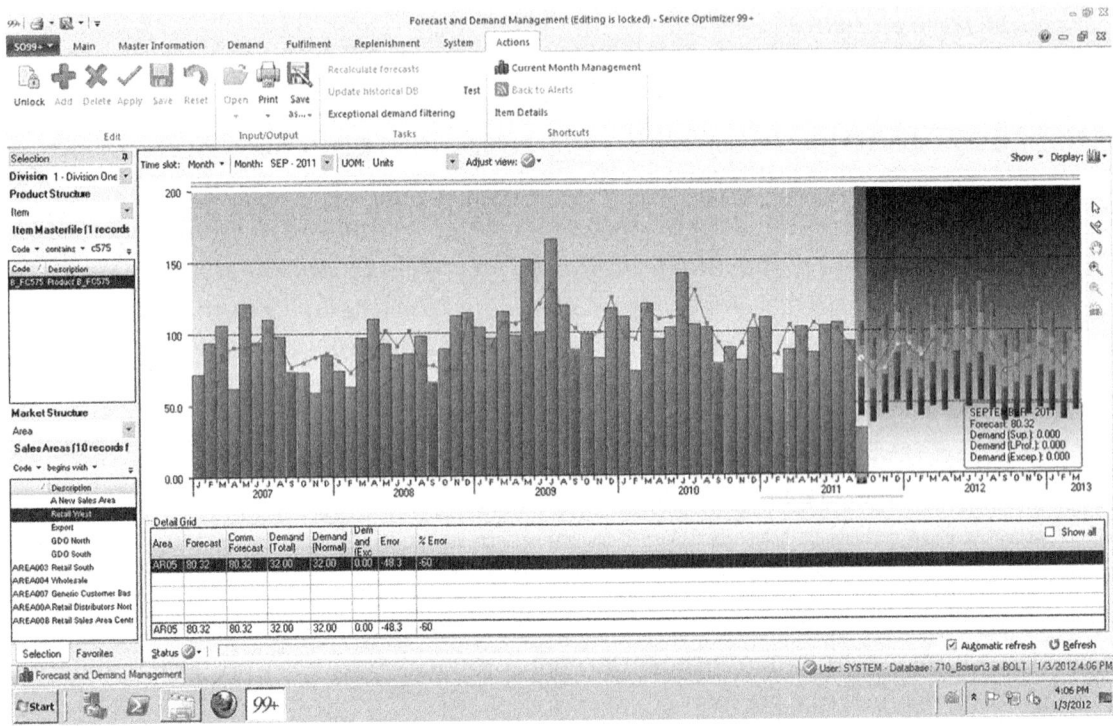

The blue bar shows the range of probable values of the forecast. The range of the probable values is represented by a probability distribution. Showing the forecast as a prediction interval rather than as a discrete point is an example of a user interface element that helps the user better understand the subject matter.

The probability distribution of the forecast prediction interval takes the form of a normal distribution for forecasts of high volume units, and a leftward leaning or Poisson distribution for low volume items (and there are several other probability distributions as well for low volume demand). The "lean" of the probability distribution essentially declares the location of the mean value with respect to the other values. The value that is selected for the forecast is simply the value with the highest probability of occurrence, based upon the historical data used and the forecast method employed. Notice the term "variation" in the definition below of inferential statistics:

> *In statistics, statistical inference is the process of drawing conclusions from data that are subject to random variation...the terms statistical interference...are used to describe systems or procedures that can be used to draw conclusions from datasets arising from systems affected by random variation.*
>
> — Wikipedia

Statistical Forecasting Methods

Now that we have described why statistical methods are statistical, it's a good time to dive into more detail regarding the various statistical forecasting methods that are available in statistical supply chain forecasting applications. There are many books on statistical forecasting methods, but the coverage of the major statistical methods shown on the following page will be different than what you are used to.

Statistical Forecasting
- Time Series Techniques
- Regression or Causal

Time Series Techniques
We will start with time series techniques, as they are the easiest to explain. There are two categories of time series techniques: simple arithmetic methods and exponential smoothing.

Statistical Forecasting Explained

Time Series Forecasting Category

- Simple Arithmetic (last period + two periods ago, etc..) Methods
- Exponential Smoothing (earlier, middle or later periods given different weights) Methods

Some of the most widely used time series techniques are also the simplest. Below are two moving averages: one a three-month moving average and the next a six-month moving average.

	Jan	Feb	Mar	Apr	May	June	July Forecast
	P-6	P-5	P-4	P-3	P-2	P-1	P = Forecasted Period
Demand History	0	0	0	4	2	6	
3 Period Simple Moving Average							4.00
6 Period Simple Moving Average							2.00

This spreadsheet shows various methods of creating a forecast with time series methods.

1. *Formula one is (Jan + Feb + Mar + Apr + May + June)/6*
2. *Formula two is (Apr + May + June)/3*

This is called a simple moving average. There are many different types of moving averages, each with a particular twist on the moving average concept.

When placed in a spreadsheet, complex time series formulas can be broken down into formulas that are much easier to understand. When I want to understand a statistical forecasting formula, rather than reading mathematical notation I simply read the formula as input into Excel. This is where buying books that come with prebuilt spreadsheet examples can very much pay off.

There are of course much more complex time series methods than a moving average; Box-Jenkins is an example. However, my purpose here is to give an overview of what the methods are doing conceptually, rather than to get into details on how each method is calculated—that would be a different type of book. In fact, there are several excellent books that just cover time series forecasting.

Exponential Smoothing

> *Exponential smoothing is the use of adjustment factors to weigh the demand history to develop a forecast. Exponential smoothing is a technique that can be applied to time series data, either to produce smoothed data for presentation, or to make forecasts. The time series data themselves are a sequence of observations. The observed phenomenon may be an essentially random process, or it may be an orderly, but noisy, process. Whereas in the simple moving average the past observations are weighted equally, exponential smoothing assigns exponentially decreasing weights over time.*
> — Wikipedia

"Exponential smoothing" is another example of exaggerated demand planning terminology. I assume the name was created to get an academic paper published or for marketing reasons (even academics market their ideas and inventions with terminology). I say this because exponential smoothing could just as easily be called "Recent Period Emphasis Adjustment," or any number of less complex terms. Unnecessarily complex terminology that does not communicate as effectively as simpler terminology, particularly if the simpler term is more descriptive is not useful. This is a good opportunity to consider a great quote from Albert Einstein:

> Everything should be made as simple as possible, but no simpler.

Exponential smoothing places more weight or emphasis on recent periods rather than past periods. The system uses parameters to control the forecast. These parameters, which also have unnecessarily complex names, are listed below:

- Alpha: Also known as the base value, this value determines how many recent periods or how many past periods should be weighed in the forecast calculation.
- Beta: Also known as the trend value, the beta value determines the degree of the ascent or descent value that should be used to adjust the forecast.
- Gamma: This is the seasonal component of the forecast. It determines how seasonal the forecast will be.

For simplification and improvement in communication, these parameters could be translated as such:

- Alpha = Base
- Beta = Trend
- Gamma = Seasonality

These parameters appear in a number of demand planning applications, including SAP DP.

32 Supply Chain Forecasting Software

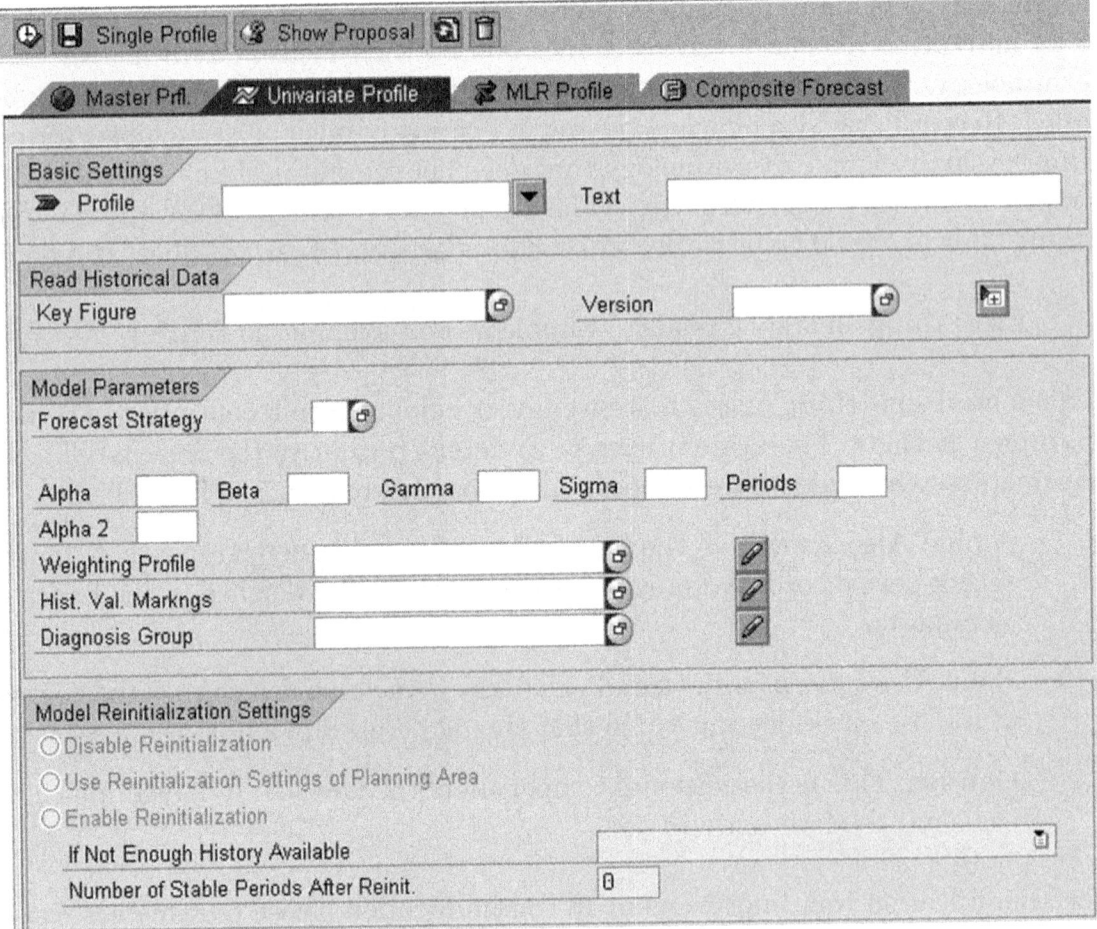

Univariate Forecast Profile

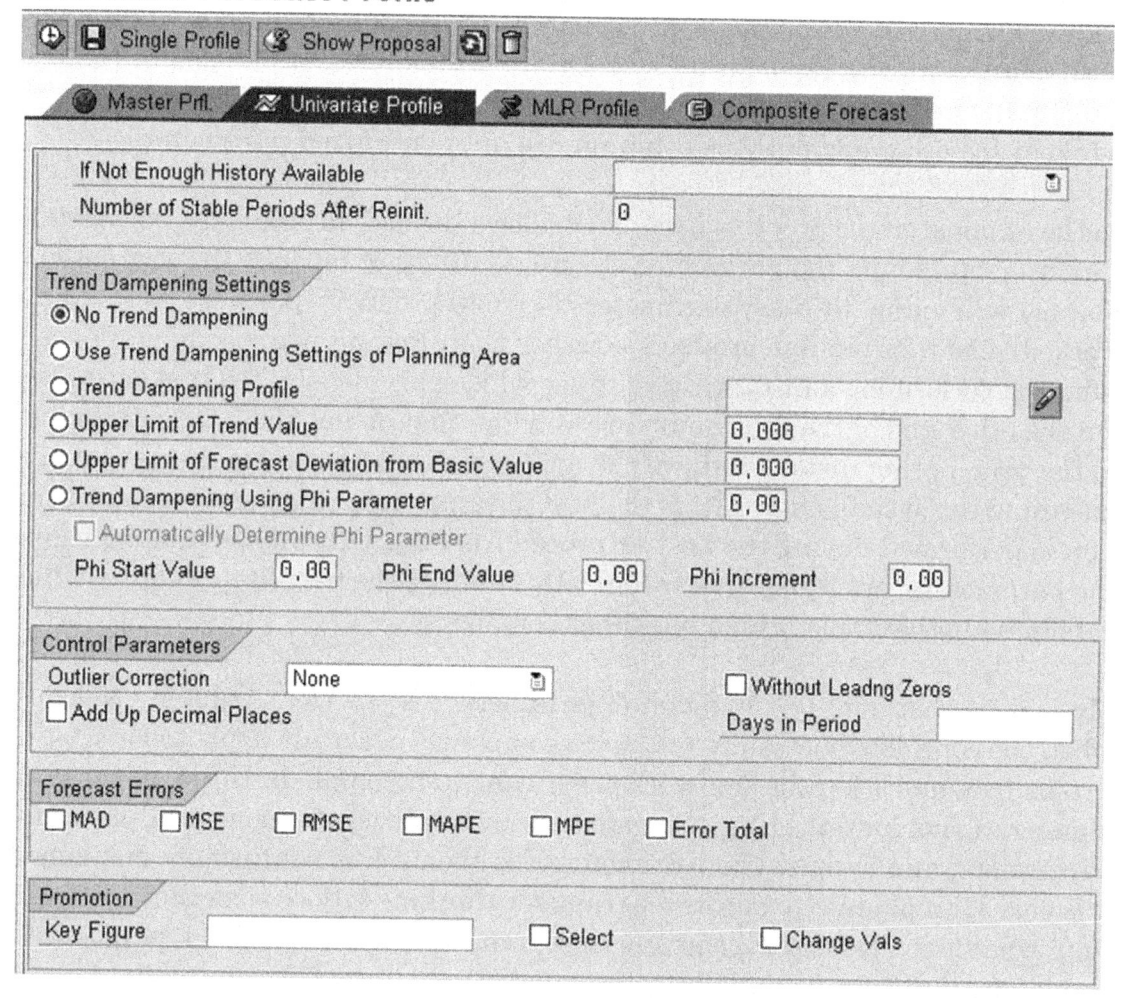

Master Prfl. | **Univariate Profile** | **MLR Profile** | **Composite Forecast**

If Not Enough History Available
Number of Stable Periods After Reinit. 0

Trend Dampening Settings
- ● No Trend Dampening
- ○ Use Trend Dampening Settings of Planning Area
- ○ Trend Dampening Profile
- ○ Upper Limit of Trend Value — 0,000
- ○ Upper Limit of Forecast Deviation from Basic Value — 0,000
- ○ Trend Dampening Using Phi Parameter — 0,00
  - ☐ Automatically Determine Phi Parameter
  - Phi Start Value 0,00   Phi End Value 0,00   Phi Increment 0,00

Control Parameters
Outlier Correction: None   ☐ Without Leadng Zeros
☐ Add Up Decimal Places   Days in Period

Forecast Errors
☐ MAD   ☐ MSE   ☐ RMSE   ☐ MAPE   ☐ MPE   ☐ Error Total

Promotion
Key Figure _____   ☐ Select   ☐ Change Vals

SAP DP allows for a profile to be created and saved. The profile can then be assigned to a product-location combination. The planner can create an unlimited number of profiles by making a small change to a parameter in a saved profile and then saving the revised profile under a new name. This is one strategy for managing parameters; we will discuss a strategy found in other applications a little further on.

However, some vendors have effectively translated alpha, beta and gamma within their user interface so that users do not have to be concerned or confused by these terms. JDA DM uses the terms "level," "seasonality" and "trend."

Manual Versus Auto-optimized Parameters

An important distinction between various forecasting systems is how they deal with changes to the exponential smoothing parameters. At one end of the continuum in forecast parameter management are manually adjustable parameters, while at the other end of the continuum are auto-optimized parameters.

In the example on the previous page, SAP allows the user to access the parameters. The user can adjust the parameters to create different models. In most cases, a planner will manually apply parameters to a new product—parameters that have worked before for similar products—rather than testing new parameters every time and performing a historical test to see which parameter is the best one to use. On the other end of the continuum are vendors that do not show the parameters to the user, opting instead to have the application auto-optimize the parameters (meaning the system auto-selects the best parameters). This auto-optimize function is performed during the best-fit procedure. SAP DP can also auto-optimize the parameters, but it requires specifically running the best fit procedure, which gets into another topic, which has other complexities.

My view is that auto-optimization of parameters is the clear winner, especially when one considers how many resources companies generally apply to forecasting versus how much forecasting work they want to accomplish. In my experience, planners do not have the time to create their own catalog of exponential smoothing parameters, and because the parameters are themselves confusingly misnamed, it is easy for a planner to adjust a parameter thinking it does something different than what it really does. A company that manually adjusts parameters must also be able to document how different parameters relate to different product types. The number of companies that document and share this information internally is extremely small. Therefore, in my view, an application that does not auto-optimize parameters is a maintenance issue and a liability for the vast majority of demand planning environments.[3]

---

[3] Again, vendors that have best-fit procedures that are difficult to run will push back on what I have written above because they will say they can auto-optimize the parameters as well. However, to determine the truth in their statement, the test to apply is whether any special procedure must be actively run, and how difficult that procedure is to run. If an application's best-fit procedure takes a great effort or is tricky to run (rather than being run automatically), then this application is not really in the classification that I am describing.

However, the question of manually-adjusted versus auto-optimized parameters in part comes down to what type of application is most appropriate for your company's structure. If planners are given the time to manage parameters, and if good documentation is maintained, then it may make sense to go with an application that exposes smoothing parameters to planners (although even here, I don't think there is much of a benefit to doing so). My experience is that most demand planning departments would do better to go with an application that hides parameters and has an easy-to-use best-fit functionality. Applications differ widely in the ease with which they allow their best-fit procedure to be run (we'll cover more of this topic a little further on in this chapter). Companies that are evaluating applications that show forecasting parameters may think they are getting more functionality, when in fact they may simply be picking up higher maintenance overhead and extra complexity that may lead to less accurate forecasts.

Regression or Causal Forecasting

The other major category of statistical forecasting is called "regression" or "causal forecasting." For those familiar with regression analysis, this type of forecasting uses a formula with an independent variable and a dependent variable. The independent variable is the causal factor, and the dependent variable is the forecast.

> *Regression or Causal forecasting (sometimes even referred to as econometric or leading indicator forecasting) is forecasting one value based on another value based upon an observed relationship between the two variables.*
>
> *— Apple Dictionary*

There are various forms of complexity with regard to causal forecasting. However, the simplest mathematical explanation is the following:

Forecasted Variable = Value x Causal + Constant

Here you can see a simple formula, which is generated by a best-fit line. The best-fit line is a straight line that is drawn and that best fits the data points. A graphical representation of a regression formula is shown on the next page:

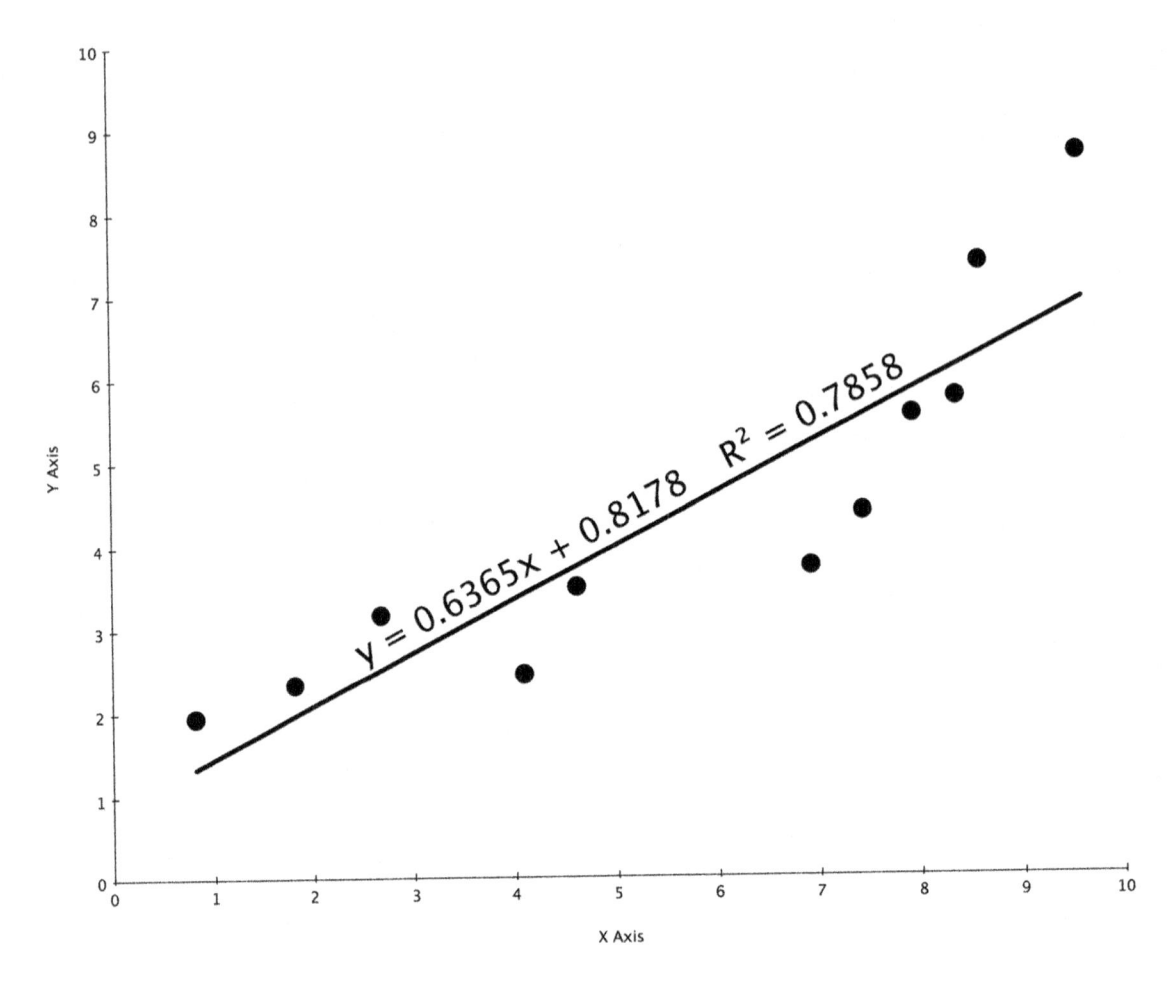

[Scatter plot with trend line: y = 0.6365x + 0.8178, R² = 0.7858]

The individual creating the causal forecast has a great deal of flexibility in choosing the independent variable. Service parts planning—which presents many opportunities for causal forecasting as its demand is dependent on the repair rate for the product in the field—sometimes uses the following independent variables to create a forecast:

1. The number of items already in the field (also known as the installed-base)
2. The usage of the item (in the aerospace field, this can be either miles flown or landings)

The Actual Use of Regression or Causal Forecasting

While causal forecasting is commonly discussed in supply chain demand planning, in actual fact it is rarely used. This is true even though causal forecasting is built into many statistical forecasting applications. However, just because the functionality exists in an application does not mean it is used. Vendors tend to predict that their software will be used at a higher level than it actually is, and sometimes functionality is added for reasons related to marketability.

Causal forecasting is rarely used in demand planning departments. I do not provide very much coverage about it in this book because there are intimidating practical impediments to increasing the use of causal forecasting. While causal forecasting is applied in a number of other fields—the most notable being finance—it should be understood that financial forecasting is quite different from supply chain demand planning. Financial forecasting is typically concerned with forecasting a fewer number of items (i.e., investment instruments versus an entire product database). Financial forecasting also receives much more in the way of resources per forecasted item than does supply chain demand planning.

There has been much written about causal forecasting, although far more by academics than by supply chain practitioners, for the reasons previously listed. The following factors explain why causal forecasting lacks wide usage for supply chain demand planning:

1. Causal models are high maintenance. They require analysis and the declaration of a mathematical relationship in the forecasting system per SKU, which is simply too much work when combined with the number of products that need to be forecasted.

2. Companies do not apply sufficient resources to the statistical forecasting process to enable more complex methods (many are overwhelmed simply trying to get time series methods to work).

3. Companies generally do not hire individuals with sufficient technical and mathematical knowledge required to work in the mathematical side of forecasting. (Even if the company does have a person who is capable of doing causal models, the person is not generally provided with a sufficient amount of time to perform this effort.)

4. It's rare for executives to be familiar with or to bring up causal models unless they work in service parts, where causal models are well known (due to the dependent nature of service part demand), but still not frequently applied.

5. Companies most often do not maintain sufficient data on the independent variables that are required to build causal models. Even if they have software that is capable or provides a simple workbench with which to create causal forecasts, the companies still cannot create causal models.

6. Some valuable independent variable data (such as weather, for example) are often difficult to predict in themselves, particularly over actionable lead times. Incorrect independent variable forecasts produce inaccurate forecasts.

Correlation Versus Causation

An important topic to bring up with respect to causal or regression forecasting is the well-worn discussion of correlation versus causation. One could observe and find a correlation between the increased use of umbrellas and the increase in precipitation even if one did not understand rain or how rain makes things wet. Observing the fact that more people carry and open umbrellas when it rains or looks as if is about to rain is called correlation. Understanding that people like to keep dry and that umbrellas are an effective device for accomplishing this goal would be called understanding the underlying mechanism for the relationship or finding the *causation*.

The majority of academic research generally starts from correlation and attempts to understand causation. Supply chain forecasting is less concerned with performing detailed research to uncover causation and is satisfied simply with discovering correlation. (Although in supply chain forecasting, the reason for the correlation is usually known.) In academics, a study may attempt to prove or forecast one hypothesis or one "thing." In supply chain forecasting, a forecast must be created for many thousands or millions of things, meaning that much less attention can be applied to each individual item. (This is one reason why being able to group items by attribute, as discussed in Chapter 4: "Why Attribute-based Forecasting is the Future of Statistical Forecasting," is so important.)

However, a strong correlation is all that is necessary to use a causal or regression forecasting formula to create an accurate forecast and to meet the supply chain objectives of producing or procuring the right quantity at the right time and keeping inventory levels low. This is true regardless of whether causation is ever proven or investigated and is different from the use of inferential statistics in academic research, where the objective is to understand causality.

High-level Causal Models

The most basic causal system to implement is the application of an overall macroeconomic variable (such as predicted economic growth or decline) to the entire product database. This type of forecast adjustment can be applied before performing any other forecasting to effectively tie future sales to the overall economy. Secondly, the forecast adjustment formula does not have to be applied inside of the forecasting system. Once the percentage change is determined, it can be applied very simply by altering the forecast with the adjustment percentage. Attribute-based systems can apply this change very easily.

As different products react differently to changes in the economy, the regression formula would have to be determined to know how much or how little to change the top-level forecast in response to economic vacillations. In some industries such as construction, companies would show a high correlation between either the overall economy or specific housing statistics, whereas companies that are in nondurable consumer products would not see a very strong correlation. An economic-based model may not be worthwhile for these companies.

MLR Profile

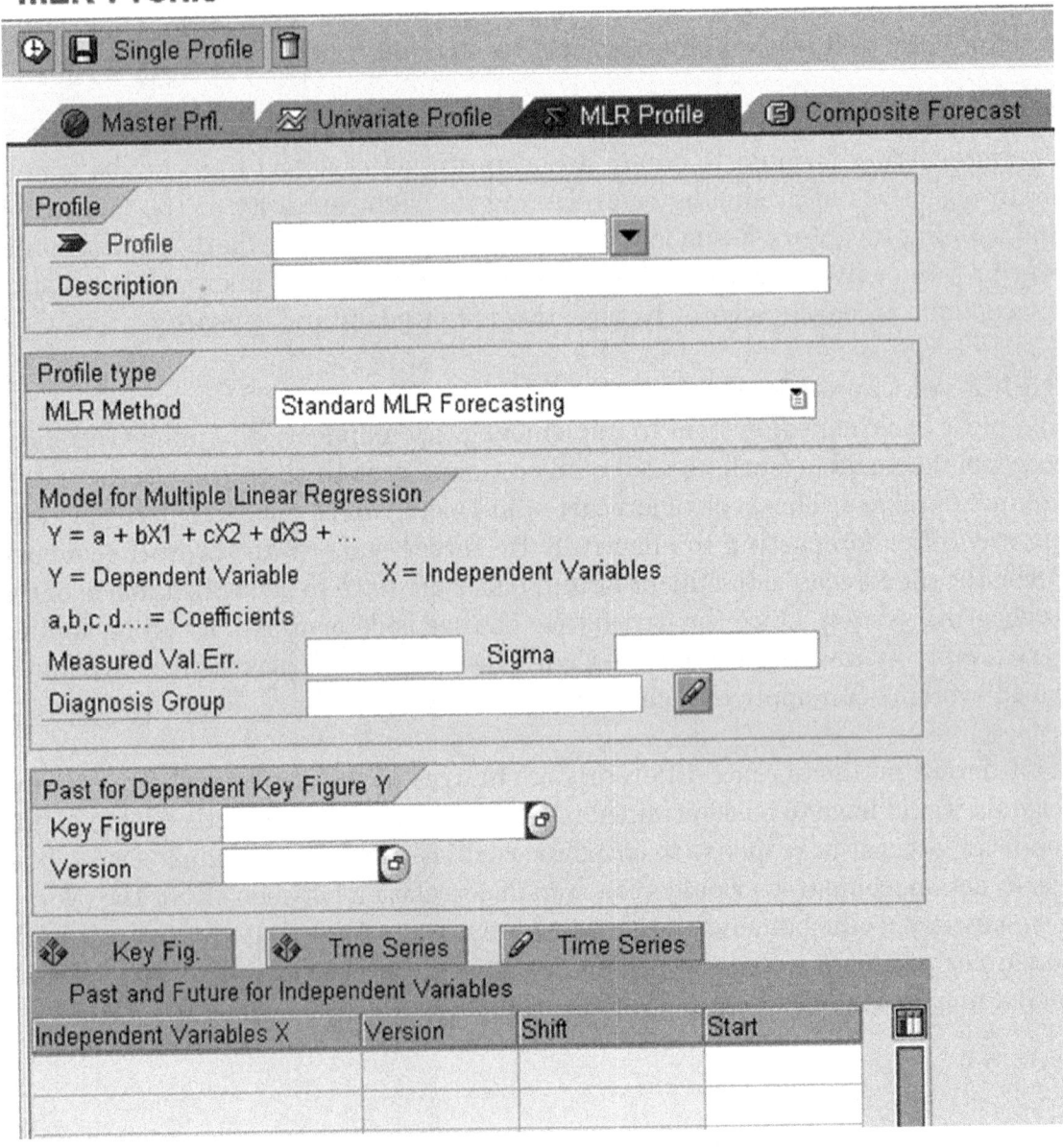

Profile
- Profile
- Description

Profile type
MLR Method: Standard MLR Forecasting

Model for Multiple Linear Regression

$Y = a + bX1 + cX2 + dX3 + ...$

Y = Dependent Variable X = Independent Variables

$a, b, c, d, ...$ = Coefficients

Measured Val.Err.   Sigma

Diagnosis Group

Past for Dependent Key Figure Y
- Key Figure
- Version

Past and Future for Independent Variables

Independent Variables X	Version	Shift	Start

Many applications, such as SAP DP above, have the ability to create causal models; however, they are rarely used by demand planning departments. As I will describe in the next paragraph, for maintenance reasons I do not recommend creating linear regression models this way.

Implementing Causal Forecasting
In order to perform this type of forecasting, three things are required:

1. The macroeconomic statistic (the independent variable)

2. Causal relationship adjustment factors (which are created through analysis and are applied to different products or product groups).

3. A method of applying the factor by differentiating between those products so that the different product groupings receive the associated increase or decrease.

Obtaining a solid economic statistic is not as easy as it first appears. The official US Government statistics have been so manipulated by successive administrations that they are not usable for building macroeconomic adjustment factors. This is highlighted by ShadowStats, a website that adjusts US Government economic statistics.

> *The CPI (Consumer Price Index) was designed to help businesses, individuals and the government adjust their financial planning and considerations for the impact of inflation. The CPI worked reasonably well for those purposes into the early 1980s. In recent decades, however, the reporting system increasingly succumbed to pressures from miscreant politicians, who were and are intent upon stealing income from social security recipients, without ever taking the issue of reduced entitlement payments before the public or Congress for approval.*
>
> *The Boskin/Greenspan concept violated the intent and common usage of the inflation index. The CPI was considered sacrosanct within the Department of Labor given the number of contractual relationships that were anchored to it. The CPI was one number that never was to be revised given its widespread usage.*

However, there are places where reliable economic statistics can be found, and this is also explained in the link below:

http://www.scmfocus.com/demandplanning/2011/12/getting-around-the-us-governments-fake-economic-statistics/

The second step involves performing the analysis to determine how an increase or decrease in the economic statistic affects the demand for a group of products (it would not make a lot of sense to create a different causal forecasting model per product); however, a causal forecasting model for a grouping of products is feasible. The first question becomes how to combine different products in the correct groupings, and this can be performed by the planners with the domain expertise over the company's products. After the product groups are selected, the demand for all products in each group can be aggregated. This aggregated value is then run in a simple regression formula versus a variety of economic statistics to see which statistic is the most predictive. This analysis can be performed in Excel alone or combined with an advanced analytical plug-in such as Oracle Crystal Ball. The result of this process should be a series of economic statistics which can be used to adjust various product groups.

In the third step, a forecast of the economic variables that have been proven to correlate with the historical demand of the product groups is applied to the product groups. It is important to have access to an attribute-based forecasting system to do so, because a forecasting system with true attribute capabilities can easily categorize each product into a group, and then apply the projected increase or decrease to the product group based upon the change in the forecast of the selected economic variables. Doing so involves much less effort and is lower maintenance than using the standard causal forecasting functionality available in most statistical forecasting applications. As I describe in Chapter 4: "Why Attribute-based Forecasting is the Future of Statistical Forecasting," not all vendors that offer attribute functionality are created equal and many cannot create models of this type in a sustainable method. Therefore, it is more valuable to research yourself whether the application you currently have can be used in the method described above than to verify with your vendor that the application can do this or seeing the functionality in the release notes or user manual.

Best-fit Functionality

Best-fit functionality is actually a procedure that compares different forecasting models. Best-fit functionality exists in every enterprise supply chain statistical forecasting application I am aware of. Best fit works by computing a forecast for previous periods and then comparing the errors versus the actuals of each of the compared models. It then chooses the forecasting model with the lowest error. The term "best fit" is derived from the quality of the fit between the forecast that is generated and the actuals, or more specifically, the fit between the two lines that would be drawn on a graph. Different forecasting applications use different methodologies to arrive at the best fit. EZForecaster describes the available approaches they use:

> *By default, ezForecaster chooses the most appropriate forecast technique by ranking three different statistical measures of Goodness of Fit: the Mean Absolute Percent Error (MAPE), the Mean Absolute Deviation (MAD) and the Root Mean Squared Error (RMSE). The Method with the lowest composite ranking is the Best Method.*

> *Alternatively, you can let ezForecaster choose the Best Method using the smallest MAPE, MAD or RMSE individually.*

Best-fit functionality automates the process of selecting the best forecasting method for a product. However, while best-fit procedures work well when the future looks similar to the past, they do not work well when this assumption does not hold. Therefore, best-fit functionality selects the forecasting method that best "fits" with the demand history, but it is not necessarily the best forecast algorithm to choose to produce a forecast. This is an important distinction.

There are several ways to evaluate a best-fit capability:

1. How good a job the software does at matching the demand history to forecasting model

2. How fast the best-fit procedure can be run

3. How easy the best-fit procedure is to use

4. Whether the procedure be run initially or the user must initiate it

There are significant differences in the best-fit capabilities of different applications, even though the functionality may appear identical. Most companies that are evaluating software ask about how good a job the software does at matching the demand history to a forecasting model, but more frequently than not leave out many of the other criteria listed above. However, these other criteria are just as important. For instance, some vendors may have a strong best-fit functionality (from a purely mathematical perspective) that is so onerous to use that it is typically only used in the early stages of the go-live. Other systems automatically perform a best fit as soon as the demand history is loaded into the application. These distinctions make a difference in whether the functionality can only be accessed occasionally or can be run in the normal course of forecasting.

In SAP DP, the best-fit functionality (either Auto Model 1 or Auto Model 2) must be actively run.

Demand Works Smoothie takes the opposite approach and runs a best fit automatically as soon as the demand history is imported into the model. Therefore, the best-fit selected method is the default that is used by the application.

Statistical Forecasting Explained

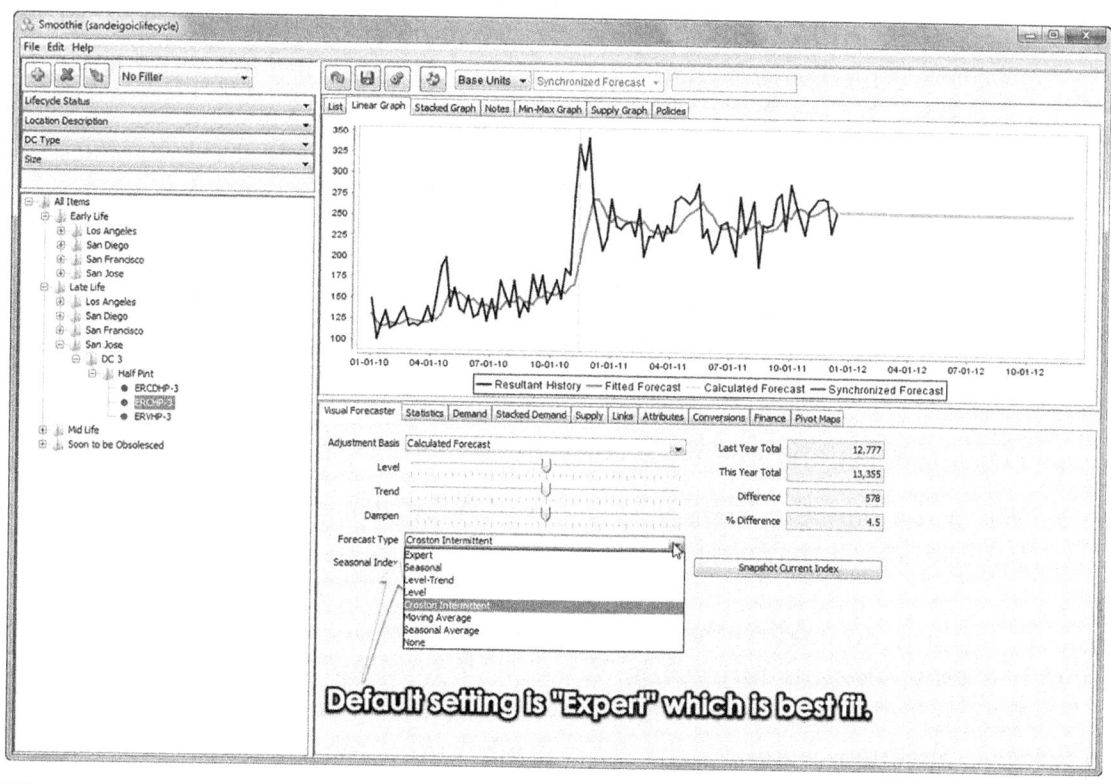

[Screenshot of Smoothie software showing a linear graph with forecast lines and a dropdown menu highlighting "Croston Intermittent" among forecast type options. Caption overlay reads: "Default setting is 'Expert' which is best fit."]

When the forecasting method or model is selected by Smoothie's best-fit functionality, it is called "Expert." In order to turn off best-fit functionality in Smoothie, it must be manually changed or overridden with a different model.

A best-fit functionality that is easy to use, runs quickly, and does not require any special initiation by the planner, is a far more sustainable functionality and is more likely to be used post go-live. It should also be mentioned that many products may not be applicable for the best-fit procedure, and it must be easy to disable the best-fit procedure in these products.

The General Confusion on Best-fit Functionality

The results of best-fit functionality often perplex companies that run it for the first time. Common comments I hear related to best fit include:

It picked a constant model for a large portion of the product database, even when the demand history was highly variable and anything but constant.

Best fit sometimes selects models that we know can be improved with a manual selection method.

Best-Fit Functionality and the Selection of the Constant Model

There are two cases when it is valid for a best-fit procedure to select a constant model:

1. When the demand history is constant

2. When the demand history is so erratic that it is "unforecastable" and a level forecast is selected.

In both of these scenarios, the best-fit functionality is selecting correctly, even though it may seem like an error. When a demand pattern is highly erratic, selecting a middle point or average between the highs and lows is rational, and in fact not much more can be done. This is where the understanding of statistical forecasting tends to break down for many people, and it's helpful to go back and review the limitations of statistical forecasting. So to review, statistical forecasting is useful *when there is some pattern in the demand history, which the software can observe, and can then apply a forecast model to copy part of the pattern into the future.* If no discernible pattern can be found in a product's demand history, any statistical forecasting system will be limited in the value that it can bring to the process. For products like this, there is, in fact, little value created by the forecast, and hence I refer to them as unforecastable. This concept of unforecastability is described in detail in Chapter 12: "Forecastable versus Unforecastable Products."

Best-fit Statistics

A good feature to look for in a demand planning application is the existence of a dashboard that shows the percentage of the product database forecasted using the various methods. This provides an "at a glance" understanding of what the best-fit procedure is doing.

Statistical Forecasting Explained   47

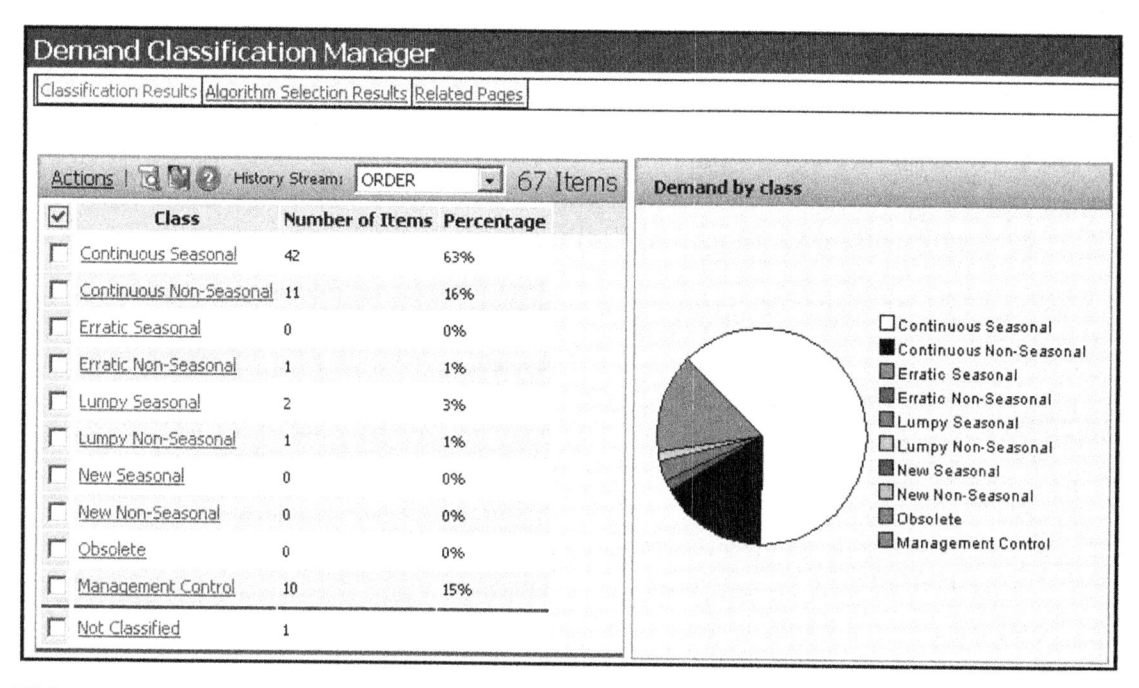

This screen in JDA Demand Management shows the high-level breakdown of the percentage of products into the different "classes" or forecast methods selected. The screen also allows the user to drill down into each classification to see the products that are assigned to the class. This is a time-saver and is consistent with an important fact about using best-fit procedures: The best fit-result must be analyzed by the demand planner. A best-fit procedure will strongly fit the past, but is not necessarily the best forecast for the future. More on this is described in the following post:

> http://www.scmfocus.com/demandplanning/2011/12/forecastability-and-over-fitting/

Visibility into what forecasting method is being applied to each product is a good starting point for planners to investigate whether they want to keep the forecasting method that has been applied by the procedure or apply a different method manually.

Manual Adjustments to the Statistical Forecast

While this chapter has focused on automated mathematical methods of producing a forecast, as any demand planner knows, manual adjustments are also a part of statistical forecasting. I have had the opportunity to work closely with a number of demand planners at various client sites, and I frequently hear from demand planners that making manual adjustments in the application they are using is more difficult than it should be.

Manual adjustments can be performed several ways. (Copy and paste or mathematical adjustment is described in Chapter 11: "LifeCycle Planning.") Here we will cover graphical adjustment with sliders.

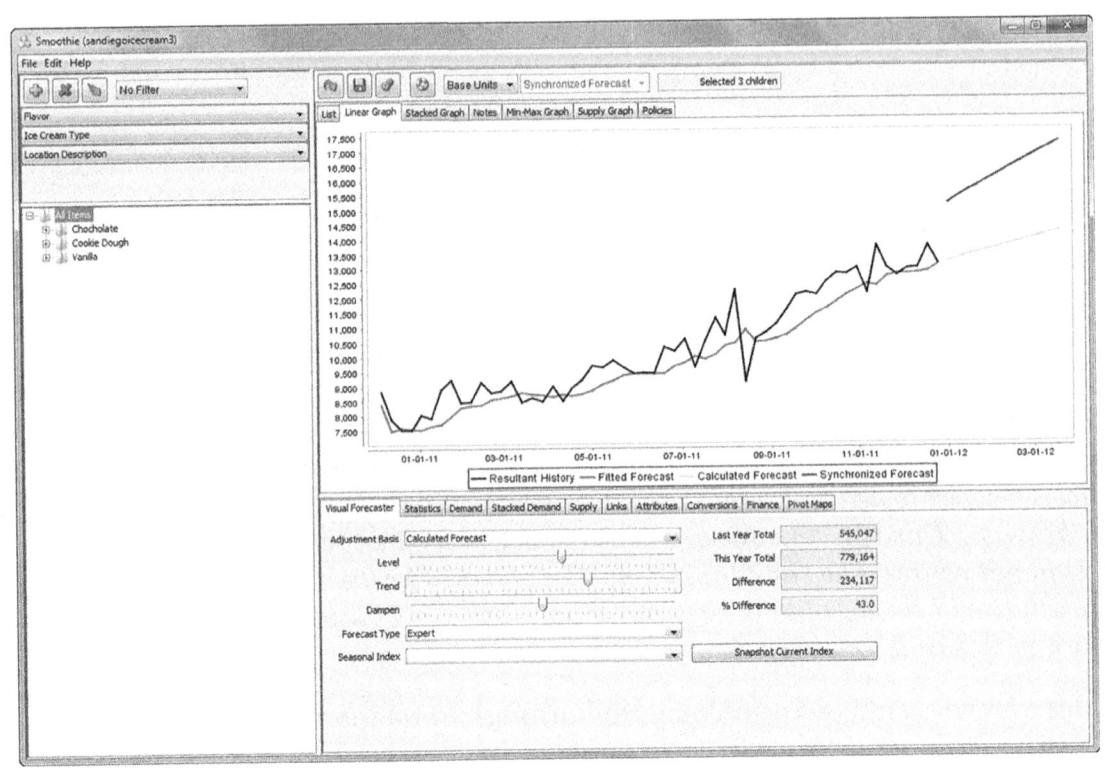

Here we can see that the forecast is brought down by pulling the slider down using the Visual Forecaster in Smoothie. There are three sliders that can be used to increase or decrease the effect of different influencing factors. The sliders are all set to the midpoint to begin. Changes can be made without affecting the actual or final forecast. To export the forecast, the Save button must be used. This is, of course, a very important step. Without the step of saving the changes we have made, the data will display in the user interface, but it will not carry through to the database or to the export. Each slider controls a different dimension of the forecast. The level controls the height of the forecast; the trend controls the rate of increase or decrease; and dampening "decelerates" the rate of change, essentially bringing the slope to zero over time.

User Adoption Issues and the Type of Forecasting System Selected

In many cases, enterprise-forecasting software is not anywhere as easy to use as it could be. Users tend to naturally gravitate away from using software that does not serve them. I was once in a meeting where the project decision makers, frustrated that the users were using Excel rather than the expensive planning system they had implemented, briefly discussed the feasibility of removing Excel from the planners' computers as a way to force them to use the expensive forecasting system.

After implementation, it is very common for management or IT to complain that the users lack the understanding of statistics to use the application selected for them. Depending upon the forecasting application selected, the user should not need to be particularly knowledgeable in statistics or even the mathematical formulation employed to use a statistical forecasting application. I know this because I have effectively trained demand planners to use forecasting software who were not particularly mathematically oriented. This worked as long as the software was well designed. Bad forecasting software, which has underperformed expectations, is sometimes defended with the argument that the planners don't know enough about statistics. However, some enterprise demand planning software requires users to understand statistics quite well as part of their design. For instance, SAS and SPSS are specifically designed for companies that want to create their own custom models. Therefore, its users need to be strong in mathematics, but not all enterprise demand applications are designed this way. The most important thing to understand in order to use most forecasting applications effectively is conceptually how the software works. This is why this book focuses on mathematical concepts rather than spending a lot of time on detailed mathematics, as this is the type of knowledge required to leverage forecasting applications. Good forecasting applications make complex mathematics easy to leverage. A good example of this was covered previously in the discussion of the ability of some forecasting software to internally optimize forecast parameters.

I have, of course, seen a poor match between the application and the skill set of the planners. Should this be considered the fault of the executive decision makers? A poor fit between planners and the demand planning application results if users are marginalized or completely removed from the software selection process. It should go without saying that selecting software without user input will decrease the acceptance of the application, for the same reason that Christmas presents are far less effective at satisfying the recipient than a purchase made by the individual for themselves (especially if the buyer does not consult the recipient on what they would like). The speed with which users gravitate to a system greatly depends upon the application that is selected. Companies should match their planners' skill sets and skill levels with the application, and the best way to do this is to involve the user community in the software selection process. However, what seems obvious often goes out the window when a software selection begins.

Increasing the success rate of IT implementation projects necessitates the improvement of the selection process in all aspects of enterprise software. Selecting and implementing a demand planning application because it is from the same vendor that makes your ERP system, or because the IT department likes it, or because a person who only does demos for a living can make it shine in a presentation is simply not working in practice. Companies that persist in following these approaches will continue to have implementation problems. Meanwhile, certain parties will continue to benefit from the current software selection approach, which maximizes the profits of the major consulting companies and the major vendors, and meets the needs of IT. It is a matter of incentives, not only a matter of a lack of knowledge.

Conclusion

Statistical forecasting has moved past the introductory stage, when it was thought by many that improving forecast accuracy would be a simple matter of implementing mathematical models into applications. An overemphasis on mathematical models—particularly increasingly complex mathematical methods—continues to negatively impact demand planning applications, as many vendors place importance on adding esoteric formulations but underinvest in the other aspects of their applications. Even with all the effort put into more complex time series forecasting models, the most common types of models continue to be moving averages and exponential smoothing. In fact, given the effort involved, these two models are some of the "best value" methods available, and although an enormous variety of time series forecasting methods are available, the treatment of the topic in this chapter was limited to these main techniques.

There is a misallocation development effort in software vendors as more complex forecasting methods are emphasized. This is because these methods do not demonstrate benefits over simpler methods. Even in a controlled or artificial environment, complex methods do not perform much better than simpler methods. Furthermore, complex methods tend to underperform simpler methods in real implementation situations, where higher maintenance implementations tend to degrade over time. When I compare the problems faced by companies that attempt to get value from statistical forecasting implementations, the issues turn out be very similar to production planning and detailed scheduling implementations, in that both software categories suffer from too many applications that are too difficult to use and have too much complexity, little of which is accessed by the vast majority of companies that implement them.

Statistical forecasting methods are called "statistical" because they do not use all of the available demand history, but instead sample the demand history and emphasize or de-emphasize specific periods that are considered more or less representative of future demand. Statistical methods use inferential statistics rather than descriptive statistics. Because forecasts deal with the future, which is inherently unknowable, all forecasts are probabilistic. The forecast that is used and sent to the supply planning system is the *highest probability value*, which is also the mean probability. However, it is nothing more than that. This is the proper frame of reference with which to interpret present statements about future events. Different probability distributions apply to different types of products, and common probability distributions are the normal, Poisson and negative binomial (which are leftward leaning probability distributions).

The statistical forecasting categories are time series and causal (also known as regression), or sometimes leading indicator forecasting. Of the two statistical categories, time series techniques are used far more frequently than causal or regression techniques. Statistical methods are the methods of choice when there is demand history with a discernible pattern to drive the forecasting mathematics. However, they do not apply for all forecasting situations and tend to be both over-applied and misapplied. Statistical methods have been implemented in software for several decades; however, adoption rates have greatly varied, and few companies get anywhere near the full value from statistical forecasting systems.

There are very important philosophical differences between the various statistical forecasting vendors, resulting in wide discrepancies between how easy or difficult their applications are to use. For instance, some vendors do not expose the users to forecast parameters, but automatically optimize parameters during the best-fit procedure. Some vendors do not run the best-fit procedure as a natural course of forecasting because it is very cumbersome or otherwise unappealing. Instead, the best-fit procedure is only run at the beginning of the implementation and may not be run again. Other vendors run the best-fit procedure as a natural course of forecasting, so unless a manual override is actively performed to change the forecasting model, the best fit, and therefore the parameter-optimized forecast, will be applied.

Case Study: Forecast Parameter Management

In this chapter we discussed the usability of various technical functions of demand planning systems. The following case study highlights an observation regarding both the use of best-fit functionality and forecast parameter optimization.

A company I consulted with set alpha and gamma values by creating different forecast models and then running best-fit functionality to choose among the different models. From this they determined different alpha and gamma values would work well for a product. However, they did not want to run the best-fit procedure during the normal demand planning runs and instead decided to hard code the parameter values. The mistake was made in *how* they hard coded the parameter values. Instead of assigning the different parameters per product, they decided to "average" the various parameters from the various products and enter them this way. This, of course, reduced the accuracy of the forecast and undermined the best-fit research, as the parameters entered for a given product-location were not what the best-fit procedure had selected. One of the important aspects of a best-fit procedure is that it is customized per product-location.

This is why choosing the correct software, or should I say software that is a match for the company's resources, is so important. Had this company used the right software for their needs, none of this would have been necessary. More advanced systems can run the best-fit procedure smoothly and with little overhead, making it unnecessary to disable the functionality except in situations where there is a specific reason to manually assign a different forecasting method to the product. The more advanced systems have the extra benefit of allowing the system to better adjust parameters to the demand history as time passes.

I run into a number of projects where optimized forecasting parameters are not being used because the companies have not figured out how to get their systems to automatically choose parameters. Any system that has a problem with parameter optimization needs to be replaced by a system that can do this, because setting parameter values in exponential smoothing or seasonal forecasting formulas is not a good use of planner resources, especially since software can optimize these values relatively easily. I am surprised how this problem persists at companies. The fact is that a number of forecasting vendors are selling antiquated technology that is simply not competitive with newer software designs.

Case Study: How Sales Teams Often Circumvent Client User Feedback

Back when I was with i2 Technologies, I worked with a sales team that had recently sold an application to a company. However, as the implementation approached, some of the users began to learn details about the software we had sold them and were asking questions for which we did not have good answers. As a consulting resource that was soon to take over the management of the impending project, I was tasked with analyzing the client's questions.

It quickly became apparent that the software we had sold them was a very poor match for the client's needs. I questioned our sales team as to why we had not engaged the user community. I was told in very explicit terms that they knew they needed to keep the software discussions secret from the users. They were only to engage at the "executive level" because they knew we had no chance to sell the software if the users were actually able to review it prior to purchase. When I questioned the sales team on the correctness of this approach, I was told that this is simply the way things are done in many sales processes. Furthermore, our competitors did the same thing. This case study is something to think about the next time a vendor pushes back on including your user community in the software selection process.

CHAPTER 4

Why Attributes-based Forecasting is the Future of Statistical Forecasting

Background

For the longest time, static hierarchical forecasting systems have dominated the statistical supply chain forecasting software space as well as the analytics software space. The reason for the embedding of approaches that are so common today is because of previous hardware and software limitations or designs. Backward technologies and approaches persist as they do in any field. Even though, historically, supply chain planning applications were adjusted to account for hardware or software limitations (and these adjustments were eventually obsolesced by hardware or software improvements), individuals tend to fall back on the old familiar techniques and use the applications to which they have become accustomed. Thus, dated approaches are perpetuated, even by some of the largest most influential companies in the enterprise space; some actually promote them as the leading edge. As a result, nationally and internationally, businesses are left with lower forecasting capability and IT departments have much more maintenance than is necessary because decision makers are unaware of better and more efficient approaches. To find out why, simply read on.

Understanding Static Hierarchies for Demand Planning

A static hierarchy in forecasting software terms means that while the hierarchy can be occasionally reconfigured, it can only represent one sequence of parent-to-child relationships between reconfigurations.

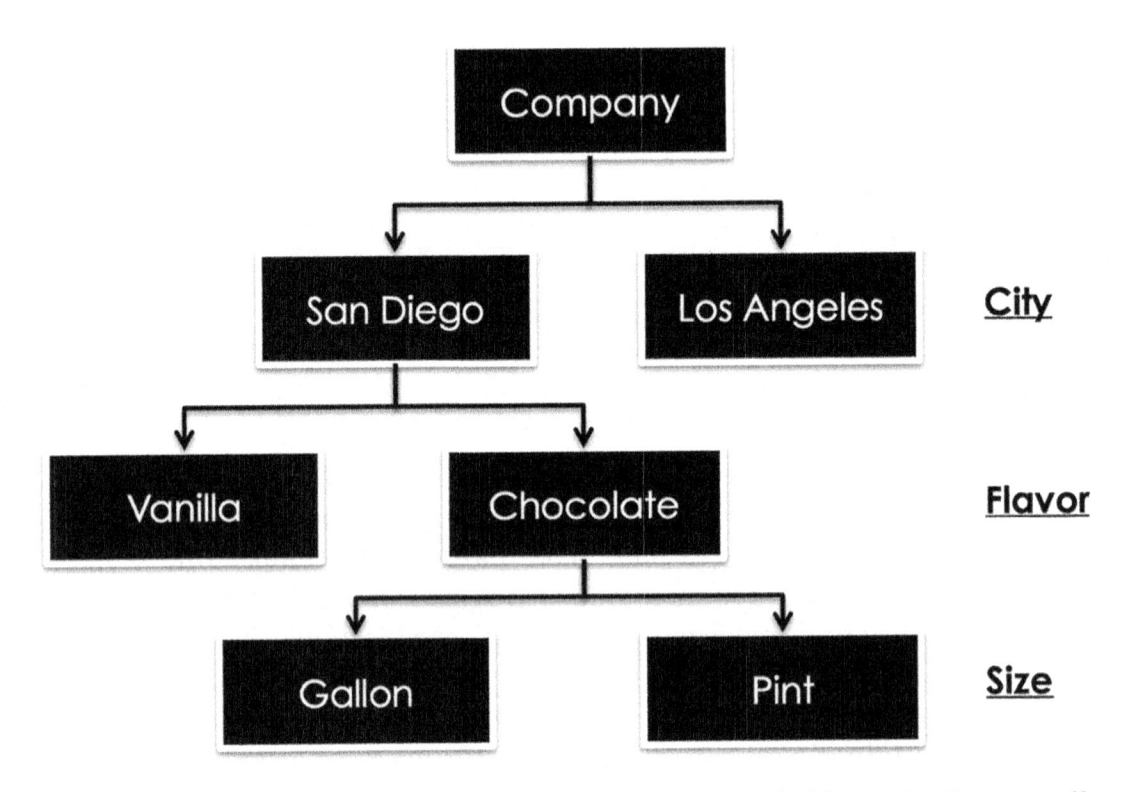

```
                    Company
                   /        \
            San Diego       Los Angeles        City
           /        \
       Vanilla    Chocolate                    Flavor
                  /        \
              Gallon        Pint               Size
```

The graphic above has a sequence of city, flavor, size. A static hierarchy does not allow the sequence to be adjusted by city, size, flavor. Therefore, one could not immediately switch the view to see the grouping of flavors within a size, rather than size within a flavor. Static hierarchies present the user with one way to see data, a hierarchy that was most likely not selected by them. That is one restriction; however, there is a second restriction. In addition to not being able to adjust the sequences of attributes, the attributes themselves are fixed. New ones cannot be flexibly added. Therefore, new attributes (i.e., ice cream type, packaging type) cannot be added to the current hierarchy without significant IT effort. This restricts the business in what it can do in both demand planning and supply planning along a number of dimensions. I will provide a detailed explanation why it is important that the business—and not IT—be in control of the attribute forecasting file.

To fully understand static hierarchies in forecasting, it's instructive to go through how static hierarchy implementations, in both forecasting and analytics, were rolled out in the past and present. During the design stage of these types of projects, consultants typically walked the client through how the static hierarchy will be set up. The consultants then asked for guidance on what that hierarchy should be. Because there can only be one hierarchy between reconfigurations, there was a great deal of hand-wringing over what that one hierarchy should be. The consultant then configured these static hierarchies as data hierarchies in the data workbench or backend of the forecasting or analytics system; the client would test them, and sign off on them.

The hierarchy would then be used for forecasting at the company, for years in many cases. When a static hierarchy needs to be changed, a time-consuming process called realignment is necessary. I cover realignment in detail in Chapter 5: "The Statistical Forecasting Data Layer." The realignment process is very time consuming, expensive in resource time, high in long-term maintenance, as well as extremely limiting for the business.

Knowing that they must choose one hierarchy, many companies are motivated to combine reporting requirements with forecasting requirements. This is why the chosen hierarchy often ends up simply being the organizational sales structure of the company. This is a real problem for the following reasons:

- Viewing the forecast by the sales organization structure is a reporting need. However, for supply chain planning, the organizational structure is not the only way, and not even the best way, for the demand planners to aggregate the data.
- The sales hierarchy is unrelated to the best hierarchy for performing top-down forecasting. A flexible hierarchy allows for the flexible grouping of products for all manner of adjustments, which a static hierarchy cannot perform.
- No company has simply one "forecast hierarchy." Different planners want to see different hierarchies, and sometimes a planner will want to see one hierarchy, and in other cases they will want to see another hierarchy. In fact, the more flexibility that is provided with hierarchies, the more power is placed into the hands of the planners, and the more control they have

over the forecasting process. As a person who has used attribute systems myself, once you gain access to one, it's very hard to go back to a static hierarchy forecasting system.

- A single hierarchy does not give demand planners flexibility, and that's just within the supply chain planning organization. This leads to the next point.

- Forecasting applications have numerous customers inside of a company. Of course, each customer wants to look at their data in a way that is most suitable for them, and each has different hierarchies that they want to impose upon the design. For instance, the sales department often wants to look at the forecast by sales regions, which are multi-leveled. Finance often wants to see the forecast by the financial reporting hierarchy as well as seeing the forecast dollarized rather than in units. No set of hierarchies can satisfy all of the customers inside of a company, making the static hierarchical systems that underlie most enterprise forecasting applications unable to achieve a flexible forecast system that can meet all the company's needs.

Static hierarchies have been the standard approach of forecasting companies for over fifteen years. Vendors often present this approach as leading edge or desirable; perhaps it was several years ago but time has passed these designs by. I will demonstrate in this book that static hierarchies are no longer necessary and are actually counterproductive for meeting forecasting requirements. This is not a matter of there being new requirements. Attribute-based planning systems could have been applied decades ago, but they simply have not become available until recently. The best way of managing the need for flexible hierarchies is with attributes that can be used to build virtual hierarchies, or hierarchies "on the fly," which is the topic of the next section.

Attribute-based Forecasting

Attribute-based forecasting is one of the most important developments since enterprise demand planning software began being used. I know this is a big statement to make, but I make it based upon research into the history of demand planning and in light of my research, I am quite confident that my statement is true. After one uses an application capable of attribute-based forecasting, it's difficult not to come to the same conclusion. And perhaps most interesting is the fact that attribute-based forecasting is still only used in a minority of companies (even though so many vendors say their applications are good at dealing with attributes).

Is the Word Out on Attribute-based Forecasting?
I cannot find a good explanation for why the term is searched for in search engines so infrequently. According to SEOMoz.com, the number of searches typed into Google per month for either the term "attribute forecasting," or "attribute-based forecasting" or other derivations of these terms is negligible. There are few Internet articles on this topic as well. Even a search through Google Books does not bring many results (this is usually a very comprehensive way to search for a topic). Attribute-based forecasting may not be used that commonly now; but I predict it will be in the future.

Attribute-based Forecasting and Virtual Hierarchies
Attribute-based forecasting is the use of a product's attributes to create "virtual hierarchies." An attribute can be anything that is associated with a product. It can be a physical product attribute such as the color or size of an item. However, it can also be any categorization of a product that the company chooses to model in the forecasting software. In the right software, adding attributes is so easy. I have experimented with performing attribute forecasting in a way I have never seen documented. In Chapter 11: "Lifecycle Planning," I demonstrate the use of attributes to categorize products by their phase of life, and to apply an adjustment to a product grouping. Another major use of attribute-based forecasting is to perform top-down forecasting, or forecasting based upon aggregations. Top-down forecasting forecasts for a grouping of products and eventually disaggregates down to the SKU based upon some disaggregation logic (which can be adjusted in some applications). Forecasts based upon aggregations tend to be more accurate, demonstrate seasonality and trends more clearly, and possess less bias. Different groups of products or channels will be optimally forecasted at different aggregation levels and/or using different hierarchies. More on this topic is provided in the link below:

http://www.scmfocus.com/demandplanning/2010/07/pivot-forecasting-renders-forecast-hierarchies-obsolete/

Attribute-based forecasting makes it possible to forecast each segment of a business with the attribute that works best for improving forecast accuracy. Static hierarchy systems can also produce top-down forecasts. However, they can only produce them along the static levels that exist in the hierarchy. In order to select the right attributes on which to perform top-down forecasting, various attributes must be tested. Static hierarchy systems are not designed to test attributes. (Attribute testing can also be performed in an external mathematical environment such as Oracle Crystal Ball, but this is done infrequently.) Therefore, the most common situation is for a company to have a static hierarchy setup, which does not include a level that improves the forecast accuracy when performing a top-down forecast. Many companies that I have worked with are simply not aware that attributes can be tested to determine which ones improve the forecast.

Attributes in Demand Works Smoothie

I have used Demand Works Smoothie in order to explain how attribute forecasting works. More information on how Demand Works performs attribute-based forecasting is provided at the link below:

> http://www.scmfocus.com/demandplanning/2011/05/flexible-attribute-selection-in-smoothie/

Smoothie can be fed data from a database when the application is being used as a live production system, or it can read data from a preformatted spreadsheet when being used on a stand-alone system. The spreadsheet is eventually imported into an SQL database used by the Smoothie application. I demonstrate Smoothie in this stand-alone mode as I am dealing with a small amount of data. This spreadsheet is easy for me to adjust and to show screen shots of the data setup along with how the attributes are shown in the user interface. Regardless of the mode in which Smoothie is used, one attribute is represented as a column. You will see multiple columns representing multiple attributes in the Smoothie spreadsheet.

Adjusting Smoothie's Virtual Hierarchy

While attribute-based forecasting does not have a static hierarchy in the database, it emulates a hierarchy in the user interface. The hierarchy is simply presented to the user as a visual element, the same way it would be presented in a static hierarchy system, except that the user has the ability to adjust the hierarchy based upon any of the attributes that have been added to the database. In Smoothie, hierarchies are only temporary because they are simply a flexible sequence of relational objects. (For this reason the term *attribute sequence* is more accurate than the term *hierarchy*. But because it is completely unknown, the term must be explained the first few times it is used.) Attribute sequences can be shown graphically, but there is really no better way to demonstrate the concept than going directly to the application.

Attributes have to be selected in the interface in order to display properly. Choose the attributes by selecting the drop down selection boxes, and then refresh by choosing the "thunderbolt" icon. This is the attribute sequence or virtual hierarchy that I have been discussing up to this point. To change the hierarchy, simply select different attributes in a different sequence, and select the thunderbolt icon again. The following screenshots demonstrate how quickly a virtual hierarchy can be changed without requiring any changes to the underlying data.

Supply Chain Forecasting Software

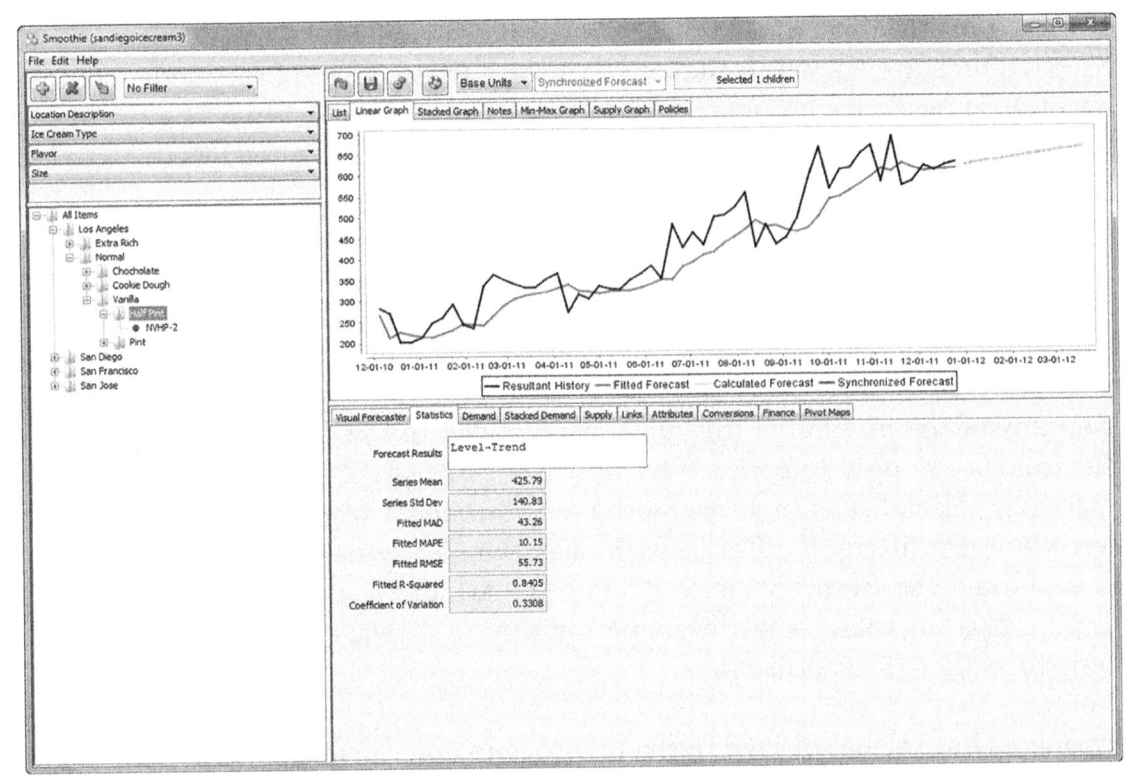

Notice the attribute sequence is Location – Ice Cream Type – Flavor – Size. This is defined in the upper left hand corner of the interface where attributes and their sequence are defined. However, the attribute sequence, as well as what attributes appear in the virtual hierarchy, is infinitely changeable.

Now, we will adjust the hierarchy by simply selecting the attribute drop down as is shown on the following page.

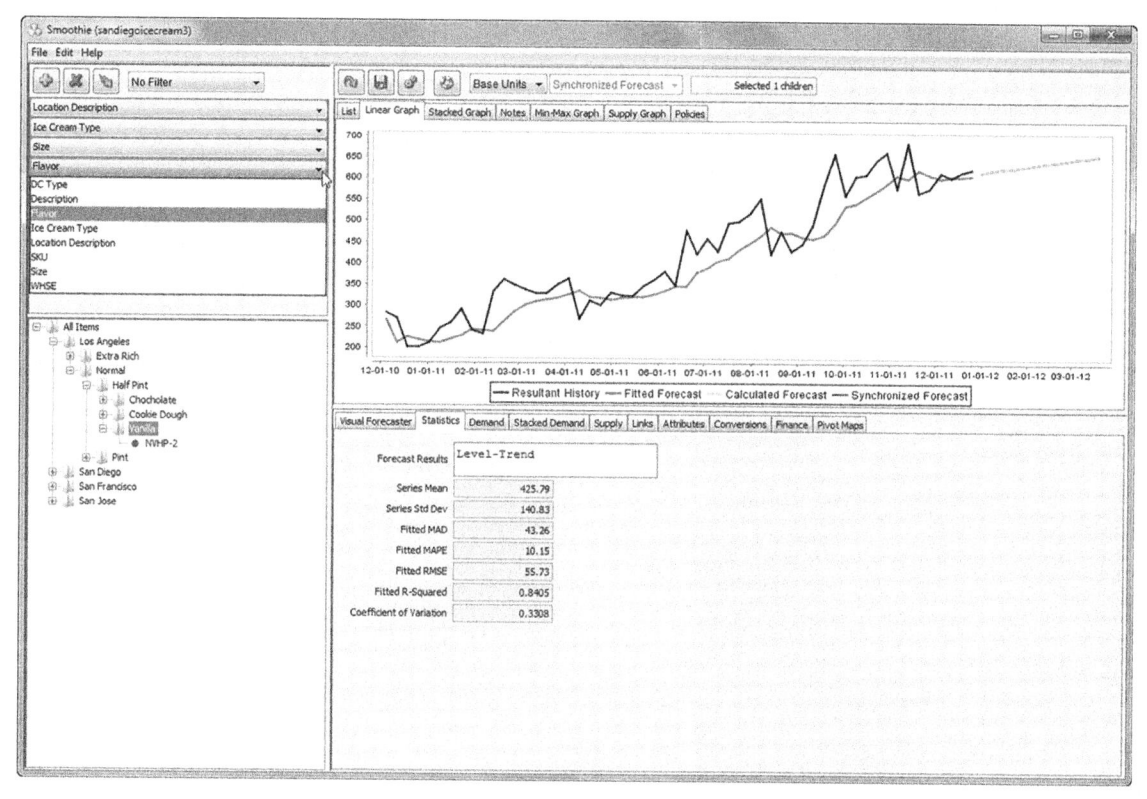

Why Attributes-based Forecasting is the Future of Statistical Forecasting

We have now "created" an entirely new hierarchy. Notice that now the attribute sequence is Location – Ice Cream Type – Size – Flavor. The Size and Flavor attributes were switched, but any attribute combination is possible.

Smoothie can have an enormous number of attributes (over two hundred), but most companies typically use between five and fifteen attributes, including product, channel or customer, organization, region and classification data. Each group of users will typically focus on a particular subset of attributes and in differing orders according to their roles. All participants and departments can use the same application and the same data files to see their own virtual hierarchies by selecting and sequencing them in the user interface. All of this can be accomplished simply and without anyone stepping on anyone else's toes. Different forecast results can also be accomplished by having different groups store their results in different measures.

Supply Chain Forecasting Software

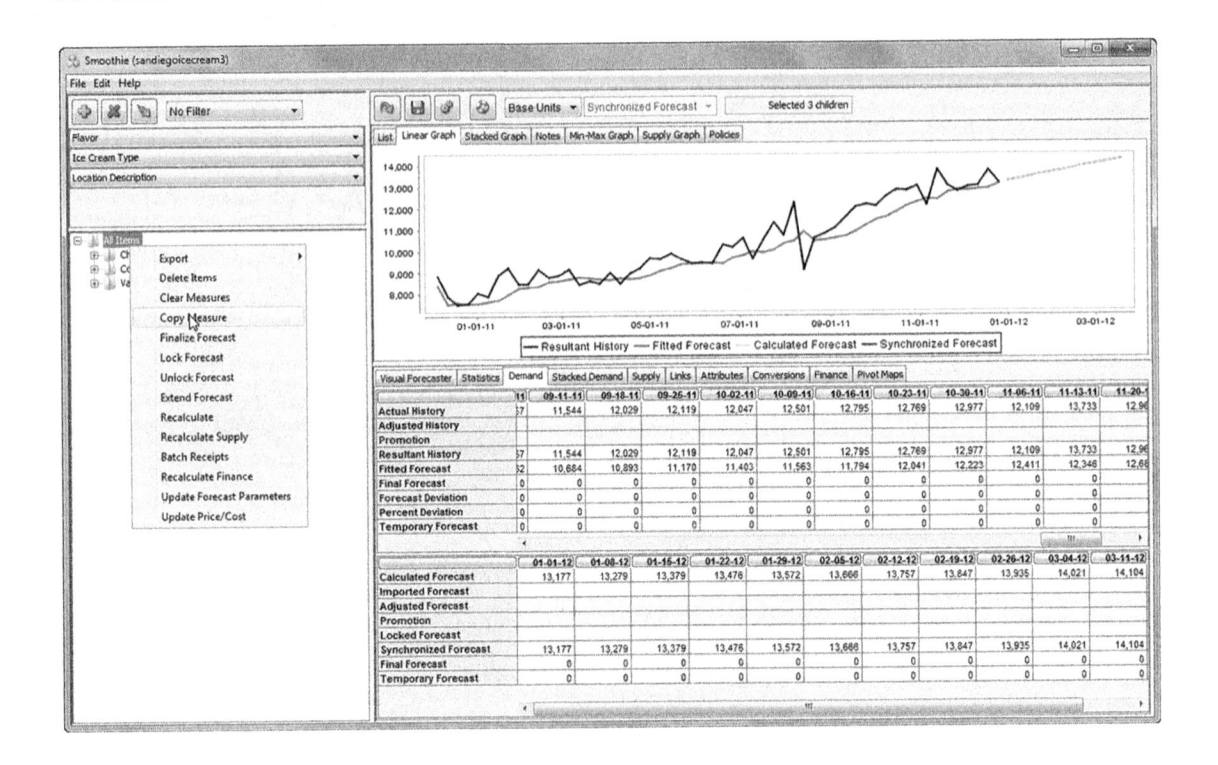

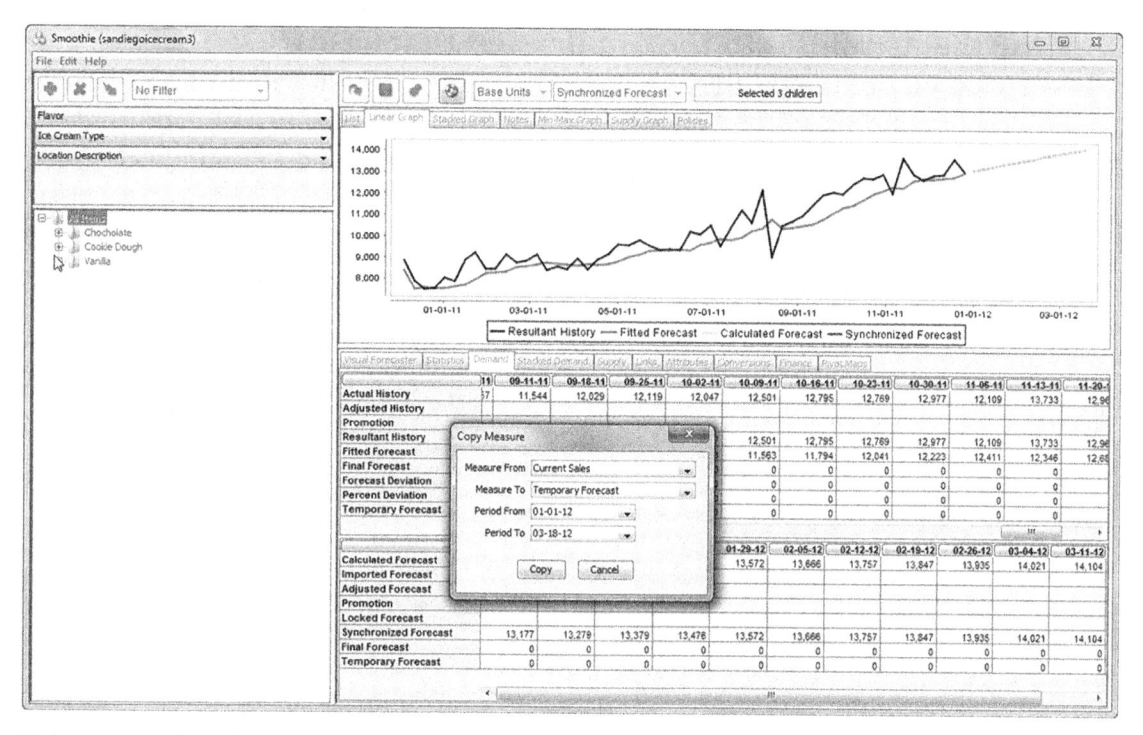

Why Attributes-based Forecasting is the Future of Statistical Forecasting

This screen shot shows a universal need across analytical systems, not only for forecasting. This is described by the analytical graphics book, Now You See It: Simple Visualization Techniques for Quantitative Analysis.

It's frequently useful to navigate through information from a high level to progressively lower levels in a defined hierarchical structure and back up again. This is what I described earlier as "drilling." A typical example involves sales analysis by region along a defined geographical hierarchy, such as continents at the highest level, then countries, followed by states or provinces, and perhaps down to cities at the lowest level. On the following page, the node-link diagram (also known as a tree diagram) illustrates a familiar way to display hierarchies.

Creating the Attributes in the Application Database

It is very simple to create attributes in Smoothie. Any attribute must be represented as a column in the Smoothie input file. The number of combinations of attributes (planning items) that can be added is limited primarily by hardware sizing. Attributes are simply added as columns in the Attribute tab of the spreadsheet (when being used in demo mode), or within a table (when used in a production environment).

	A	B	C	D	E	F	G	H
1	SKU	WHSE	Description	Location Description	DC Type	Ice Cream Type	Flavor	Size
2	NVHP	1	Ice Cream	San Diego	DC 1	Normal	Vanilla	Half Pint
3	NVP	1	Ice Cream	San Diego	DC 1	Normal	Vanilla	Pint
4	ERVHP	1	Ice Cream	San Diego	DC 1	Extra Rich	Vanilla	Half Pint
5	ERVP	1	Ice Cream	San Diego	DC 1	Extra Rich	Vanilla	Pint
6	NCHP	1	Ice Cream	San Diego	DC 1	Normal	Chocholate	Half Pint
7	NCP	1	Ice Cream	San Diego	DC 1	Normal	Chocholate	Pint
8	ERCHP	1	Ice Cream	San Diego	DC 1	Extra Rich	Chocholate	Half Pint
9	ERCP	1	Ice Cream	San Diego	DC 1	Extra Rich	Chocholate	Pint
10	NCDHP	1	Ice Cream	San Diego	DC 1	Normal	Cookie Dough	Half Pint
11	NCDP	1	Ice Cream	San Diego	DC 1	Normal	Cookie Dough	Pint
12	ERCDHP	1	Ice Cream	San Diego	DC 1	Extra Rich	Cookie Dough	Half Pint
13	ERCDP	1	Ice Cream	San Diego	DC 1	Extra Rich	Cookie Dough	Pint

Being able to store, manipulate and upload product and attributes files from a single spreadsheet with multiple tabs is in my view a best practice and is described in the post below:

http://www.scmfocus.com/demandplanning/2011/05/a-better-way-of-importing-data-into-forecasting-and-analytic-systems/

To find out more detail on this topic see the link below, which shows Smoothie's capabilities in this area, and how it enables flexible management of attributes.

http://www.scmfocus.com/demandplanning/2011/05/flexible-attribute-selection-in-smoothie/

Forecasting by Customer

As stated, an attribute can be any categorization that one wants to associate with a product. An attribute can also be a customer. There are several ways of associating a customer with a product. Coding the product per customer would not make a lot of sense, as only one customer per product would be allowed and nothing would be aggregated. The following three coding methods would work much better:

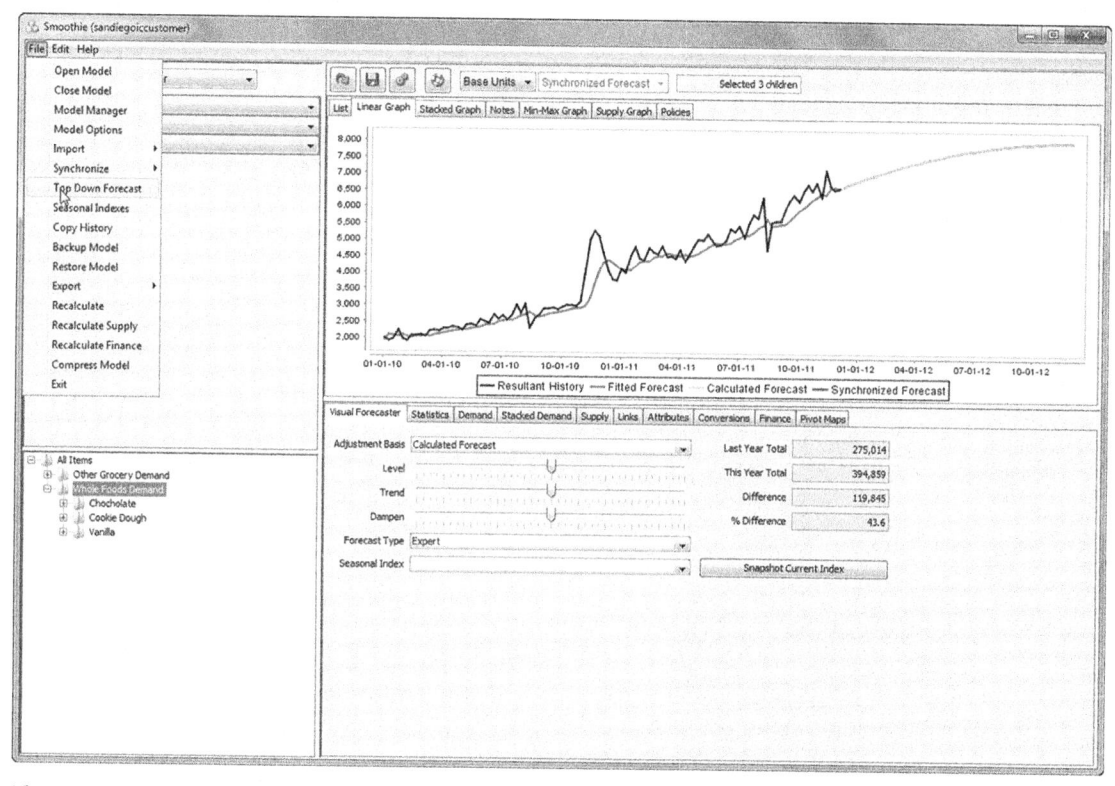

Above we have assigned two attributes, one for Other Grocery Demand and one for Whole Foods Demand. As this company sells fifty percent of its product to Whole Foods, it makes sense to develop a forecast and an attribute for just this customer. Using multiple customer attributes would allow for aggregated forecasting by customer. Not every customer would necessarily be entered into the attribute columns—possibly only critical or large customers. The maximum number of attribute columns required would be the maximum number of customers that would be applied to any product. The second method, customer groups, would require less attribute setup but would also provide less flexibility. It would only allow aggregation based upon a grouping of customers and not just one customer. The third method would focus on breaking out only large customers.

Performing the Top-down Forecast

In addition to viewing the forecast by the attribute, top-down forecasting can be performed by any attribute. This is accomplished in Smoothie from the menu I have selected **File –> Top-Down Forecast** in the screen shot below. Next, select the attribute and then the measure where you want to place the forecast.

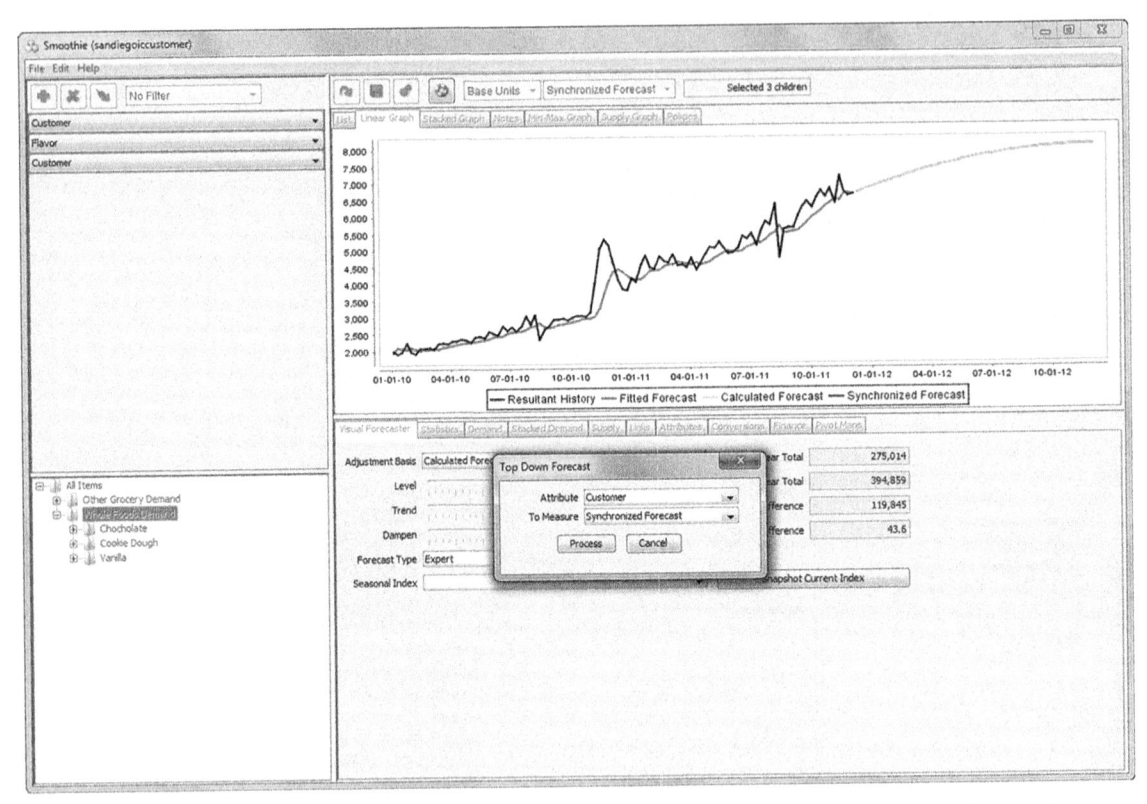

This is a very simple way to perform a top-down forecast. Creating a top-down forecast on the basis of attributes is highly recommended because the attributes are so flexible, and attributes other than those that are "officially recognized" can be used. "Customer" was used as an example, but any attribute can be used as is demonstrated in Chapter 11: "Lifecycle Planning." *Being able to alter and add attributes in this flexible manner is a tool that demand planners can adjust and improve their usage of over time.*

There are options for different levels of detail when creating a forecast in this way. For instance, an attribute coding system can be created for the largest customers, while the other customers are nondifferentiated. Differentiating between customers can be very beneficial if larger customers have significant differences in their behavior and forecast accuracy than smaller customers. Having the ability to forecast by attributes allows these types of modeling questions to be asked. And, this modeling flexibility applies to all attributes.

Forecasting by the Customer and Service Level Agreements

One benefit of attribute-based forecasting is that it allows a forecast and forecast aggregations to be created by customer or customer group. This forecast can later be recombined into a single line item per product location for use in standard supply planning applications. Doing so synchronizes the forecast aggregation type with how the supply plan is managed.

The ability to forecast by customer supports a growing trend in industry of managing the supply plan by customer. Many companies are contractually obligated to manage the supply plan by customer through something called "service level agreements," or SLAs, which define a specific service level to a customer for a specific level of compensation. SLAs are branching out from where they first developed in service organizations and are becoming popular in finished goods companies. I cover SLAs and their impact on supply planning in the book, *Inventory Optimization and Multi-Echelon Planning Software*. Inventory optimization and multi-echelon planning software is the only category of supply planning software designed to control the supply plan on the basis of the customer. Forecasting by customer can be an important complement to inventory optimization and multi-echelon planning on the supply side.

Can Multi-attribute Forecasting Be Performed?

Different attributes or aggregations can be beneficial for different products. Smoothie allows different products to be forecasted by different attributes. Top-down forecasting can be performed for an attribute subgroup by using the Visual Forecasting tab, selecting the Calculated Forecast measure (even if it is already selected) as the adjustment basis, and then selecting the Save button. The top-down forecast is created for the selection. Next the forecast can be locked so that subsequent top-down forecasts using other attributes will not change these original forecast values. The product database can be sectioned off by previously-forecasted items and new forecast attributes used. That is the easy part. The complex part is performing the attribute testing to know which attributes work for which product groupings. This means segmenting the product database and testing attributes for the different segments.

Forecast Disaggregation

Every statistical forecasting vendor that I am aware of states that they can perform forecast aggregation and disaggregation; however, there is a large gap between statistical forecasting vendors in terms of capability. This functionality is too important for clients to simply accept the statement from a vendor that "our product can do that." In fact, aggregation and disaggregation should both be extensively demonstrated and tested by the company's planners prior to selecting an application for purchase, in order to discern how easy the aggregation functionality is to use in competing systems. Aggregation and disaggregation capability cannot be an afterthought. Instead these capabilities must be designed into the application from the database layer up. The following quote on this topic is instructive:

> *The allocations are according to each item's forecast which can be modified (to give them a larger or smaller share of the top-level changes) or locked (so that changes are only allocated to non-locked items). It's the way it's supposed to do it. The trick with Smoothie is the flexibility, ease and speed that we can handle these types of changes.*
>
> — Bill Tonetti, Demand Works

A comparison of forecast aggregation and disaggregation in two forecasting systems can be found at the link below:

http://www.scmfocus.com/demandplanning/2011/03/forecast-disaggregation-in-smoothie-vs-sap-dp/

Being able to aggregate effectively has many implications, some of which are not obvious. The following quote relates to how top-down forecasting supports improvements in the forecasting of seasonal products:

Statistical forecasts generated at a low level tend to have a positive bias. They can also miss seasonality and trends that are apparent at the aggregate levels. Patterns that are obvious at aggregate levels are masked by the stochastic behavior of demand at lower levels. The Top-down function prepares automated forecasts by aggregating demand streams according to any attribute in the model. As a result, they are much more useful as a comparative statistical baseline than only calculating and comparing the forecast at the base.

—— Smoothie Help

Increasing or Decreasing the Forecast for a Product Group by Attribute

I have described how to perform a top-down forecast on the basis of an attribute. However, attributes can also be used to categorize products and then to apply changes, increases or decreases to things like trend or level, to the entire attribute grouping. Because attributes can be flexibly created and assigned, the grouping can be literally anything. For instance, let's say a company provides a variety of products that also includes storm gear. The forecast is for better weather. The company can isolate the storm gear products from the other products, and categorize and decrease them by a percentage, which is the expected decline of their sales. The regression formula can be created outside of the application in Excel, and the change in weather can be shown to decrease sales by a certain percentage based on the regression formula. This percentage increase or decrease can be applied to the attribute grouping. Applying some causal forecasting to products is far less maintenance than switching products to complete causal forecasting.

Conclusion

Companies that move to virtual or attribute-based forecasting software can expect not only superior forecasting, but also better data visibility, as well as far lower maintenance costs. Attribute-based forecasting is far easier to understand and implement than static hierarchy systems, and even eliminates the need for some of the unnecessary forecasting terminology that is based upon the older and less efficient way of forecasting, as discussed in the post below:

http://www.scmfocus.com/demandplanning/2011/12/why-middle-out-forecasting-does-not-apply-to-attribute-based-forecasting-systems/

Attribute-based forecasting can allow different groups and departments to perform forecast aggregation as *they* are interested in seeing the data, and does not require that one single static hierarchy be used for all users. As was shown in screen shots in this chapter, attributes can be easily added to files, and virtual hierarchies can be quickly created and adjusted in the user interface, if the system, like Smoothie, has the ability to perform attribute-based forecasting. An important aspect to understanding virtual hierarchies is that they are actually *flexibly alterable sequences of attributes*. Some vendors that follow static hierarchical data structure designs have added some attribute capabilities to their applications; however, attributes are too important to be tacked onto an old design. Doing so is very easy from a development perspective but doesn't necessarily result in functionality that is usable or implementable. Rather than added as an afterthought, or as a defense measure against more innovative applications (and to confuse executive decision makers),[4] companies that really want to leverage attribute-based forecasting should choose applications that have been designed from the ground up to perform attribute-based forecasting.

With attribute-based forecasting systems, the implementation approach for forecasting and analytic projects, which currently focuses on the technical details of complex database setup, can be changed. Instead of explaining the concept of realignment and spending seemingly endless hours debating what the "one" static hierarchy should be, that time can now be refocused onto determining and explaining how the business can get the most out of the forecasting application. This is an enormous benefit to forecasting system implementation projects, which have tended—along with many other supply chain planning software implementations—to become overly technical affairs with more emphasis on meeting deadlines and IT objectives than on adding value to the business.

Attribute-based forecasting systems not only improve forecasting capabilities, but also provide the flexibility to customize the forecast based upon customers, customer groups or other attributes. However, as with any other type of attribute, there are many alternatives for setting up the demand history file. The various scenarios should be tested to ensure that the complexity required sufficiently enhances the

---

[4] Although interestingly, most executive decision makers do not know to ask for attribute-based forecasting functionality.

forecasting process and is worth the effort to maintain. This type of forecasting can also support SLAs and can be used for companies that do not use SLAs but prefer to manage their supply chain by customer. This is related to service level planning in the supply planning domain and is enabled by applications that have the ability to perform inventory optimization and multi-echelon planning.

Many vendors say they offer attributes in their applications; however, not all attributes-based forecasting systems are created equal. The largest vendors tend to offer the oldest technology. They might like their customers to see the older designs they offer, which try to emulate more innovative applications offered by other vendors by grafting attributes onto their static hierarchy systems. Their customers are easily convinced, as quite often they themselves are invested in old approaches, in some cases by their own IT departments. Adding to the situation is the lack of publicly available information on the real distinctions between forecasting applications. Most hired consultants do not see the distinction. Furthermore, consultants have no leeway to recommend these systems as the companies they work for have signed agreements or are partners with vendors that offer lagging-edge demand planning products. Usually the policy on recommendations comes from the top of these organizations.

Many decisions on software purchases are made on the basis of brand, without scratching below the surface of the various demand planning applications. However, companies that choose true attribute-based forecasting applications can transform their forecasting process. If you are reading this and work in demand planning for a company, it is most likely that your present system does not have the type of attribute-based forecasting capabilities that I have described in this chapter. However, fully attribute-capable applications can be acquired at a very reasonable cost (either by purchasing an application or by using an outsourced forecasting service), and combined with the present forecasting application. Furthermore, forecasting applications have the benefit of being the easiest of all supply chain planning applications to integrate.

Case Study: Attribute-based Forecasting

My first exposure to attribute-based forecasting was actually by accident. I accepted a consulting contract to help a company improve the implementation of SAP

Demand Planner (DP). Having worked with SAP DP several times previously, I knew that we needed a good prototype environment because making changes in SAP DP is cumbersome. I also needed to test the results from SAP DP's best fit (which the client had questions about) against another system.

A method for hypothesis testing in systems implementation that is greatly underused is the use of an external forecasting system to prototype and compare against the live forecasting. In fact, most supply chain professionals are not aware of this method. A prototype environment can be an application that can be run as a production system, but is used for testing and hypothesis development, allowing for a comparison between the live system and the prototype system.

The best way to understand the benefits of a prototype environment is to understand how it differs from a live or production system. A prototype allows the testing of concepts in a lower cost and more flexible medium. Automobiles are initially designed and reviewed on a computer or in clay before they are fashioned in metal. Prototypes are usually not built with the materials that would be used in the final production item. However, by creating a reasonable semblance of what the final product will look like, the designers can take input and make changes, and do so early in the process when the costs of making changes is lowest. This same principle applies to the testing and implementation of software.

I felt I needed a prototype environment for this particular project because the client wanted me to review issues they were having with SAP DP best-fit functionality. I needed an external forecasting application that could also perform a best fit and compare the results to DP's best fit. The company's previous approaches to resolving the DP forecasting issue had, up to that point, centered on solving all of the problems in DP without triangulating its results against any other system. That approach had failed to gain the company any improvement.

This led to me finding Smoothie by Demand Works, which I tested and selected as the prototype environment for the project. At the time I felt the product met all of the short-term requirements related to the product's ability to create a prototype environment, and it had the potential to be used by the client after the prototyping was complete. In the end, I was right on both counts. I began using Smoothie and performing best-fit comparisons with DP. However, I then discovered its ability to flexibly add attributes and to perform top-down forecasting on the basis of these attributes. I certainly did not expect to find any of this functionality.

Because of Smoothie's capabilities with respect to attributes, the project took an interesting turn. We decided to test the attributes that the company thought would improve the forecast, but which they had never actually proven would improve the forecast.[5] The client was able to come up with fifteen attributes. I tested them all by comparing one attribute to another and removing the lower-performing attribute. I continued this process until I had tested all fifteen of the attributes. We eventually found two attributes that made a significant improvement to the forecast accuracy.

Something important to recognize is that one attribute will not necessarily work for the overall product database. My tests used a single attribute for the entire product database, but testing of different attributes for different segments of the database would likely have shown some segments to be a better fit for some attributes over others. This gets into the topic of multi-attribute forecasting which is probably better left to a second stage of testing after the company has mastered single-attribute top-down forecasting. Determining the best attribute per product would have required further testing. However, as the project was nearing its end, we decided to table that analysis and simply go with the single attribute that made the largest contribution to forecast accuracy, on average, for the entire product database.[6]

---

[5] Subsequent projects demonstrated to me that many companies perform forecasting with a static hierarchy on the basis of an attribute that they have not demonstrated mathematically will improve the forecast.

[6] Smoothie allows you to forecast different sections of the product database by different attributes, so it is not necessary to select a single attribute for all products.

Through this project, we were able to quantify how much the aggregation category improved the forecast by performing a top-down forecast for these attributes. No static hierarchies needed to be built, and there was nothing permanent that needed to be created in order to use the aggregation category going forward. All of the testing was performed in Smoothie, and the only data tool I needed to set up all the models was Excel. Roughly 75,000 product locations were tested and the tests were performed on a MacBook Pro and an iMac (both in Boot Camp mode running Windows as Smoothie does not run on Mac).

New attributes were easily added through the addition of a single column to the import file used by Smoothie to create the model. What was really nice was how quickly attributes could be changed before simply reloading the entire data file into Smoothie. After working with onerous static hierarchy forecasting systems from the big ERP software vendors, the project was a revelation to me.

Using a prototype environment as a point of comparison allowed us to effectively compare DP's best-fit functionality and find the issue related to running best fit in a particular way, which could then be changed. We documented how to run DP so that the best-fit functionality could work properly. Other aspects of this project will be described in the sections where that functionality is discussed.

CHAPTER 5

The Statistical Forecasting Data Layer

Background

The screen shot examples of attribute sequences that were just shown in the last chapter are the user interface elements, which are the main way that planners and other users interact with the attributes. This forecasting functionality is supported by a specialized database configuration. This specialized database configuration is employed to create relationships in the data layer. There are several options in this area. Therefore, I wanted to follow the chapter on attribute-based forecasting with a chapter on the data side of forecasting. Before we discuss the specific innovation that supports attribute-based forecasting, it's important to first understand the two major categories of specialized database configuration available to forecasting systems.

The Importance of the Technology in the Data Layer for Forecasting

Of all the supply chain planning applications, forecasting is the most data intensive. It is the only area of supply chain planning that requires years of history to be held, and it is the only area of supply chain planning that does not use a standard relational database. A standard relational database would not provide the performance necessary for the large amount of data and the relationships between data elements. Demand planning intersects with analytics and uses the same data back-ends that were developed to speed the association of various data elements. For instance, SAP DP and SAP BW (SAP's data warehouse) both use the same data back-end. The twin database innovations of ROLAP/star schema and MOLAP were originally designed for analytics and were later adopted for forecasting. For this reason, most of this chapter applies as much to analytics as it does to forecasting.

OLAP, ROLAP and MOLAP

The need for high performance associative capabilities in the data layer is the reason for a host of technologies that underpins conventional Online Analytical Processing (OLAP). OLAP was developed after the term Online Transaction Processing (OLTP), which are databases that have been normalized (redundant data has been removed) and that are used to support transaction processing systems. For instance, ERP systems are primarily OLTP systems. While OLTP databases are optimized to store transactions, OLAP (analytical and forecasting databases) are optimized for data retrieval.

The "online" portion of OLAP essentially means that the analytical results are either real-time or near real-time. The twin database technologies of Relational Online Analytical Processing (ROLAP) and Multi-Dimensional Online Analytical Processing structures (MOLAP) are the primary methods for providing online analysis. ROLAP is also known as a "star schema" because the tables in the database are conceptually organized in a star formation. MOLAP structures are a completely different design from a star schema and are not based in a relational database. Let's get into each method in more detail below.

What is MOLAP?

Unlike relational databases, which must build relationships based upon an SQL query, MOLAP databases are specialized databases that use prebuilt relationships in a batch process. The batch process is most often scheduled when users do not require access to the application (i.e., over a weekend). By prebuilding all the relationships, which are called "intersections," before the planner enters the query, the system's users can receive real-time responses to their queries. The data structure that results from completing the intersection/relationship building is called a "cube." The term "cube" was probably developed because cubes are an easy concept to grasp, as the intersections are built in three dimensions. However, the visual provided by a three-dimensional cube is not, in fact, accurate. Intersections can be built in more than three dimensions, and MOLAP cubes are almost never actually logical cubes, but take on different shapes depending upon the intersections of data that must be built. Therefore, thinking of a MOLAP "cube" as an actual physical cube is really just an oversimplification of something that is difficult to conceptualize if accurately described. Many demand planning and analytic applications have cubes that look more like miniature Rubik's Cubes in the user interface.

MOLAPs are highly specific databases that are only used for analytics and forecasting or any other application that requires fast data retrieval. Because the business relationships are prebuilt, MOLAPs are quite fast, but because they must be prebuilt they cannot be accessed 24/7 as they must have downtime to allow for processing. They cannot be easily manipulated, and they scale poorly (that is they are limited in their ability to support a very large number of intersections). Because they are so complex, in practice MOLAPs are used much less frequently than ROLAPs.

What Is a ROLAP / Star Schema?
ROLAP stands for Relational Online Analytical Processing. A ROLAP is based on something called a star schema, which emulates MOLAP cubes. Star schemas describe logical relationships that are created by associating a specialized set of tables in a very particular way, which could be conceptualized as a "star" pattern in a relational database. The star schema design has a number of wide, but shallow, "dimension" tables (many rows, few columns that store the data to be queried) that connect to narrower, but deeper, "fact" tables (few rows, many columns). The fact tables hold measurement values and serve as a central reference object. As with any relational database, each request is still an SQL query. However, because of the table and relationship configuration, a query run on a relational database in a star schema can run much faster than on a relational database with a table configuration designed to save transactions (an OLTP design). The ROLAP design turns a relational database, originally designed to enforce transactional integrity for applications, into a relatively fast retrieval

system. Although slower than MOLAPs, ROLAPs are, however, more scalable than MOLAPs, simpler to configure and are the predominant database technology for forecasting and analytics today.

Even though star schemas create no permanent relationships (as a MOLAP does), many applications that use them still call the star schema "cubes." Therefore, a forecasting or analytic system that uses the term "cubes" within the user interface (often with the graphic of a cube icon) does not necessarily use a MOLAP cube. And of course, the MOLAP cube, as I just discussed, is actually not itself a three-dimensional cube, as it is frequently represented pictorially.

MOLAPs and ROLAPs / Start Schemas in Both Forecasting and Analytics

For more than fifteen years, MOLAPS and star schemas have been the primary methods of creating relationships between various data elements in forecasting and in analytics that allow for fast reporting on element combinations. The following quote on cubes encapsulates the current view of the technologies:

> *Here is where things get really exciting. Because the cube contains all of your data in an aggregated form, it seems to know the answers in advance. For example, if a user asks for total sales by year and city, those numbers are already available. If the user asks for total sales by quarter, category, zip code, and employee, those numbers and names are already available. If it helps you to understand them, think of cubes as specialized small databases that know the answers before you even ask the questions. That is the big advantage of a cube. You can ask any pertinent question and get an answer, usually at warp speed. For instance, the largest cube in the world is currently 1.4 terabytes and its average response time to any query is 1.2 seconds.*
> — Microsoft

MOLAPs and star schemas were a response to, and an improvement on, relational databases for analytics. When I worked at i2 Technologies in the late 1990s, our demand planning applications used a MOLAP cube, and had a static hierarchy. After using i2's Demand Planner product, I gained exposure to SAP DP, this time based upon a star schema. By working on multiple SAP projects, I was also exposed to SAP BW, a data warehouse and analytics platform with the same data backend as SAP DP.

Common Problems with MOLAPs and ROLAPs

More than fourteen years after my initial exposure to static hierarchy forecasting and analytical systems, the disadvantages of these approaches and the advancement in hardware capabilities have made the limitations and overhead of many MOLAPs and ROLAPs apparent.

1. MOLAPs and ROLAPs as implemented by many vendors are inflexible and expensive to maintain. Most MOLAP cubes and star schema cubes must be realigned when relationships between any of the data elements are changed, making it a major effort to make changes to relationships and thus something that people are reluctant to do.

2. Some relationship adjustments are actually never designed to be permanent, so the company that uses this technology will often decide not to perform the adjustment because the relationships can be too complex to manage efficiently. Thus external objects are developed that also require maintenance.

3. Because the data side of forecasting applications are mostly not maintainable by the business, the business becomes completely reliant on IT for maintenance, meaning the business must go through IT for adjustments and changes.

So while MOLAPs and ROLAPs are fast, many of them are also quite inflexible and difficult to change.

The following quotation from the BIBW Directory provides insight as to why the older approaches to ROLAPs and MOLAPs continues to be so prevalent.

> *Basically, the traditional OLAP is provided by the biggest worldwide companies like IBM, Microsoft and SAP. They have managed to develop a great and complex structure for OLAP users, which was time and money-consuming. Thereupon, no one should be surprised with the fact they're not the first that turned to a new technology.*

That is why in-memory OLAP has been developed mostly by smaller vendors, like Qliktech, Applix, Hiqube, Tibco Spotfire, Panorama Software, Information Builders and others.[7]

And that is how it often works in enterprise software:[8] the solutions that most often get recommended and selected are not necessarily the best solutions, but instead are the applications that the largest vendors happen to have in their portfolio. The advisory apparatus and the major media outlets then wrap their coverage around the message of the major vendors, at some times seeming to re-release press releases from the major vendors as in the Gartner article which is described in this post:

http://www.scmfocus.com/scmbusinessintelligence/2011/11/is-gartner-now-distributing-sap-press-releases-as-analysis/

At many companies, the maintenance required by their forecasting and analytical applications in contrast to the value delivered by them is truly a sad state of affairs. In many IT departments in the US that support demand planning projects or live systems, tedious discussions frequently take place regarding data structure issues such as "characteristic value combinations" (CVCs). (With attribute-based forecasting, this would translate to attribute combinations.)

Sometimes people will point out that a company has a certain—usually large—number of CVCs, and people are often very impressed by this fact. Forecasting

---

[7] Finding a quote like this, however, is extremely rare. Most of the major media outlets in enterprise software write articles praising the largest vendors regardless of the quality or competitiveness of their product. It is not coincidental that the major vendors are also large advertisers in these same media outlets.

[8] This leads to the topic of the basic efficiency level of the enterprise software market, which is quite poor. While the US has many economists, very few of them cover or know anything about the enterprise software market. Far more economists cover other industries and write articles on them. The *Economist* magazine has occasionally written articles on enterprise software. These articles read as "puff pieces," which view the entire enterprise software market as an overly simplified outcome of the actions of major vendors. The writers for the *Economist* also make the false assumption that most of the innovation in enterprise software comes from the major vendors. The *Economist* has access to any economist in the world, and the weakness of their articles is indicative of how few economists concentrate on this area. Enterprise software market efficiency is covered in this post below:
http://www.scmfocus.com/enterprisesoftwarepolicy/2011/11/29/how-efficient-is-the-market-for-enterprise-software/

and analytics data management seems to thrive on unnecessary jargon. I can say that most of this jargon is a waste of time, and much of it is no longer necessary if the software is well designed. The best attribute-based software allows for a zero-maintenance ROLAP, where all of the relationships in the data back-end can be managed by a business resource. With the right applications high quality forecasts can be created without the need for complicated database jargon, because the best applications hide this complexity and made all changes to the data layer easily understandable. This is a positive in many dimensions, but one being that complicated jargon is also an impediment to implementing a maintainable forecasting solution. Let us now see how easy forecasting relationship data management can be with the right software.

Getting Data Into the Forecasting System with Attribute-based Forecasting and Specially Tuned ROLAPs

Something that is often overlooked about various forecasting methods and applications is how to actually get data into the forecasting system. The differences between systems are quite striking in this respect, and the topic does not get nearly the attention it deserves during software selection. Those experienced in forecasting software feel the subject is quite important. In fact, "data preparation" was one of the principles tested for in the research paper, *Diffusion of Forecasting Principles Through Software,* which is covered in the post below:

> http://www.scmfocus.com/demandplanning/2012/02/how-well-are-forecasting-principles-applied-to-software/

Important considerations for the data layer of forecasting include the following:

1. What is the speed of the data layer in every-day querying?
2. When a design change is made, how much time does it take for the system to be accessible to users again?
3. When a design change is made, is realignment necessary?
4. What is the scalability of the data layer? (As I have described, there are tradeoffs. MOLAPs are less scalable than ROLAPs; however, not all ROLAPs are the same.)

5. How adjustable is the data layer, how easily is it adjusted, and what specialized skills are required to perform the adjustment? (This is probably the most overlooked aspect of the data layer. A good question to ask is whether the data layer can be managed by a business resource, or must it be managed by an IT resource.)

Some forecasting applications require a great deal of support from the IT organization. Generally speaking, the more the business has to go to IT, the less responsive the forecasting system will be. This is an ever greater problem with so much support now being outsourced to India where the external outsourcing organization lacks the incentives and quality of internal IT organizations. Addressing issues can often be a secondary focus, with the main focus being providing the illusion of support. If your forecasting system has such a complex data layer that it requires an IT resource, there may also be significant maintenance issues.

However, there is no longer any reason to accept these conditions, as there are a number of applications that enable IT to be removed from the data management process, except for a very simple upload of a flat file extract from Excel to the application database. As discussed previously, I ran Smoothie in a prototype mode without any IT support, because I managed all the data myself. Because of this I was able to skip all the banal conversations about characteristic value combinations and the language barriers of dealing with an outsourced support resource. This is a best practice in data management, which I discuss in more detail in the post below:

http://www.scmfocus.com/demandplanning/2011/05/a-better-way-of-importing-data-into-forecasting-and-analytic-systems/

What I did worked for 75,000 rows of data, but larger data sets are possible as well. Unlike my experience, most companies have to jump through many hoops to get their data into their forecasting and analytic systems. If I had been required to go through the company's IT organization, I never would have been able to test top-down forecasting by fifteen attributes and determine which of them were effective at improving forecast accuracy in the time allotted for the project. Most organizations cannot experiment with their data design because IT controls the data and because so many forecasting data layers lack flexibility.

With attribute-based forecasting systems and the right ROLAP back-end, (data management) is a simple two-step process. First, select the attributes to be used. Second, enter them as rows in a spreadsheet or table, which assigns a different attribute value to the product. These steps are not technologically difficult and can be performed by a business resource. With the business resources in "control" of the attributes file, they can change the attributes as they see fit. Under this scenario, to allow the greatest ease in testing, it would make sense to run one production system with the agreed-upon attributes and then use a parallel test system run off of a spreadsheet on a laptop. After the attribute changes have been agreed to, they can be migrated to the production system by updating the production database table. This is the part where IT support will be required, but with very minor effort on IT's part. They will simply need to perform an update from a .csv file exported from Excel to a database table.

Some people may see a flaw in this design as Excel's row capacity could be exceeded with the number of product-location combinations in the file. However as of Excel 2007, the row limitation has been extended to one million. For companies that exceed this limit, Microsoft makes a free Add-in for Excel called PowerPivot, which extends Excel's row capacity to millions of rows. For large data sets, a powerful desktop computer would be required. More on PowerPivot can be read at the post below:

http://www.scmfocus.com/supplychainmasterdata/2011/04/master-data-management-using-excel-and-powerpivot/

With PowerPivot, even the largest companies can manage their entire attribute file in Excel. This is a very positive development, as planners should have the ability to add attributes that help them plan their products. Smoothie can hold two hundred attributes. This does not necessarily mean that every planner gets to create and add their own personal attributes (although depending upon the number of planners it may be possible), but the planners should be able to jointly agree on attributes that all or many of them can use. As discussed in Chapter 4: "Why Attribute-based Forecasting is the Future of Statistical Forecasting," attributes can be global, or can be custom-developed for individual planners to be used as navigational aids. This design I have described is possible as of the publication of this book, and has the ability to transform forecasting at companies.

Historical Adjustment

Historical adjustment is one of the most important functionalities in forecasting software, yet it tends to be overlooked during software selection, not coming up until after the software has been implemented.

Historical adjustment is a simple concept: it is the movement of demand history from a place it was incurred to a place where it was not incurred. This place can be a location or a product or both.

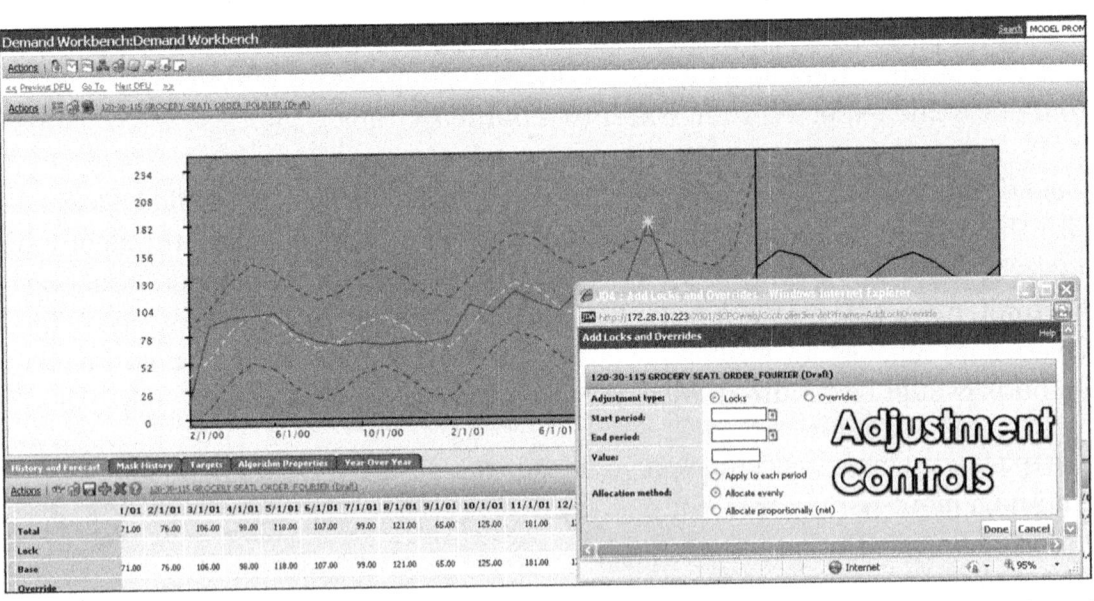

Historical adjustment moves demand history (in the application) to locations where it did not in fact occur. JDA allows for flexibility in the copying of demand history.

There are a number of reasons for historical adjustment, a few of which I include below:

1. When a new product is introduced and the demand history of a pre-existing product is applied to it

2. When a product is moved to a new location for stocking (and the demand history must follow along with it)

3. When a new location is added to a supply network

4. When products are trans-shipped

5. When there is a direct shipment from a plant to a location that is not part of the normal supply network flow (in this case the forecast must be moved from the plant to another location depending upon how the company wants to recognize the sales)

This is just a sampling; in fact, it can be difficult to guess all the reasons why a company may want to perform historical adjustment. However, with historical adjustment functionality, a company has the ability to address a range of issues and to do so easily, and without the necessity of involving IT.

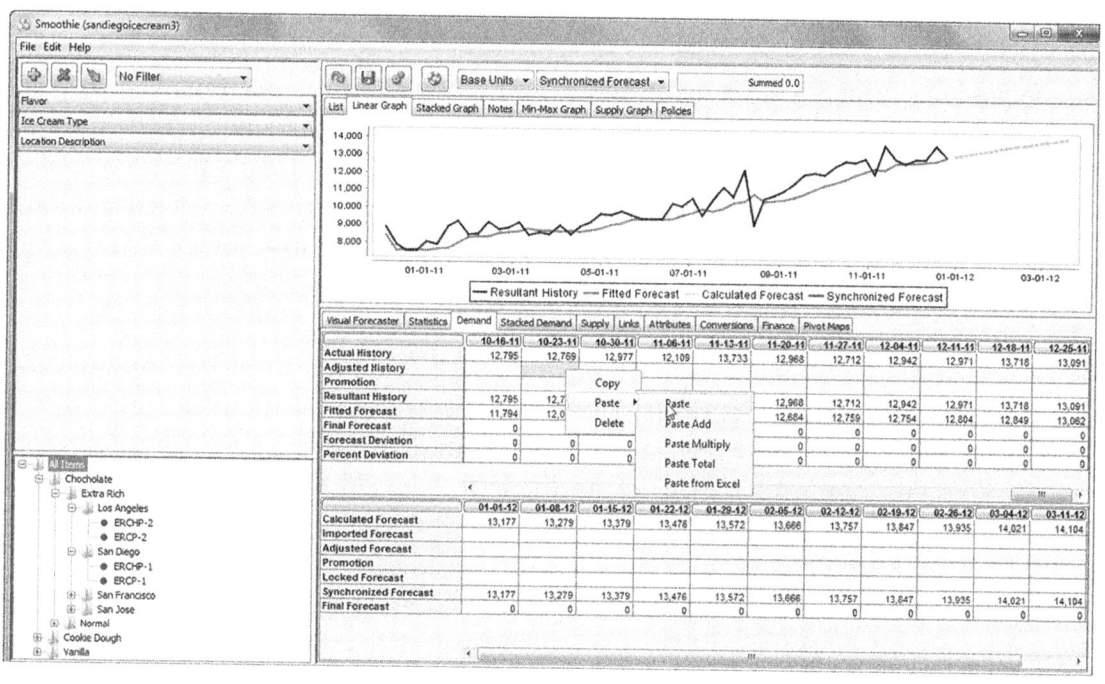

Smoothie can represent the historical adjustment in a measure (which is a row). The adjustment is shown in the application but does not affect the actual history file. Adjusted history is stored in a separate table.

Historical Adjustment in the Demand Planning Application

Historical adjustment can be accomplished two ways:

1. Within the application
2. By making adjustments directly to the database so that the original demand history is changed

For an application to claim historical adjustment functionality, it must be able to perform the adjustment within the application rather than using an external custom table or requiring realignment. Any forecasting application can accommodate historical adjustment by changing the database, but such a solution is less sustainable, far less desirable, and means higher maintenance. Software should be able to hold all historical adjustments. Having this ability has many benefits, for example, allowing a company to, with ease, move a product wherever it wants in the supply network and to bring the history along to the new stocking location.

It is extremely important that the historical adjustment be managed in the forecasting application. If historical adjustment cannot be performed in the demand planning system (and performed efficiently), the issue of unreflected location adjustments will quickly find its way into the supply planning system, which is not where this issue should be addressed. The place to account for location adjustments is at the source, which is the demand planning system.

Historical adjustment is a pervasive requirement, but it is often left unaddressed in many forecasting applications. This inability to adjust demand history efficiently degrades forecast accuracy and is a major maintenance item for many companies. The demand planning application should be able to represent, in effect, multiple versions of the past; one version is the real demand history and another version is the overlay that we want to place on demand history in order to meet future objectives. The forecasting system should be able to maintain these historical adjustments for the full demand history, and they should be easy to adjust and to move around. Demand Works has this to say on the topic of historical adjustment:

> *Smoothie has the ability to forecast using history that is different than what actually occurred. The Adjusted History measure is where adjustments to history can be made. This is useful if you would like to ignore early demand, or adjust for non-repeatable events.*
>
> *Background History adjustments are particularly useful for simulating history that may be copied and rescaled from another item, or correcting for unusual events using an approach that will not influence forecast calculations at aggregate levels.*
>
> — Smoothie Help

Smoothie has an Adjusted History Measure, which is a row in the Smoothie spreadsheet. It allows the history be moved in the interface. The forecast can then be based upon this adjusted history while the history stays where it is in the data file. This is particularly beneficial for history that has to be moved multiple times. For instance, there are scenarios where it is necessary to move the demand history back and forth between two locations every few weeks. The following quote brings up the relationship of historical adjustment to the topic of promotions:

> *We use "promotions" for this, too. They're additive and the advantage of this approach is that the effects of promotions are utilized at other levels of aggregation. History adjustments don't aggregate since there would be a risk of duplicating history while working with aggregations. Having both additive and absolute adjustments is an important and differentiating feature in Smoothie.*
>
> — Bill Tonetti

Some vendors turn historical adjustment into a maintenance headache, but a company should be able to move demand history as it desires, and the technology currently exists to do this. Historical adjustment is something that a vendor should be able to perform on the fly in the demonstration. I run into too many companies that cannot manage this simple process in their system, and even one that allowed the problem seep into their supply planning system, which is not the system to address this issue.

Conclusion

Forecasting software is based upon a high performance data layer that is distinct from other supply chain planning applications. Modern forecasting software leverages the developments in analytics by adopting data layer techniques that were originally developed for analytics (the analytics software market is larger than that for forecasting). This means that forecasting software is currently based upon either a MOLAP or ROLAP, with the ROLAP implemented more frequently. However, just as not all attributes-based forecasting systems are created equal, not all ROLAPs are created equal. Some ROLAPs are difficult to maintain and provide inadequate flexibility to perform many of the activities described in this book. Unfortunately, most large companies are locked into expensive and poorly performing software with very high maintenance costs. Below are some very reasonable expectations that can be placed on a demand planning application:

1. It should be simple to load data into a demand planning application, and easy to manage once inside.

2. New relationships should be easy to create and easy to delete.

3. Demand history should be easily moved as required by the business.

4. No external tables should be required to make any adjustment. If a vendor states that their application must be connected to external tables in order to meet requirements, their software has a dated design.

5. There is no reason for IT to be involved with structuring the relationships in demand planning data, setting up technologically-dated hierarchical data structures, or engaging in esoteric discussions about characteristic value combinations.

You may have found this chapter to be painful (or enlightening) to read, as you may have recognized many or all of the problems described in this chapter in your own company. The truth is, most companies have these problems. Very few companies have selected the best software for their needs (this is addressed in Chapter 13: "Why Companies Select the Wrong Forecasting Software"). When I consult with companies, they often think that their problems are somehow exclusive to them.

This is common, because most companies have very poor access to the problems faced by other companies using the same software. I actually maintain one of the few blogs that posts problems as well as positive aspects with various applications. The best way to ensure your success and popularity in the field of supply chain enterprise software is to uncritically republish information from vendor promotional literature. If you consult, this should also extend to your consulting advice. Selling out the interests of your readers and clients to software vendors is one of the surest way to build partnerships and gain access to choice consulting contracts. Deloitte and IBM do it, and in fact most consulting companies down to the smallest companies do the exact same thing.

Relying upon vendor provided information about their software will always engender an overly rosy opinion into the experiences that other companies have with the software. When I arrived at clients and tell them that several other companies are having the exact same problems as them, they sometimes accept this fact, and sometimes reject it. That is how powerful is the effect of software marketing on the minds of decision makers. The difference between forecasting applications in terms of capability is both very large and greatly dependent upon the competency of an application's data layer. Most vendors, regardless of their data layer competency, all claim identical or superior capabilities to other forecasting vendors. Unfortunately, most consulting companies cannot help clients differentiate among claims because they are trying to select applications for which they can bill resources.[9]

There are many factors at play when selecting forecasting software, many of which have little to do with how the application will improve the forecast, or whether the planners actually want to use the application. However, while there are many actors conspiring against a company's efforts to make a good forecasting software selection, there are ways of getting better software into your organization. It is important for companies to understand that some high capability attribute-based

---

[9] Some companies, like IBM, try and are often effective in taking over a company's technology decision-making process in a way that benefits IBM, which means buying IBM products or products that IBM directly benefits from. This, of course, has nothing to do with helping clients pick the best software for their needs.

forecasting applications are quite reasonable in cost, and that forecasting systems can be integrated relatively easily. I would like to be able to write that software with weak attribute capabilities and a dated data layer can be adjusted with techniques; however, this is simply not the case. Software with the right capabilities is necessary to perform many of the functions described in this book.

CHAPTER 6

Removing Demand History and Outliers

As discussed in Chapter 3: "Statistical Forecasting Explained," the reason statistical methods are actually statistical is due to the fact that the demand history is sampled. (If you have not read Chapter 3 yet, or can't remember that concept as a main point of the chapter, you may want to review the chapter.) The subject of why statistical methods are statistical naturally leads into the topic of this chapter: when historical sampling is used independently of the forecasting model. We will talk about two of the main ways of removing demand history: historical removal and outlier removal. We will cover historical removal first, which is very different from historical adjustment explained in Chapter 5: "The Statistical Forecasting Data Layer."

Historical Removal

Statistical forecasting is made up of mathematical models, which compute the expected future demand based upon demand history. One approach to the demand history is how to remove history in a more active manner; this approach is rarely taught. As a person who was educated in the traditional knowledge of forecasting, it was surprising to me to find out that one of the more effective techniques for improving forecast accuracy had nothing to do with the forecasting model chosen, but had to do with historical period removal.

Methods of removing history can include the following:

Historical Removal

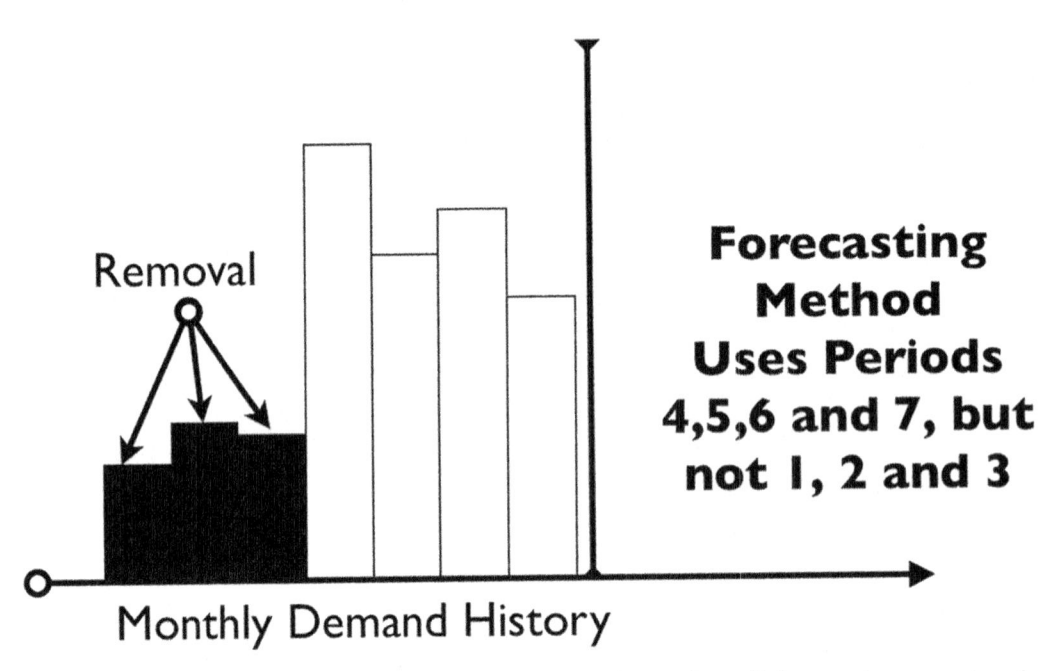

Removal

Forecasting Method Uses Periods 4,5,6 and 7, but not 1, 2 and 3

Monthly Demand History

It should be noted that historical removal would only work well for environments where recent history is more representative of future demand than older demand history.

To perform historical removal, start at the beginning of the demand history and remove either one or several months of demand history. Test the results against the known actual demand, for instance, for the past six months. Some demand planning applications, which I will discuss a little further on in this chapter, can automate this process.

The determination of which demand periods should be removed is accomplished by comparing a control versus a test.

1. **The control:** The *control* is the forecast, which includes all the historical demand periods.

2. **The test:** The *test* is the forecast with the first periods removed from the forecast system.

Very simply, if the forecast is improved by removing the earliest periods, the next periods in the sequence can be removed and compared against the forecast with fewer periods removed. This iterative process is performed per product-location combination and can be repeated until the further removal of periods no longer improves the forecast. When the calculations have been performed for the entire product database, at that point, the company has the subset of overall data history that it can use for creating the actual forecast.

After a period of time has passed and more history has accumulated, the test should be repeated to see if the oldest history should be kept or removed from the system. There are no guidelines that I can provide as to how old demand history should be before it can be safely removed; demand history removal must be tested per product location to determine what to keep and what to remove. Some product locations work best from three months of history, while others work best from three years of history.

What Happens to the Demand History Data?

It's important to remember that the history does not actually have to be removed from the demand data file. Historical removal can be performed in Smoothie without changing the data file; this is true of many demand planning applications. Essentially, historical removal comes down to altering the "begin date" used for the demand history. Demand planning applications allow a number of demand history periods to be loaded into the application database, but the "begin date" tells the application to only use a subset of the available periods. As an example, in Smoothie, historical removal is performed by changing the Number of History Periods in the Model Options screen as shown on the next page. Additionally, the date that the system considers to be "today" can be turned back, meaning that forecast results can be tested against months that have already passed.

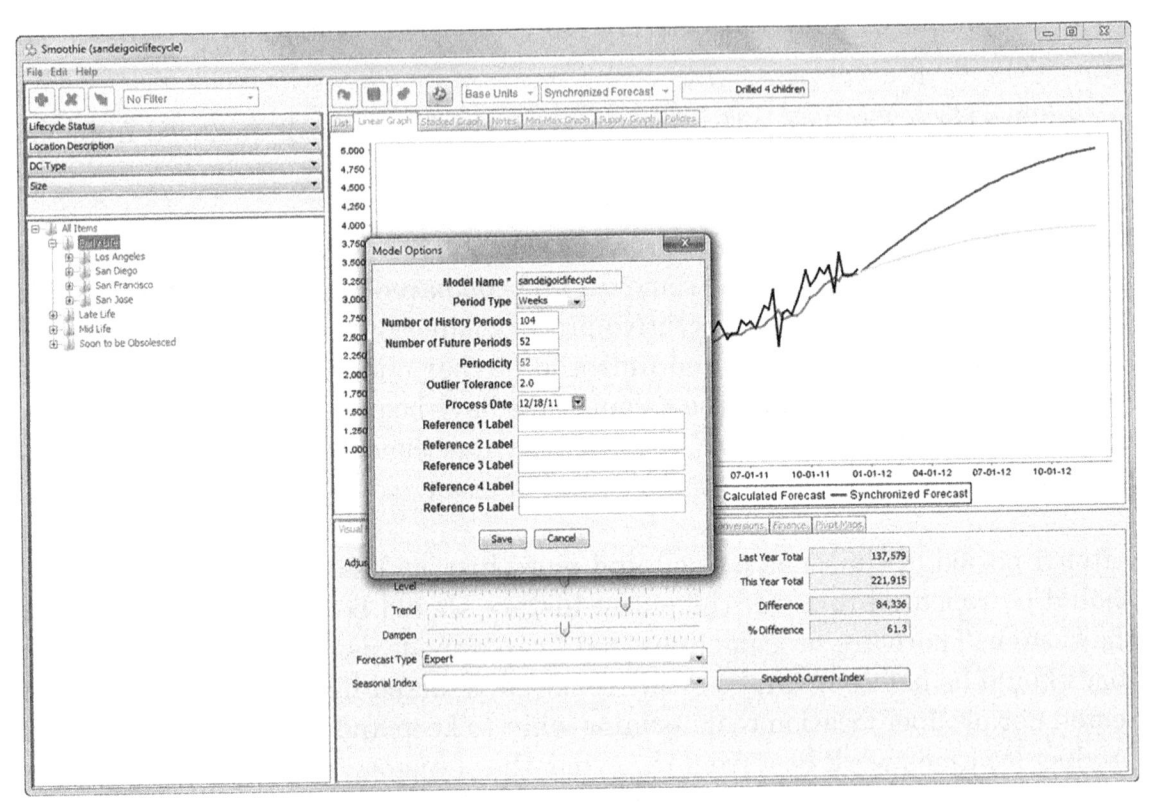

Two important features of the Smoothie demand application are controlled in this screen. One is the date that the application should consider to be "today" (therefore, the date when it should begin creating a forecast). This is the "Process Date" above. The second is the time period for the application to begin using demand history (this is the "Number of History Periods," above).

Historical removal is not used frequently and is rarely discussed or written about (readers can check this themselves by using Google to search various phrases related to removing historical periods from the forecast). One of the few references I was able to find was in a book related to tax-base forecasting called, *Government Budget Forecasting: Theory and Practice.*

The counties see revenue decline because their tax base is shrinking. This effect is not because of decline in economic activity, but because there is literally removal of taxable units as they are attributed to other jurisdictions. Forecasting future economic activities on the remaining jurisdiction is best accomplished by removing the data from the now irrelevant units from the historical record. Where the historical record is no longer relevant, there are data for correction; correction should be made.

Corrections can also be made in the opposite direction, where two municipalities merge; historical records should be brought together in the most reasonable way possible for forecasting.

Historical removal is also built into the JDA Demand Management (DM) product. JDA DM uses different terminology and instead calls its functionality "Time Weighing." However, it is essentially historical removal, although a slightly different take on the concept. I quote from the JDA DM training material:

Time weighing enables you to place more emphasis on recent history when producing a model. The system uses a least-squares regression to find the best-fit model. When using time weighing, the system produces multipliers using the time weight coefficient and applies these multipliers to errors. The value of multipliers decreases as the model moves back in time, and these multipliers in turn make the error smaller for earlier history periods. JDA also has the ability to mask unrepresentative history from being used by the forecasting model.

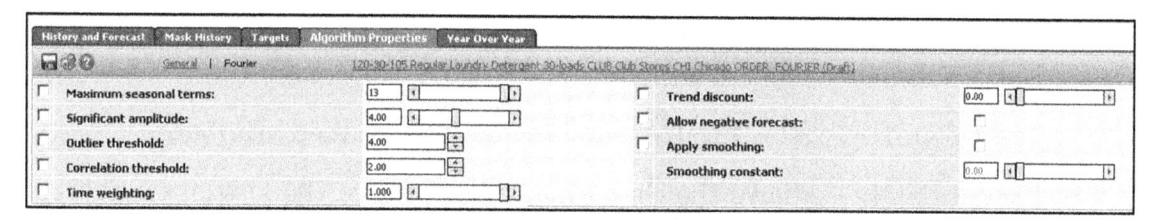

Above, the time weighing factor can be seen. Time weighing can reduce the influence of older demand history. While this is a very convenient way of essentially performing historical removal, one still has to determine whether and how much history should be removed. Once known, this setting in JDA DM can help implement the historical removal, or historical time weighing.

How to Perform Historical Removal Testing

The test to determine whether a company can benefit from using historical removal should be run independently of any other test. I typically run historical removal tests with a product-location level forecast, comparing the entire product database forecast with all demand history versus various iterations with different historical periods removed. However, this is not the only way of doing this type of test. Another way is to identify the products that have significantly changed in demand history over the years, and perform the test for only those products. As a forecast method, I typically use the best fit for both the non-historically removed and the historically removed or complete demand history.

Automating the Historical Removal Test

What I have described up to this point is a manual historical removal process. However, the process can also be automated. I have not tested other demand planning applications for this, but I know it can be automated in Smoothie. Smoothie can run on a desktop or laptop computer without any interaction with a server. All data files can be kept locally on the computer, and this is the approach I have followed when using Smoothie as a prototype environment rather than as a production system. The server version of Smoothie is called Smoothie Mambo. Smoothie Mambo allows the calling of any procedure that would ordinarily be run through the Smoothie interface, but without going through the user interface to do so. It offers APIs (doorways into the application) that allow Smoothie procedures to be run by program, and for a series of programs to automate actions within Smoothie.

Here are some examples of APIs that could be used to enable historical removal:

- ImportODBC – Imports a model from any ODBC-compliant database
- Top Down Forecast – Produces a forecast by a defined attribute
- Execute SQL – Allows the Smoothie tables (where the forecast is stored) to be interrogated
- ChangeDate – Changes the current process date in order to shift the calendar into new future periods

Mambo can produce successive forecasts for different historical ranges, which could then be compared against a smaller historical range to determine the best number of periods to use for the forecast.

Now that we have covered the topic of removing historical periods, it is time to move to another type of historical data point removal, which is related—but more targeted—and performed much more frequently.

Outlier Removal

Outlier removal is a very interesting and controversial topic and in my view should be even more controversial than it is, considering that it is a major technique of falsifying forecasts. Outlier removal is the removal of historical data points that are in significant variance with the other historical data points. Most statistical demand planning applications have a field for outlier identification or removal. One example can be seen on Smoothie's Model Options screen.

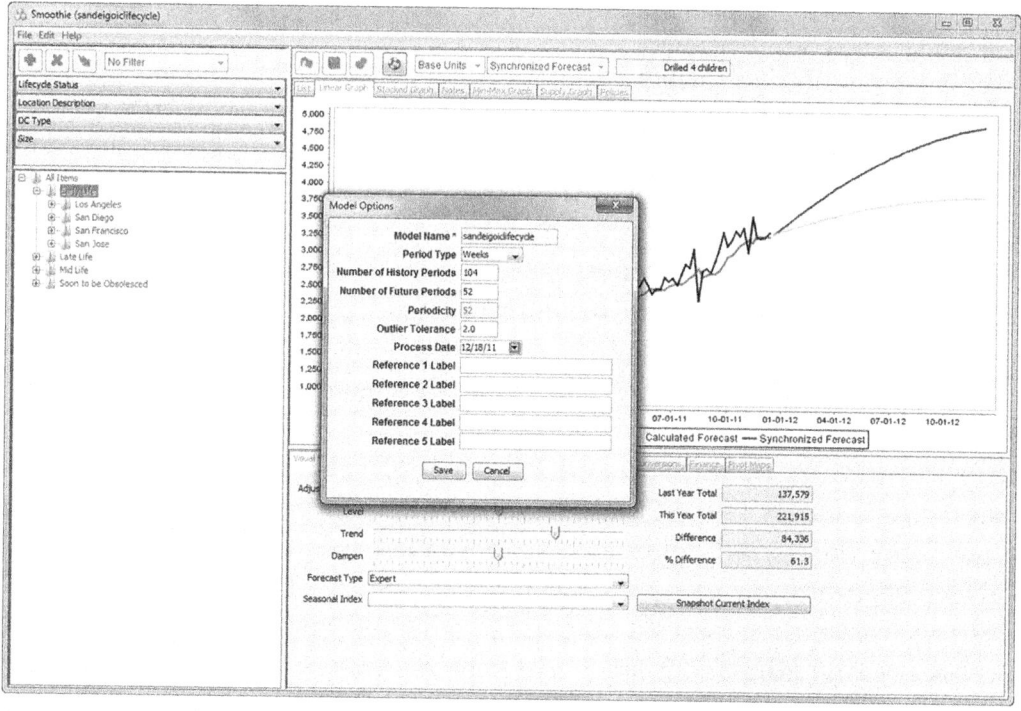

Here the outlier tolerance is set to 2, which is two standard deviations above the mean. If a demand history data point is greater than this, it will be flagged by the system.

Outlier removal is often used by financial advisors to make returns look better than they are in order to produce results that make investments appealing to unsuspecting investors. Outlier removal is also very common in medicine to gain approval for drugs and food additives that are simply too dangerous to be approved without the removal of negative observations. When one questions how so many dangerous drugs get to the market, outlier removal is a major reason. More detail on this can be read below:

http://www.scmfocus.com/demandplanning/2010/07/outlier-removal/

Outlier removal was a primary reason for the results of Hurricane Katrina, as the Army Corp of Engineers simply removed storms of a much worse level than Katrina in order to develop a standard of levee construction it was interested in building (and then added further incompetence by not building to that standard). Removal of outliers contains considerably less intrigue in supply chain forecasting than in finance or medicine and food additive testing, if only because the supply chain organization is only using the forecast internally. Forecasts that are consumed internally tend to have less bias than those produced for external consumption, as there is less incentive to produce a forecast that will be positively received by the forecast's customers. It is a general rule that internally used forecasts tend to be more accurate than forecasts that are produced for external consumption or are sold. However, while internally consumed forecasts are "better" and more reliable than externally consumed forecast, there are still a great deal of problems with the internally reported accuracy measurements of forecasts that the forecasting department reports to the rest of the company. This is discussed in more detail in the Chapter 10: Effective Forecast Error Management.

Outlier Management in Demand Planning Systems

Outliers can be easily tagged by the system and can be removed in a way that does not alter the actual demand history loaded into the model. Instead, it is stored as a separate row along with another measure—the adjusted history. The forecasting system then forecasts using the adjusted history, and in that way, the actual history and adjusted history are kept separate.

Removing Demand History and Outliers 101

In Smoothie, outliers can be identified based upon the number of standard deviations away from the mean. The higher the standard deviation, the higher the tolerance is set for outliers. However, Smoothie does not remove outliers based upon this selection; rather, it merely identifies them for the planner. JDA DM also will identify outliers in the interface. Exactly how this appears is shown on the following page:

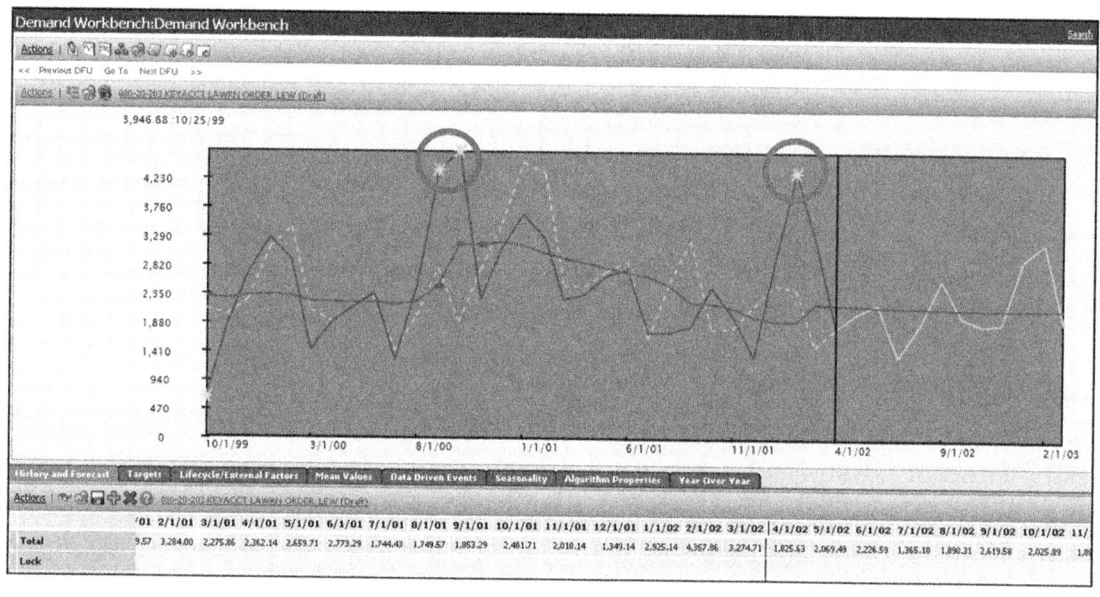

In JDA DM, the yellow stars in the interface identify the outliers. Outliers can be observed as high or low points, but the identification with a graphical element (a star in JDA's case) is a good practice so that the planner can see when their outlier threshold is exceeded. The outlier threshold is set below:

Determining Whether Outliers Should be Removed

Outlier identification is the easy part; outlier removal is where the real work begins. Outlier removal requires planners with domain expertise to make the decision as to whether the outlier should or should not be included in the demand history and used by the forecasting system. This requirement for judgment based upon domain expertise is one reason why it is not a good practice to automatically remove outliers based simply upon their distance from a mean value. Historical data periods can be far from the mean and yet still be valid data points to use for creating a forecast.

The central premise of outlier removal is that one-time events should be removed from the demand history in order to prevent them being used to produce a forecast biased by events that will not be repeated. The determination of what is and what is not a one-time event is often a sea of disagreement, even among different individuals with the same amount of domain expertise.

Conclusion

Historical removal and outlier removal attempt to remove periods to produce a better forecast. Historical removal eliminates periods that are further back in time under the premise that older demand history is less representative of the future than more recent demand history.[10] Outlier removal, on the other hand, is designed to eliminate one-time events. Historical removal can be automated, which means that an automated test is performed to determine when the forecasting system should begin using the demand history. Outliers can be identified using a system, but an individual with the appropriate domain expertise should only remove the outliers after an evaluation.

---

[10] Which also happens to be the premise of several statistical forecasting methods.

CHAPTER 7

Consensus-based Forecasting Explained

Background

Judgment methods tend to predominate in consensus-based forecasting (CBF). CBF is often discussed or introduced conceptually as something that brings together input from different groups, resulting in a better forecast. Many stories on CBF seem to center around efforts to get more people to participate, as if unmoderated participation has been proven to generate high-quality forecasts.

The real story about CBF is considerably more complicated. In fact, CBF is very much a process of receiving input and then performing analytical filtering to remove or reduce the impact of individuals or groups with poor forecasting accuracy. This part of CBF is underemphasized, probably because it's not as appealing as the story of simply increasing participation. The next logical question is, "Who is going to get their input reduced?" which then begs the question of how this topic is raised during the implementation of CBF projects.

Where Consensus-based Forecasting Originated

What we now consider CBF was first formally studied at the RAND Institute and was called the Delphi Method. This project was named after the city of Delphi in Greece, the location of the Oracles who were consulted by the Ancient Greeks and Romans among many others. The Delphi Method is now just one method of CBF. RAND's research into the Delphi Method goes back to 1943 and they performed a number of studies on this topic. The original intent of the research was to obtain better group judgment, for example, by performing research into how the effect of strong personality types on groups can be mitigated (the research had the participants isolated from one another). Since then, CBF methods have been studied in a number ways and applied to a wide variety of disciplines. The majority of academic research in CBF is outside of supply chain management and is concentrated in areas such as finance and, specifically, trading.

The Rise of Prediction Markets for CBF

One of the most fertile areas of study in CBF is the field of predictive or prediction markets, where speculative markets are set up for the actual purposes of making future predictions. In fact, several of the CBF vendors that I will discuss have their origins in predictive market research. An example of a prediction market, unrelated to supply chain management, can be checked online at the Hollywood Stock Exchange. This is a site where people buy and trade different actors and movies.

Consensus-based Forecasting Explained

The Avengers (AVNGR)

H$405.13 ▼ H$9.38 (2.26%)
CURRENT VALUE   CHANGE TODAY

Shares Held Long on HSX: 459,646,898
Shares Held Short on HSX: 14,707,891
Trading Volume on HSX (Today):   21,400,426

TRADE AVNGR Advanced »   Quick Trader

Qty | Buy | Sell | Short | Cover

Here, information about trading for individual movies is listed.

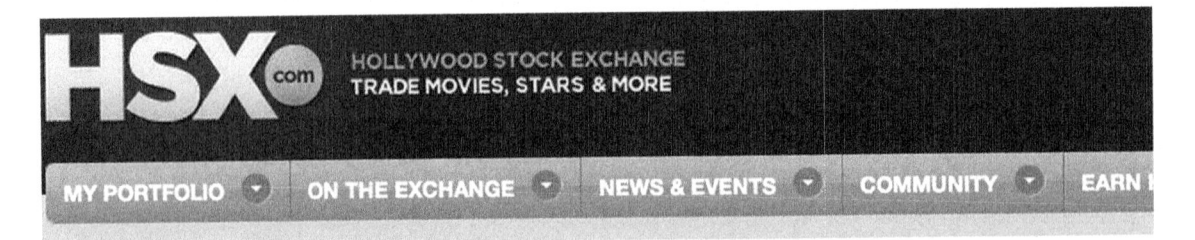

Weekend Box Office
WEEKEND OF FRIDAY, APRIL 27, 2012

< Previous Week | Next Week >

Rank	Name	Symbol	Week Gross	Total Gross	Week	Price
1	Think Like a Man	TLKAM	$17,604,141	$60,472,199	2	H$86.04
2	Pirates! Band of Misfits	PIRTS	$11,137,734	$11,137,734	1	H$29.75
3	The Hunger Games	HGAME	$10,814,271	$372,019,021	6	delisted
4	The Lucky One	LUCON	$10,808,023	$39,409,719	2	H$56.06
5	The Five-Year Engagement	5YENG	$10,610,060	$10,610,060	1	H$29.79

At the Hollywood Stock Exchange, which is an example of a consensus-based forecast system (albeit outside of supply chain management), recently released movies all have prices and trading activity.

Prediction markets use information obtained from many individuals to create a better future forecast than could be obtained with information from any one individual. They come to supply chain from finance and are based in many of the concepts that are the backbone of trading systems. Wikipedia has the following definition of prediction markets:

> *Prediction markets (also known as predictive markets, information markets, decision markets, idea futures, event derivatives, or virtual markets) are speculative markets created for the purpose of making predictions. Assets are created whose final cash value is tied to a*

particular event (e.g., will the next US president be a Republican) or parameter (e.g., total sales next quarter). The current market prices can then be interpreted as predictions of the probability of the event or the expected value of the parameter. Prediction markets are thus structured as betting exchanges, without any risk for the bookmaker. People who buy low and sell high are rewarded for improving the market prediction, while those who buy high and sell low are punished for degrading the market prediction. Evidence so far suggests that prediction markets are at least as accurate as other institutions predicting the same events with a similar pool of participants.

— Wikipedia

A Different Model for Obtaining Consensus Input

If you are familiar with supply chain demand planning software, prediction market-based software is completely different from what you are probably used to. When I saw the first few demonstrations of this software, it took me some time to understand what it was doing. While supply chain demand planning applications tend to be about managing demand history by applying factors to trend lines and phasing in or phasing out products, prediction market-based applications look more like web trading platforms, and in fact, that is essentially the concept on which the vendors based their software designs.

In essence, prediction markets set up different forecasters or forecasting groups with different amounts of money that they can use to "bid" on forecasts—what they think the forecast will be. The forecasts are in a way "stocks" that go up and down based upon the forecast bids of the different players. Consensus Point is one software vendor that offers software based upon prediction markets. A look at a few screen shots shows that Consensus Point is not typical product forecasting software.

Supply Chain Forecasting Software

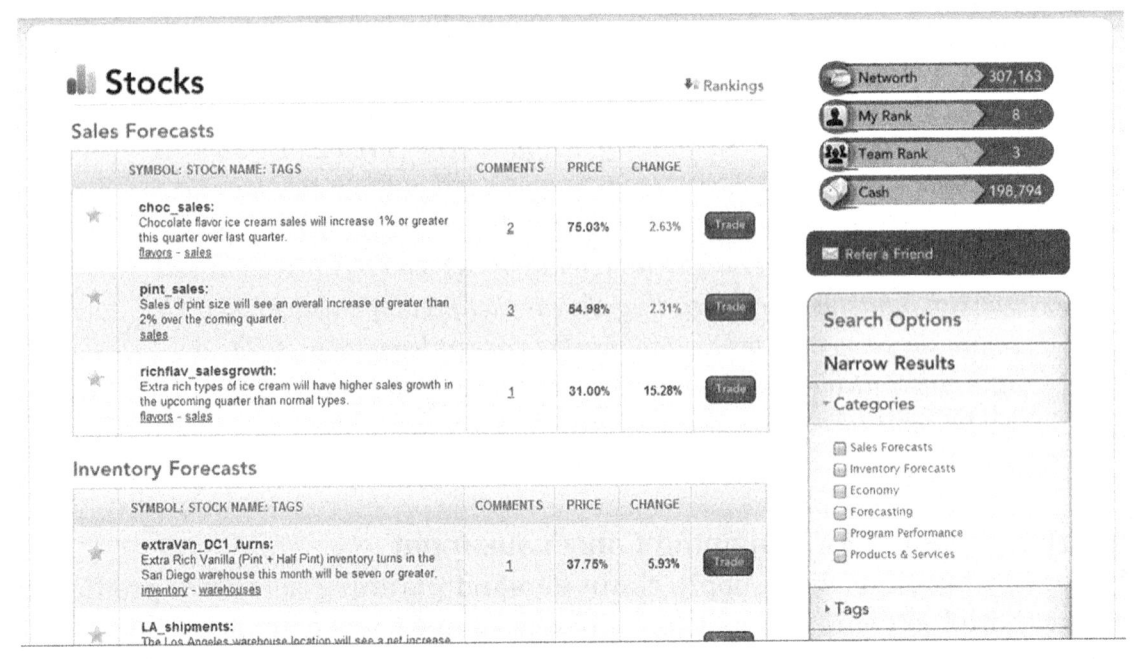

This screen shot shows how the Consensus Point interface allows for easy viewing of the status of different forecasts and different inputs to the forecast (different individuals have different weights to the inputs they can give to changing the forecast, so-called "votes"). The participants are forecasting the quantity of sales.

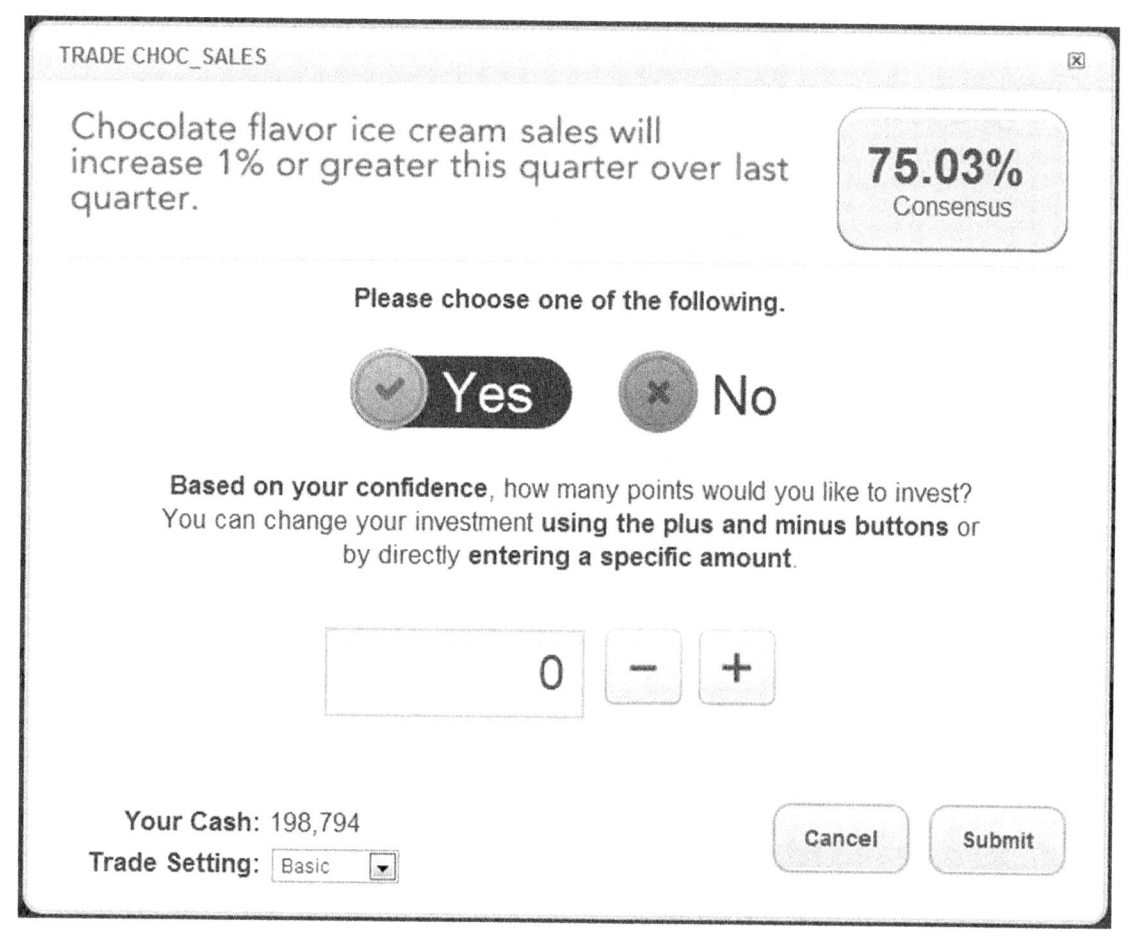

The user can then "bid" on the forecast using the points that have been given to them. The more points they use, the higher their confidence in their forecast.

Supply Chain Forecasting Software

TRADE EXTRAVAN_DC1_TURNS

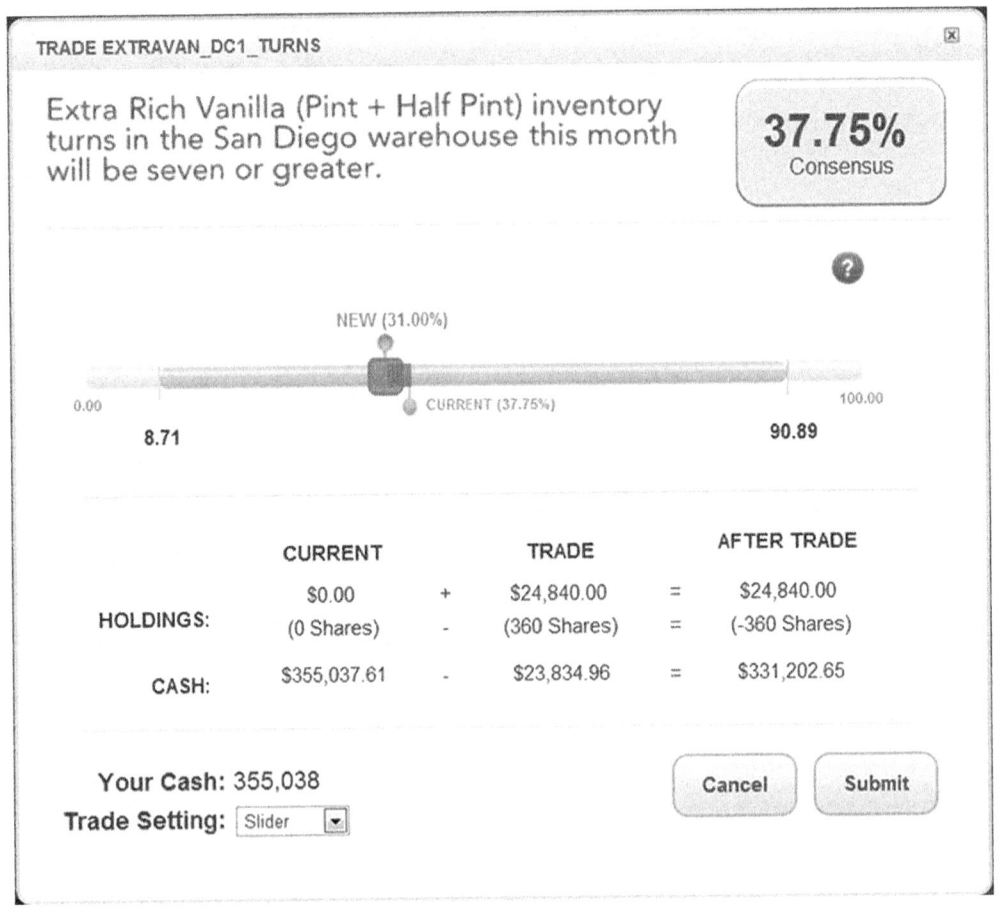

Extra Rich Vanilla (Pint + Half Pint) inventory turns in the San Diego warehouse this month will be seven or greater.

37.75% Consensus

NEW (31.00%)

0.00 — CURRENT (37.75%) — 100.00

8.71   90.89

	CURRENT	TRADE		AFTER TRADE
HOLDINGS:	$0.00 (0 Shares)	+ $24,840.00 (360 Shares)	= =	$24,840.00 (-360 Shares)
CASH:	$355,037.61	− $23,834.96	=	$331,202.65

Your Cash: 355,038
Trade Setting: Slider

[Cancel] [Submit]

A slider allows for quick and easy entry of the user's forecast. It also shows the user the allowable range within which their forecast must fall.

Decision Dashboard

SYMBOL	CURRENT	CHART	TREND 5 DAYS	15 DAYS	30 DAYS
[-] Sales Forecasts					
pint_sales	54.98%		+15.75%	-9.96%	-4.28%
choc_sales	75.03%		+10.47%	-5.52%	+25.32%
richflav_salesgrowth	31.00%		-29.19%	-15.28%	-6.57%
	86.99%		+5.46%	+5.46%	+10.70%
	58.66%		+9.16%	+23.49%	0.00%
extraVan_DC1_turns	37.75%		0.00%	0.00%	-11.30%

Callout: Extra rich types of ice cream will have higher sales growth in the upcoming quarter than normal types.

The decision dashboard provides a miniature graphic and a different view on how the forecast or the forecasted items are changing over recent past.

Aggregation Using Consensus Point

As with most CBF applications, Consensus Point is not designed to perform specific SKU forecasting; instead, it is designed to perform high level/aggregated forecasting which could then be used to augment the statistical forecast.[11] A logical way to integrate Consensus Point with the statistical SKU forecast is to use Consensus Point at a product group or geography, and then disaggregate the forecast to the SKU level selectively by increasing or decreasing by percentage points. This would all be handled in the integration between Consensus Point and either the planning or execution system.

Making SaaS Work and Enabling Collaboration

In talking with Consensus Point, I was surprised to learn that a high percentage of their customers are on their hosted solution. This is true even though many

---
[11] Consensus Point is used for many forecasting applications, many of which do not require disaggregation, so I am speaking here of using Consensus Point for supply chain demand planning.

vendors in the supply chain space receive weak interest from customers for software as a service (SaaS), as is described in the post below:

http://www.scmfocus.com/supplychaininnovation/2009/11/why-is-cloud-computing-taking-so-long/

SaaS is when the application is hosted, normally by the vendor, and the customers don't actually need to buy any hardware or install any applications or worry about upgrades. The best example of SaaS that is used by most people is Google Docs. Google Docs is hosted at Google and the service requires no hardware or software on the part of the user to leverage Google Docs. In fact, a person could use Google Docs without having a permanent computer, by simply logging into Google at a library. SaaS's advantages have been considerable for some time, but it is just starting to grow relatively more rapidly. SaaS tends to be concentrated in CRM and less so in supply chain planning, but the opportunity is also quite high in supply chain planning. Nevertheless, many supply chain planning vendors have had difficulty in getting their customers interested in SaaS. However, Consensus Point is not having a problem convincing customers of the benefits of going with a hosted SaaS solution. Software accessibility, for which SaaS-based applications are specifically designed, is one of the most important factors in obtaining the desired level of collaboration. In fact, SaaS vendors routinely seem to produce applications that are better at collaboration than vendors that are not SaaS-based. This is true regardless of the supply chain domain. For instance, Arena Solutions, which provides BOM management software, is one of the best collaboration systems in any supply chain domain and also designed their solution to be delivered via SaaS.

Consensus Point brings both an engaging and easy-to-use user interface to companies that want CBF. However, conceptually and from a design perspective, they are also bringing a different approach for obtaining consensus input. Because it is different, Consensus Point (and other vendors based upon prediction markets) must deal with the hurdle of getting clients comfortable with this concept. The software will be new for the vast majority of people who work in supply chain and who are used to forecasting software that simply looks and behaves differently.

Vendors who base their software on prediction markets do not sell their software only into the supply chain space. The same software is sold to universities and media/broadcasting companies among many other non supply chain areas. In fact, supply chain forecasting is one of the slower growing areas for the prediction market vendors.

Disaggregation with CBF

What can be helpful in obtaining buy-in to this type of software is to explain how the high-level consensus-based forecast eventually drives to the lower levels of the product. In demand planning, the demand plan is eventually sent to the supply planning system, where it is broken down to a forecast at a product-location combination. Unlike statistical forecasting systems, CBF systems are generally not designed to go to the level of detail of an exact product-location combination. Therefore, how the data is disaggregated is quite important.

Companies have traditionally used a single enterprise demand planning application, with offline analysis and aggregated SKU-level forecasting performed in spreadsheets. This simplified (and not particularly effective) approach has, for the most part, kept companies away from the question of how to effectively blend multiple demand planning applications. This is true even though most companies use a single demand planning application that does not meet their business requirements.[12]

A question in regard to blending demand planning systems is how to combine the aggregation in one system with disaggregation in a receiving system. This issue applies equally to statistical forecasting as it does to CBF, and I describe it in more detail in the following article:

> http://www.scmfocus.com/demandplanning/2012/02/combining-the-hierarchies-of-two-different-demand-planning-systems/

---

[12] Specifically, it does not meet the business requirements in actual usage. Many applications may be seen to meet the business requirements if their hypothetical functionality is presented as the actual reality of the implementation.

Inkling Markets

Inkling Markets is a vendor with a similar heritage to Consensus Point. Their application can be used to obtain input on aggregated forecasts for both forecasting types (consensus and collaborative). With the following screenshots, I demonstrate how to set up a forecast question in Inkling Markets.

For example, if we asked 1 person how many jelly beans are in a jelly bean jar, they probably wouldn't be close in their guess. If we asked 100 people and averaged their answers, they *collectively* would likely be within a few beans of the right answer.

This is the wisdom of a crowd at work.

Inkling Markets offers the following explanation of predictive markets, which is a good place to start. I will demonstrate how to set up a question to which others will then provide their input.

After signing up with Inkling Markets, a question can be set up. The questions can require simple "yes/no" answers or can have multiple-choice answers among others.

For a supply chain forecast, the question could be whether the forecast will be short of, exceed or match a numerical value. In setting up my question, I keep my question simple by asking a yes or no question.

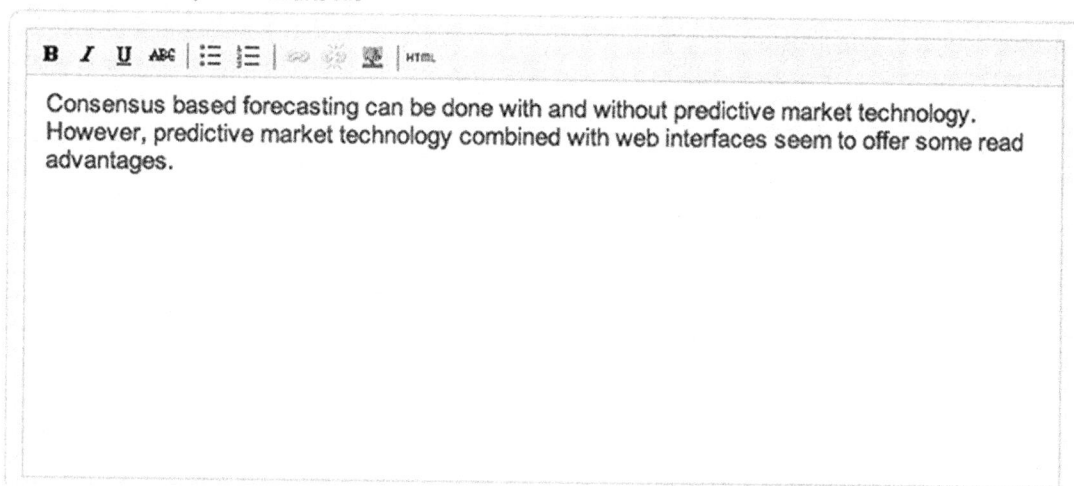

Detailed Description what is this

> Consensus based forecasting can be done with and without predictive market technology. However, predictive market technology combined with web interfaces seem to offer some read advantages.

The question is what is being forecasted.

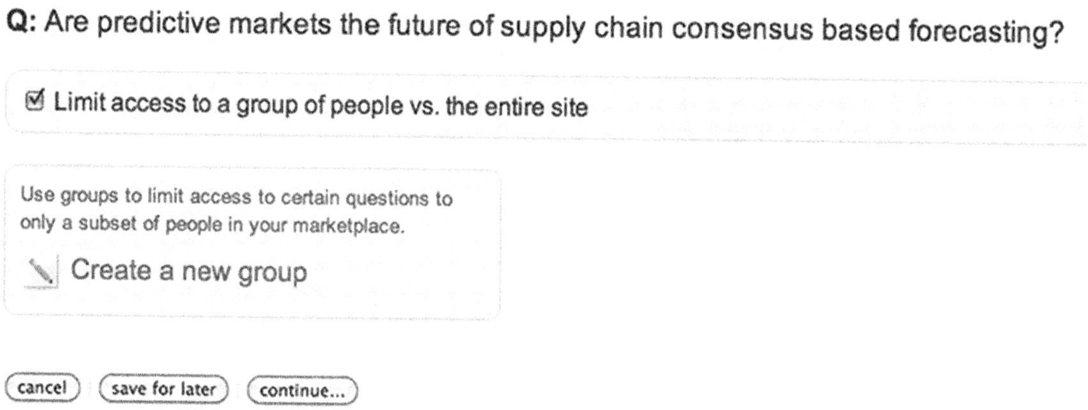

Q: Are predictive markets the future of supply chain consensus based forecasting?

☑ Limit access to a group of people vs. the entire site

Use groups to limit access to certain questions to only a subset of people in your marketplace.

✎ Create a new group

(cancel) (save for later) (continue...)

If I want, I can also set up the question to be open to the entire site or limited to just the people that I designate.

Questions
A list of all questions, possible answers, and current results.

Are predictive markets the future of supply chain consensus based forecasting? 50.0% unchanged today

Trades: 0 • Supply Chain Planning • Creator: supersnapp • Ends: Mar 28, 2010 @ 01:23 PM PDT

Next the question is published and is available on a site, which the individuals that are part of the forecasting group can access. The group can be within one organization or across an unlimited number of organizations.

Are predictive markets the future of supply of consensus based forecasting?

Do you think:

▲ Chances are **higher** than 50.00%

▼ Chances are **lower** than 50.00%

Patiently awaiting your clicks...

The individuals invited to the forecasting group then have the opportunity to "vote." The vote moves the forecasted value by the weight assigned to the voter in the system. Again, not all individuals in the group need to be given the same voting power. Those with a

better forecast accuracy history should be given more votes or influence than those with poorer forecast accuracy histories. This is a consistent best practice that has been picked up by all of the consensus-based forecasting vendors showcased in this book, which is an area where they lead statistical forecasting vendors.

What should also be discussed is the pricing on this application. Most of Inkling markets plans are less than a dollar per month per user, and it is a 100 percent SaaS solution so there are no software maintenance or hardware costs. Therefore, an application like this can be an inexpensive addition to a much more expensive statistical forecasting application. The price of an application like this makes it especially illogical to attempt to perform consensus-based forecasting in a statistical forecasting application.

The Current Thinking on CBF

In most areas of supply chain management currently, the pendulum has swung away from statistical forecasting and toward CBF, although this does not necessarily reflect reality. In practice, companies still spend far more time and money on statistical efforts, but the current thinking indicates where many executives see opportunities for improvements. (As we will see, this has as much to do with a widespread sentiment of disappointment in statistical forecasting as with the actual opportunities in CBF.)

Generally, there is a great deal of misunderstanding about CBF in terms of its effective practice, as well as how it relates to the sales forecast, S&OP and other forecasting methods. In terms of CBF itself, the following statement approximates the line of reasoning regarding why consensus-based methods should be the focal point:

> *Many of the statistical methods have not improved the forecast accuracy as much as had been hoped, and the real improvements in forecast accuracy come from getting more people involved in the forecast.*

While this perspective is appealing, it does not accurately represent how CBF fits within the overall forecasting "infrastructure" of a company. The statement also misinterprets the forecast accuracy that can be expected from different methods.

In fact, I have a direct quote from an article in *CIO* magazine that is representative of a number of articles that cover this topic.

> *'There's been a change in the technology for demand planning,' says AMR Research Vice President Bill Swanton, who declined to address the Nike case specifically. 'In the late '90s, companies said all we need is the data and we can plan everything perfectly. Today, companies are trying to do consensus planning rather than demand planning.' That means moving away from the crystal ball and toward sharing information up and down the supply chain with customers, retailers, distributors and manufacturers. 'If you can share information faster and more accurately among a lot of people, you will see trends a lot sooner, and that's where the true value of supply chain projects are,' Swanton says.*
>
> — CIO Magazine

http://www.cio.com/article/32334/Nike_Rebounds_How_and_Why_Nike_Recovered_from_Its_Supply_Chain_Disaster

The above quotation is problematic in terms of understanding the history of statistical forecasting. While many statistical forecasting systems were oversold, this quotation exaggerates the level of the claims that were made. Secondly, the quotation adds confusion by placing CBF as an *alternative to demand planning*, when in fact, CBF is a subset of demand planning. (Demand planning is interchangeable with the term "forecasting within a domain." For instance, forecasting for demand is one of many types of forecasting, and therefore describes all efforts to predict future sales.) I have a definition for demand planning at this link:

http://www.scmfocus.com/demandplanning/2012/02/what-is-demand-planning/

It would have been more accurate for the quote to state something like the following:

> *Companies are trying to focus on consensus planning rather than statistical forecasting. Companies (or at least some companies) have come to believe that more opportunity lies in the CBF area.*

It's not the first time that I have heard this said. In fact, I have heard repeatedly on projects that "getting more inputs into the forecast" rather than improving the use of statistical forecasting is where most of the opportunities reside for forecast improvement. I have even heard estimations that between sixty and seventy percent of the opportunities to improve forecasting accuracy lie in the CBF versus statistical realm. Interestingly, in searching through scholarly sources I found no research that compared CBF to statistical methods or compared their accuracy improvement, much less attributed a specific percentage improvement to each forecast category. Where are people that make these statements getting their information? Scholarly research is still trying to prove the effectiveness of consensus methods and is nowhere close to making a proposal as to where the majority of forecasting improvement opportunities currently lie. However, the quotation is valuable because it does describe the viewpoint of many decision makers in this area.

The Origins of Forecasting Myths

Up to this point, we have discussed three forecasting myths:

1. Simply using statistical forecasting software would significantly increase forecast accuracy.

2. More complex statistical forecasting methods would improve the forecast over simpler methods.

3. Consensus-based forecasting is where the majority of the opportunities lie for improving the forecast versus statistical methods.

All three myths are at the heart of the current trend in forecasting: trying to get more inputs into forecasting systems. Software companies and consultants promulgated the first and second myths in order to make sales (or sell business on their software). These actors were able to convince industry to invest in complex software by promising better forecasts, but without ever proving that these more complex solutions would improve forecasts.

The third myth is primarily a reaction to the first two myths. Since the more advanced methods did not improve the forecast (so the argument goes), statistical methods are now less important than getting the input of more groups to improve the forecast. This myth resulted, in part, from not understanding why statistical methods failed to meet the lofty expectations that were placed upon them.

A More Accurate Way to Think About CBF

Many of the ways that CBF is described and discussed in relation to statistical methods are simply inaccurate and not particularly functional or helpful. A more accurate way of thinking about CBF is as follows:

> *CBF is a forecasting method that is used in conjunction with statistical methods. It is important that CBF is performed effectively.*

Both statistical and CBF forecasting are important, require investment, and must have software designed specifically for each process in order to work properly. If one were starting from scratch designing an enterprise application to support CBF, it would look quite a bit different than an application designed for statistical forecasting. This fact is well known by anyone familiar with both processes, and yet, statistical forecasting applications continue to be used for CBF.

The best approach is not to think in terms of "either statistical or consensus," but to think in terms of using both. The financial benefits of more accurate forecasts will pay for the cost of implementing and maintaining both consensus and statistical software and processes. Simply put, companies should strive to be good at both consensus and statistical forecasting.

The Historical Problem with Consensus Methods

Much like the optimism on statistical methods and software in the 1990s, the current thinking on CBF oversimplifies the challenges inherent in this process.

In fact, many of the conversations I have had and articles I have read on this topic have convinced me that the majority of companies that implement CBF in the coming years will waste a large amount of their budgets implementing CBF forecasting systems. There are two primary reasons for this:

1. Most decision makers selecting CBF software are unfamiliar with the distinctions between software designed explicitly for CBF and software designed explicitly for statistical forecasting and *the best solution is almost always a different vendor for each.*

2. The difficulty of implementing CBF processes is being greatly underestimated. CBF requires the same type of executive backbone that, when lacking, has doomed countless master data management projects. An effective CBF process means *filtering out less effective forecasts and elevating the better forecasts based upon historical performance and without regard for the point of origin of the forecast input.* If a company is not willing to do this, even the most outstanding CBF software will not make their project a success.

Because of the current state of knowledge regarding CBF, it is quite likely and even predictable that in the future, the pendulum will swing back to statistical methods as being considered a better opportunity to "improve the forecast" over consensus methods, the reputation of which will be sullied by a number of failed implementations. It is well known in the cognitive sciences that recent history is more powerful at controlling interpretation of future threats and opportunities and there is a strong human nature to fight the last battle. However, a studied analysis of demand planning software from its beginning paints a very different picture than the current general consensus on this topic.

CBF and Bias

Incentives are very important to understanding CBF. In fact, judgment methods of forecasting have always been problematic due to the motivations of the individual creating the forecast. One of the best examples of this is the sales forecast, which often ends up being a salesperson's quota. Salespeople obviously have an incentive to keep their quotas low so that they can eventually exceed their quotas and collect their bonuses. In another real life example, which I witnessed at a client's site, regions within the company competed with other regions in order to receive an allocation of inventory, which was based upon the forecast. In this particular company, compensation is tied in part to the size of the forecast, even if it is unrealized by future sales. Certainly, the many people reading this book can find similar perverse incentive schemes within their own companies; schemes that interfere with the development of unbiased forecasts.

Any forecast that can affect the compensation of its creator in a significant way is going to have a bias. This is an example of a conscious forecast bias; there is also unconscious bias. People thinking that they are better forecasters than they actually are is a good example of unconscious bias. This is well documented and is as true of the everyday worker as the leadership in organizations (as several studies have demonstrated, including one that showed a negative correlation between the performance of the stock market and a CFO's predictions of the stock market).

There are several ways to setup a CBF process so that bias is reduced:

1. Limit the forecasting group to those that have domain expertise.
2. Adjust inputted forecasts consistent with their previous error level.
3. Use the error reports as a tool for counseling the forecaster.
4. Reduce the contributor's forecast to the final forecast.

All of these techniques are much more difficult to implement than one would think, because poor quality forecasts sometimes come from politically powerful parts of the organizations. These stakeholders generally don't want their input reduced, and will fight—and often win—the right to perpetually provide bad forecasts. Companies are made up of individuals with differing objectives and incentives. If bad forecasts can be produced that hurt the company but are of some advantage to certain individuals, these individuals will continue to submit bad forecasts. On the other hand, some individuals produce poor quality forecasts because they have no real interest in forecasting and don't put very much effort into the process. It is desirable to remove these forecasters from the process as is brought up by Michael Gilliland in the following quote:

In some cases, it may be possible to improve performance with some education or technical training for the participants. In other cases, the only solution is to eliminate the problematic step or participant from the process. Most people are not going to complain when they are excused from the forecasting process. There aren't that many people who actually like being responsible for forecasting!

If this is the case with some of the people in your organization and their forecasts are not adding value, then they are, of course, the first people to remove from the forecasting process.

The Sales Forecast

The sales forecast is a consensus forecast created among different salespersons and sales leaders, and is developed by the sales organization. This forecast is then entered as part of another consensus forecast to become part of both the S&OP and the operational forecast. Sales forecasting is so specialized that at least one best-of-breed vendor only focuses on sales forecasting, and a number of other vendors address sales forecasting as distinctly separate from other types of forecasting.

The sales forecast is generally considered the least accurate of all the inputs to the consensus-based forecast. The inaccuracy of the sales forecast is related to how the sales forecast is used to set quotas for salespeople (as was discussed earlier in this chapter). According to a survey by Right90, a leading sales forecasting vendor, only twenty-seven percent of companies are either *very* or *highly confident* in their sales forecast. They report that they do not trust the forecast for the following reasons:

- Forecast inaccuracy
- Lack of details
- Management judgment is too subjective
- Incompleteness of forecast
- Forecasts are not timely
- Too many versions (of the sales forecast) in spreadsheets

Not surprisingly, operation departments within companies have the lowest confidence in the sales forecast. I can speak to this first hand. When I worked for a software vendor, I never found the salespeople's projections of what account would sell and what wouldn't to be reliable. I don't think the salespeople were misleading me; I think they actually thought the probability of any prospective client becoming a real customer was higher than it actually was. However, when it comes to committing to a forecast number, their "forecast" changes; salespeople will often set the minimum acceptable number as the forecast, an action that is called "sandbagging" the forecast. When sales forecasts are compared against historical data of actual sales, I am not sure that most sales forecasts actually meet the definition of a forecast, which is why I sometimes place the word "forecast" in quotation marks. In fact, after a review of forecaster bias in a variety of fields, it would seem that the quotation marks are the most appropriate way of describing forecasters' proposals about the future.

Below is a quote from the head of AIG Financial Products, the company that provided credit default swaps, or insurance to mortgage-backed securities. The quotation is just prior to the mortgage-backed security meltdown, which resulted in hundreds of billions in losses on the exact financial instrument being described by Cassano below:

> *It is hard for us, without being flippant, to even see a scenario within any kind of realm of reason that would see us losing one dollar in any of those transactions.*[13]
>
> — Joseph J. Cassano (at an August 2007 Conference)

---

[13] Many companies are unhappy with their forecast accuracy. However, if we are charitable and assume that Joseph Cassano could have seen a scenario where AIG could have lost ninety-nine cents (he said he could not see AIG losing a dollar) on all of their credit default swaps, his forecast error is more than a hundred billion percent. Let's just say Joseph Cassano is not someone I would want involved in any consensus-based forecasting process. The fact that Cassano was providing a forecast on something which he was so involved in creating and in which he had a great personal financial and reputational stake invalidated the value of his prediction.

The research firm, Gartner, provides more insight to this topic. Gartner is on record as stating that sales and marketing input into the S&OP process is one of the lowest quality inputs (and most biased) of the overall S&OP process. According to Charles Chase of SAS and many other specialists in the field, the sales forecast typically has the highest degree of bias and is the least accurate. Bias is the most extreme in sales forecasts, but bias is found to a lesser degree in all forecasting inputs. For instance, the marketing forecast often has the opposite bias from the sales forecast, as the marketing forecasters have a tendency to think the market opportunities are greater than they are. (Again, salespeople tend to be strongly optimistic, but what they put down as a forecast is strongly influenced by the incentives that are presented to them.)

In Charles Chase's book, he recommends that the weight sales forecasting should receive depends greatly upon the following considerations:

> *The key to success is to ask the sales and marketing departments to look at macro trends in the marketplace by account and channel and hold them accountable for measuring and improving forecast accuracy. In some industries where there is a great deal of available upstream data (consumer packaged goods, apparel and automotive manufacturing), the sales department will have less input, with the marketing department having more input. However, in industries where upstream data are limited (telecommunications, heavy manufacturing, and semiconductor), the sales department will play a key role in the demand-driven forecasting process.*
> — Demand Driven Forecasting

Supply Chain Forecasting Software

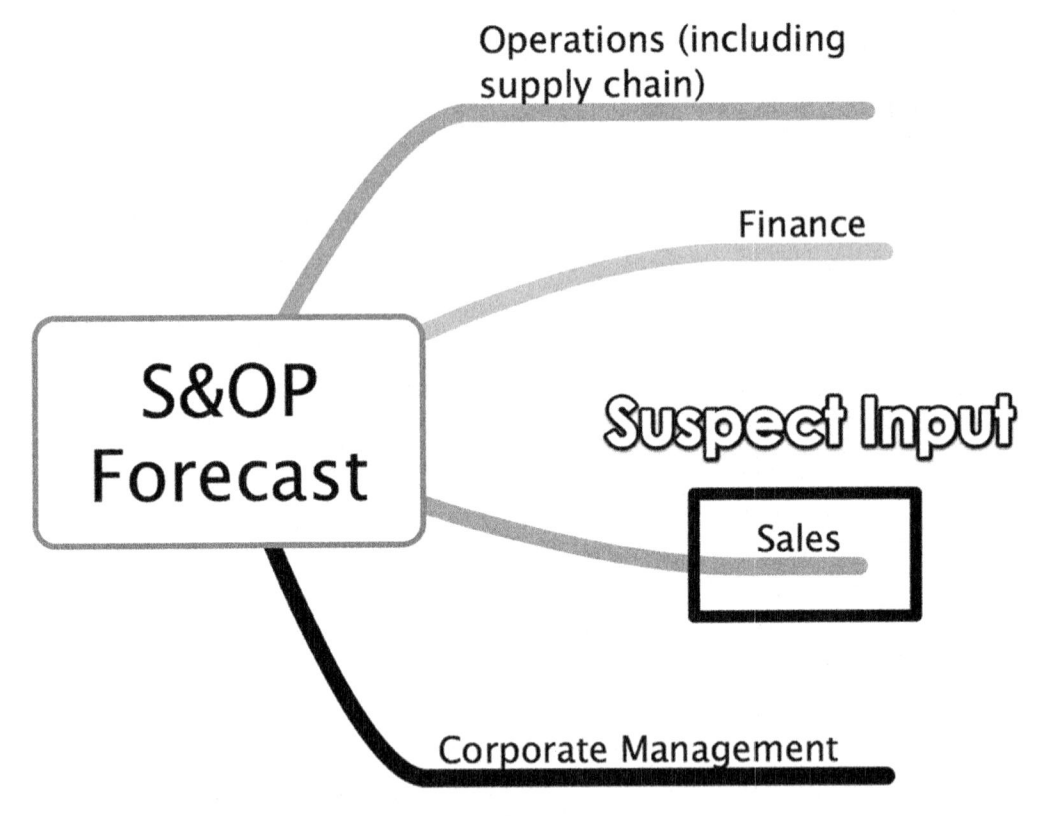

Operations (including supply chain)

Finance

S&OP Forecast

Suspect Input

Sales

Corporate Management

Of the different forecasting inputs, the sales forecast is more often than not the most suspect.

Consensus-based Forecasting Explained

Right90 Forecast Factors = Trust Factor

- Accuracy
- Bias
- Completeness
- Consistency

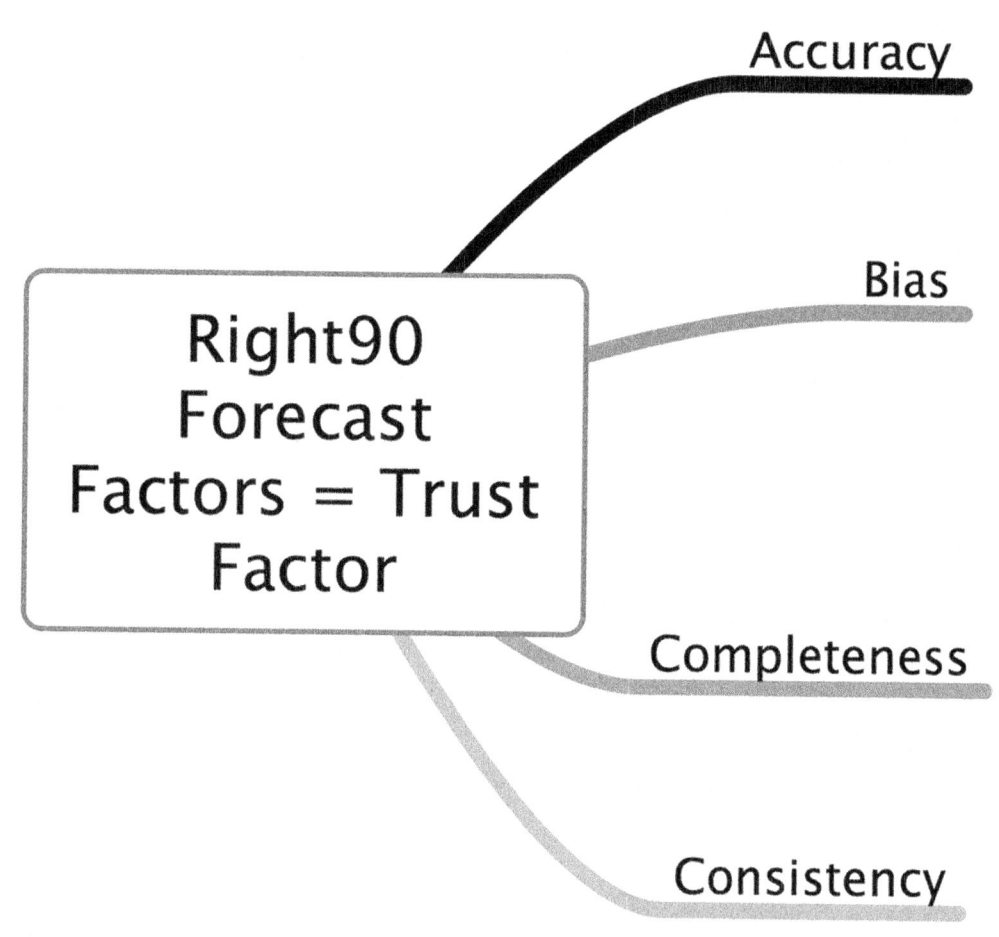

Above: Right90's trust factor is a combined statistic.

Right90 brings up the following good point regarding sales forecasts:

> *This concession by executives to allow the forecast to be dynamic has a flip side as well. Sales reps who game the system and make artificially low forecasts but raise them at the last minute look like heroes should not be tolerated. Companies need to track forecasts over time and watch for patterns of abuse. Some companies offer incentives for forecast accuracy (not too high or too low) as a carrot, and set quotas higher as a stick to discourage this kind of behavior.*
>
> — Right90

However, Right90 proposes that sales departments are, in fact, starting to be held more accountable for the quality of their forecasts. They are the experts in this topic; however, if this were the case, I would argue that the sales forecast accuracy issues would not persist. To be optimistic regarding such a long-standing problem like this (as people are predisposed to positive projections), I would need to see quantitative improvements.

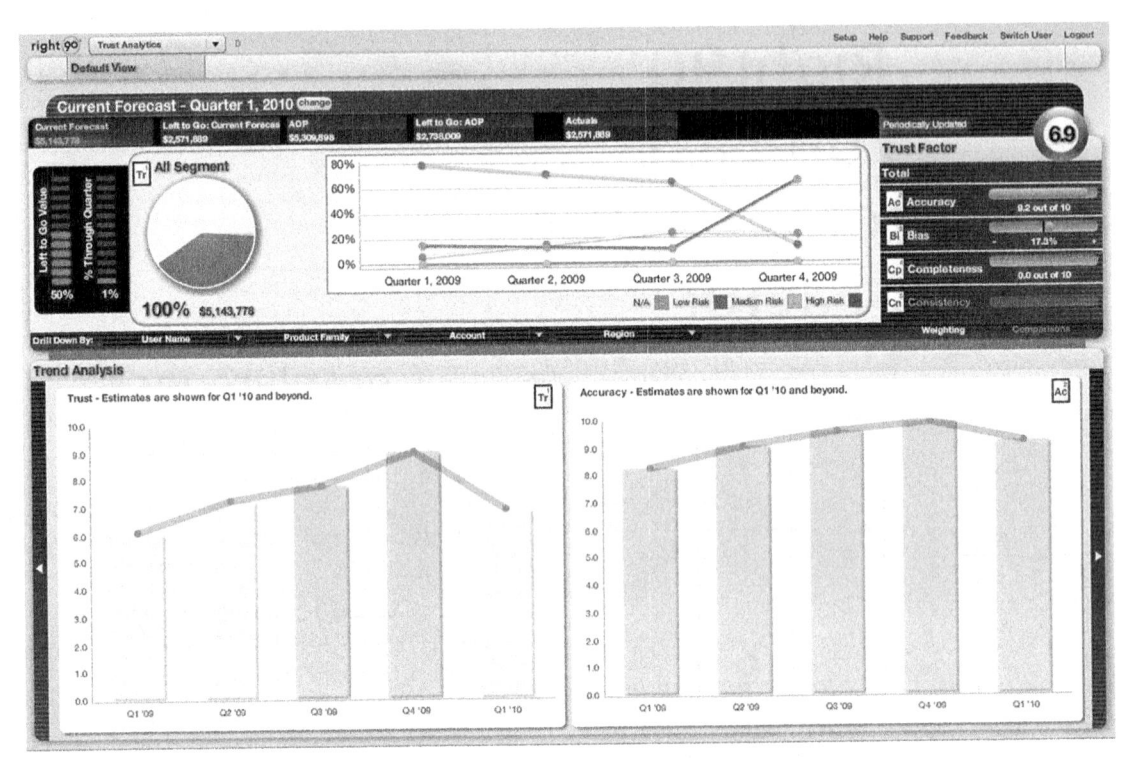

The Trust Factor is made up of multiple values, all which measure accuracy, bias completeness and consistency. Right90 provides a time phased view of these factors as the screen shot above demonstrates.

The sales forecasting process does not necessarily have to be included in the supply chain planning forecast. If the sales forecast continues to have such bias, it should be isolated within the sales department and used by the sales team for the purposes of sales quota setting and so on.

The S&OP Forecast

S&OP forecasting is a highly aggregated subcategory of CBF and is performed primarily by the leaders of the company. S&OP has a very strong finance overlay, and S&OP forecasts tend to be stated in dollars. This dollarization of a forecast is performed within the application and calculates the following formulas:

1. **The Product's Forecast in Units x the Unit Selling Price = Unit Sales**
2. **The Product's Forecast in Units x the Unit's Cost = Unit Costs**
3. **Sales – Costs = Profit**

All of the above are often analyzed at different levels of aggregation by different categorizations during the S&OP process, which is why an application that can perform attribute-based forecasting is very helpful. The per item dollarized values above is then combined with operating costs to help finance understand how much funding is required in the future periods. S&OP is a common focus of complaint and is an area of software that many companies always seem on the brink of implementing. It is not uncommon to hear complaints like this within companies:

> *This company has no S&OP process; it's simply whatever sales thinks we can sell.*

This quote reinforces what I have witnessed: operations is generally not given an equal place at the table with sales and finance in S&OP, and therefore at many companies, S&OP could more accurately be called S&FP (Sales and Finance Planning), leaving the "O" for operations out. The suggestion that operations have as equal a place at the table as sales and finance is not borne out by anything I have seen, but is endlessly accepted as an assumption by author's of books and articles on S&OP. If a company refuses to balance the inputs from the different groups in a company, there is not a lot a software solution can do, and an S&OP process which is managed in this way will always lack the feasibility aspect.

The MPS and S&OP

Research into the history of supply planning for the book *Supply Planning with MRP/DRP and APS Software,* has led me to conclude that at least some of the role of the master production schedule (MPS) has merged into the S&OP process.

(I speak here of the term MPS as its original meaning, not what it has often come to mean as simply the initial planning run.) See more on this topic below:

http://www.scmfocus.com/sapplanning/2011/06/18/why-mps-is-misnamed-in-sap-erp/

However, MPS works backward from supply and production planning, while S&OP begins at the opposite end—at the forecast. How MPS, which is one of the older terms in supply chain planning, became both part of and adopted by S&OP is an interesting story, which I describe in the article link below:

http://www.scmfocus.com/scmhistory/2011/10/how-mps-changed-through-time/

S&OP Software
From the software perspective, vendors that specialize in S&OP are still relatively new. Of all the vendors, Steelwedge is probably the one most often associated with S&OP. However, few companies actually use an enterprise S&OP application. Due to its highly aggregated and abstract nature, S&OP (unlike other types of forecasting) can be performed reasonably well with spreadsheets, although not optimally. S&OP software is dependent upon data supplied by the demand and supply planning systems and the production planning system. Because S&OP forecasts are dollarized, the price for each product must be extracted from the pricing system, and this allows companies to deal with both units and prices.

Why Forecasting Software is Only One Part of an S&OP Analysis
Whether experts in S&OP like it or not, the S&OP process has become overwhelmingly associated with forecasting. But, a complete S&OP process means going beyond forecasting, it means having a mechanism for understanding *the benefits along with the cost of increasing capacity.* Funding is the capacity that is often a focus of discussions about S&OP. Funding is the ability to pay for things that are required to meet the consensus sales forecast, such as inventory. However, a second important part of the funding question is the capital improvements that can be required to meet the consensus forecast. Capital improvements are

an example of constraints, and are much more complicated to estimate than the effect of carrying different levels of inventory.

Constraint Evaluation

S&OP planning is different with respect to how it deals with constraints from other supply chain planning processes. Supply planning and production planning systems accept constraints as restrictions, and attempt to move demand around constraints. To "level the load," the S&OP process is partially designed to determine which constraints can be "relaxed" or which capacity areas can be increased permanently in order to enable demand to be more efficiently handled, or simply for more demand to be handled. Doing so requires an understanding of the most restricting constraints, which can be done by analyzing the information from the demand, supply and production planning systems, combined with information from operations and finance regarding the costs of increasing different capacities.

Sensitivity Analysis

Sensitivity analysis is a method that can be used to identify and evaluate constraints and the cost of increasing the constraints (investing in larger warehouses, more production capacity, etc.). Some of this analysis can be performed by the supply and production planning software used to support the company's planning, depending on what that software is. Generally speaking though, enterprise supply and production planning software is not designed for constraint analysis, and in many cases it is more effective to model constraints in a separate application that specializes in this type of aggregated analysis and is designed to produce sensitivity analysis output. A detailed explanation of this topic is covered in the post below:

> http://www.scmfocus.com/supplychainsimulation/2011/10/25/a-sensitivity-analysis-approach-for-supply-chain-optimization/

In sensitivity analysis, the objective is to find ranges of change where the solution is "sensitive" to changes in the variables. I do not want to give the impression that sensitivity analysis is performed with much regularity. In fact, I cover this topic in much more detail in my book, *"Supply Planning with MRP/DRP and APS Software."* Sensitivity analysis is one of the major benefits of optimization, but it is not part of the standard supply planning process because supply planning is designed to accept rather than evaluate the constraints. Instead, sensitivity analysis is (or rather should be) part of the S&OP process or any strategy process in the company where the assumptions are laid out for evaluation. Supply planning works within the constraints, while S&OP (and strategic planning generally) observes constraints and then determines if it is profitable to increase the capacity of the system through investment.

Because of this dichotomy between S&OP and standard supply planning, enterprise vendors that offer optimizers within supply planning applications do not direct the development of their applications toward sensitivity analysis. On the other hand, most companies do not use general optimizers to perform sensitivity analysis, even though they can be quite effective at sensitivity analysis (common examples of this being CPLEX, MATLAB, or Frontline Solver). Instead, strategic decisions regarding constraints are, by in large, done without sensitivity analysis.

Even without sensitivity analysis tools in enterprise solutions, companies have several good options for performing sensitivity analysis, two of which are listed below:

1. Create a simplified optimization model in a general solver.
2. Run the enterprise optimizer in simulation mode and gather the solution points to develop a graphic for a particular variable/constraint to output combination.

Shadow Prices

Sensitivity analysis produces something called shadow prices, which are comparative across the different constraints that are modeled. The shadow prices can then be compared against the costs for increasing each constraint as provided by finance. While sensitivity analysis is the term used to describe the overall process of analyzing the relationship between constraints and the objective function, the shadow price is the specific change in the objective function that would occur if changes to constraints were made. Such an analysis can provide quantitative support for things like investing in certain areas of the business in order to increase specific constraints.

For more on this topic see the post below:

http://www.scmfocus.com/supplychainsimulation/2011/11/08/the-shadow-price/

Demand Side S&OP

The S&OP process can mean looking at both the demand and supply side of the equation. On the demand side, two important characteristics of an S&OP forecast differentiate it from a typical supply chain planning forecast:

1. It is aggregated.
2. It is dollarized.

The most common approach to the demand side of the S&OP process is to export forecasts from the demand planning application to spreadsheets or to an S&OP application. However, this is extra work and introduces more complexity into the process. What if S&OP forecasting could be performed inside of the same application that performs the normal supply chain demand planning? It turns out that this can be done in some applications. Demand Works' Smoothie is one of them. As described in Chapter 4: "Why Attribute-based Forecasting is the Future of Statistical Forecasting," Smoothie is very effective at forecasting aggregation and can do so along any attribute that is coded in the attribute tab in a spreadsheet or in Smoothie's attribute table.

That takes care of the aggregation requirement. As for the second requirement, Smoothie can dollarize the forecast by applying the price of the product by its unit forecast, and can display this in a tab called the Finance Tab, which can be seen on the following page:

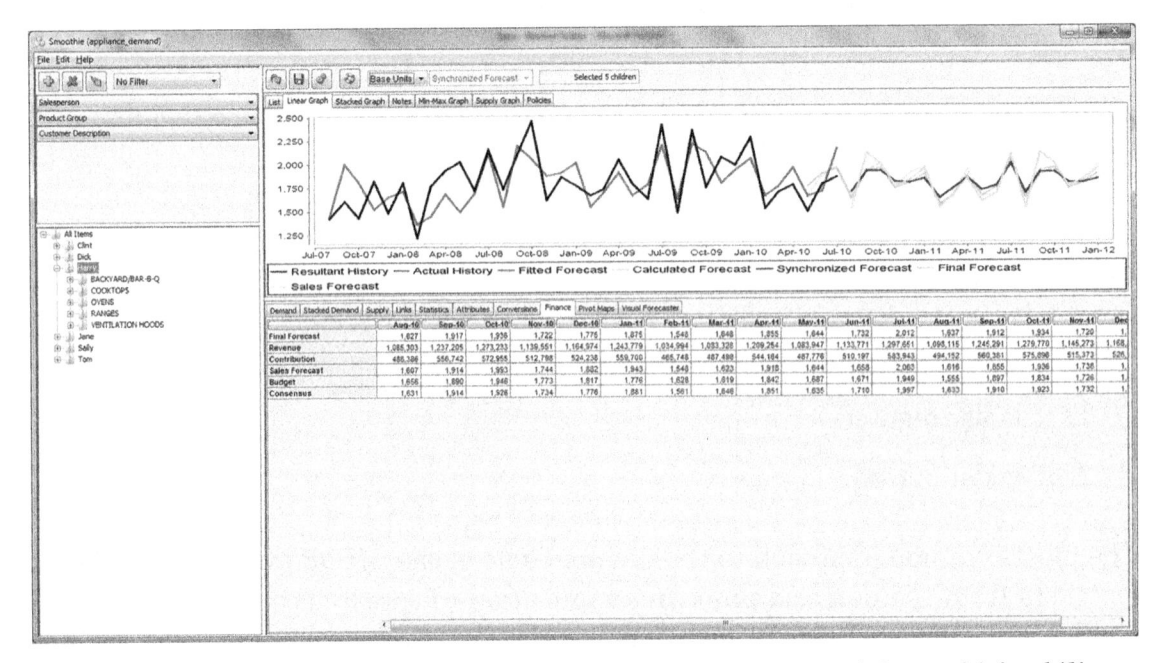

The finance tab interoperates with the Smoothie graphics, and Smoothie's ability to manually adjust the forecast (using the sliders) as described earlier in this chapter. This screen is good for screen-shared enabled conference calls where different forecast scenarios can be debated, and the consensus arrived at by all members having a visibility into the different scenarios produced by the application.

Smoothie is one of the few applications that can switch so effortlessly between traditional demand planning and S&OP.

Companies Steered to Inappropriate Solutions by the Major Consulting Companies

The vast majority of companies are using software that is inappropriate for managing their CBF process. Let's look at a typical scenario. A company has a statistical forecasting application in-house already, and their software vendor and consultants tell the company that CBF can be performed in a statistical system. The natural inclination is to "get more from the current system." Because the company is not aware of the different options in this area, it should not be a surprise that they listen to this flawed advice to use the systems they already have.

More often than not, the large consulting companies provide their clients with inaccurate information both on what CBF is and what solutions exist to meet the needs of a CBF process. Because the large consulting firms do not have relationships with these best-of-breed CBF vendors, and do not have resources trained in these applications to staff any project that might result from the purchase of new software, and as their personal financial benefit taints every recommendation they give, they simply won't recommend CBF software applications. The large consulting companies will recommend software from the large enterprise software vendors that they have relationships with and around which their consulting model is built, regardless of the appropriateness of the solution to the requirement. If consulting companies were providing accurate information, they wouldn't get their clients to stick with the wrong applications. However, this will not change, so companies must seek advice outside of the major consulting companies that are at this point, little more than implementation arms of the major software vendors.

Companies that use inappropriate applications have many challenges. Even just getting input from the necessary departments is a challenge, much less adjusting the results. If companies continue to do this, eventually CBF will decline as a trend, and the pendulum will swing back to statistical forecasting in terms of where the opportunities to improve the forecast are perceived to be. I could easily see this happening. The only evidence that would be necessary would be reported failures by companies that used statistical applications to perform CBF. That is literally how unscientific this process of switching the pendulum can be.

Where Major Vendors Stand with CBF

Innovative areas of the supply chain software market, such as CBF-specific software or inventory optimization and multi-echelon planning software, are a concern to the major vendors because their model is to put as little development effort as possible into their applications. Instead, they try to change the perception of their products through slick marketing. They will attempt to co-opt (often successfully) any area that is new and potentially attractive with a combination of the following powerful tactics:

1. Salesmanship
2. Marketing/Advertising

3. Leveraging their pre-existing relationships with existing clients and major consulting firms

4. Targeted acquisitions

This is the luxury enjoyed by large vendors due to their monopoly power. They can wait for innovation to be generated by the smaller vendors, and then co-opt it after it starts to become popular. They want to convince their customers that they already have anything new and innovative in their suite, meaning that it's pointless for customers to look elsewhere. If they can convince companies that a one-size-fits-all approach will work in every domain of the supply chain, then they win. While they may acquire a best-of-breed CBF vendor after this book is published, currently I do not see a true CBF solution from any of the major vendors. As of now, they have little need to acquire a best-of-breed CBF vendor as they are quite successful at getting their clients to use statistical applications for CBF.

http://www.scmfocus.com/sapplanning/2010/03/27/how-sap-dp-should-not-be-used-for-consensus-based-forecasting/

Conclusion

CBF forecasting covers a wide variety of forecasting types and involves combining forecast inputs from individuals in multiple departments within the company. Major types of CBF include, but are not limited to, sales forecasting and S&OP. CBF can be merged with statistical forecasting in any number of ways. There are significant CBF opportunities at all companies I have consulted with, but there are significant knowledge limitations that can hinder the success of CBF software implementations.

The sales forecasting process is one of the major types of CBF. Sales forecasting is one of the trickiest areas of CBF as the sales forecast tends to have the strongest bias. Therefore, the most important feature for this type of software is controlling for the sales forecast bias, which of course varies by individual salesperson. Right90, a vendor that specializes in sales forecasting, has strong measurements for bias and an administrative dashboard that allows for the identification of bias and the ability to adjust for bias within the application.

S&OP is a high-level process, which is both a type of CBF and incorporates requirements for estimating both the costs and benefits of constraint adjustment. The S&OP process is highly dependent upon planning systems for input. S&OP is both extremely aggregated and dollarized and tends to involve the most senior members of a company. The focus of S&OP tends to be on the demand side, and this is certainly where the process begins in its analysis. However, capacity evaluation is necessary, as well as integrated discussions with finance, in order to determine whether it is profitable to increase capacity.

One technique for determining the costs of various constraints is called sensitivity analysis. The costs of different constraints are not linear, so it is important to obtain the shadow price as well as the range of the shadow price. A range is necessary because, after a certain amount of capacity is added to one constraint, most often, another constraint then becomes the lowest cost constraint in which to invest. There are numerous books written on S&OP forecasting and it is currently a very hot topic of conversation. Although most the coverage tends to be management rather than software oriented.

Recently, very capable CBF software applications have been introduced, but few companies that could benefit are familiar with these vendors or are implementing these applications. Software designed for statistical forecasting continues to be used for most CBF processes. I have witnessed numerous projects like this and it is very difficult for a CBF project to achieve its goals when this basic mistake is made. Secondly, because the forecast is so central and political, CBF implementations are more political than statistical forecasting implementations. By and large, companies receive poor quality information on CBF from the major consulting companies. As this situation does not seem likely to change, companies must take the lead in educating themselves as to the best solutions for their CBF needs.

Case Study: Product Database Segmentation

Dividing the product database and treating the segments differently allows for a better use of demand planning resources. This strategy is very effective as different groupings of products benefit from different forecasting approaches. Most companies already have this segmentation set up, and products that typically start out as sales forecasted items, over time, become statistically forecasted items. The line between sales and statistically forecasted is not unchanging. Products can migrate back again to become a sales forecasted item if there is a product promotion.

However, I found a company that did not segment their database in this manner. I discussed with them using a formula, similar to the spreadsheet and formula I developed with another client for forecastable and unforecastable products. This formula splits the database into sales and statistical items. The formula uses the length of time a product has been in existence and uses the product's statistical forecast error. Items that have been in the product database for some time and have a lengthy demand history could become sales forecasted items if they are on promotion. Essentially, any known one-time event could switch an item from statistical to sales forecasted. The spreadsheet can be coded for events like promotions, and any item that is coded as having an upcoming promotion would be set as a sales item, regardless of any other factor. The formula can have a variety of "OR" functions; that is, if any of the criteria are met, the item moves from statistical to sales.

CHAPTER 8

Collaborative Forecasting Explained

Collaborative Forecasting
Obtaining input from outside the company creates collaborative forecasts. The most common collaboration partners are a company's customers or suppliers. Very little software has been developed specifically for collaborative forecasting, and in fact, most collaborative forecasts are shared through files rather than within an application. One of the issues with collaborative forecasting is that partners must share an application that usually is implemented by a company external to their own. Not participating in the selection and implementation of the system eventually becomes an impediment to learning about the system and to the system's uptake by the partners.

Several of the applications under the "supplier collaboration" category (for example, SAP SNC) have demand collaboration capability in addition to several other collaboration workflows. However, there are few successful implementations of these applications in this way, which is one reason why I provide very little coverage of collaborative forecasting in this book.

Those individuals that promote the benefits of collaboration tend to ignore the fact that customer and supplier relationships are not merely collaborative, but are also competitive. The buyer is trying to get the lowest price and the best service and terms, while the seller is trying to get the highest price, offer the lowest service and obtain the best terms for themselves. Secondly, not all companies have equal power. Larger companies will often push around or "Wal-Mart" smaller companies and wring concessions out of them that they never could if the companies were more equally matched. Many suppliers don't actually like dealing with their customers, and do not trust them and vice versa. The reality of the business world is not a series of buyers and sellers simply getting along, all united in their dedication to fairness and to improving supply chain efficiencies. Authors that describe the situation as if companies are neutral entities just waiting for an MBA with technology in tow to improve their collaboration are wasting their reader's time. This competitive dynamic is often glossed over by those more interested in promotion than in describing the reality of business relationships, a point that is illustrated by Walt Grischuk in his book, *Supply Chain Brutalization: Handbook for Contract Manufacturing*.

> *Even though the OEM (original equipment manufacturer) may share the forecast with the CM (contract manufacturer), nothing (transactional) typically happens until the purchase order is placed. The forecast is a nice planning tool—for discussion only. Anyone in the downstream supply chain aligning inventory or capacity to support the forecast does so at their own risk.*

Contract manufacturing is one of the lower "trust" environments. How often companies actually use shared forecasts remains an open question. Most authors who wish to sell the potential of collaborative forecasting pick up consulting business for themselves (which often means convincing companies that they are missing out on something), or stay away from controversial topics, or have generally trumped up forecast collaboration. Therefore, the real level of forecast collaboration is much less than the best-case scenario often presented in the literature. Collaboration projects are generally quite challenging; their challenges come from multiple areas and are generally greatly underestimated. More on this is covered in the following post:

http://www.scmfocus.com/supplychaincollaboration/2010/10/why-collaboration-projects-are-like-herding-cats/

Electronic supply chain collaboration between companies generally has been strongest for the objects that initiate a sale or are a notice for the impending receipt of a product, such as purchase orders (POs) or advanced shipment notifications (ASNs), which are a signal for a product to be sent between companies. Electronic supply chain collaboration is the weakest in areas that are informational in nature or internal, including forecasts. I would like to say that this will change in the future; however, there is no evidence that it actually will. Companies have been talking about increasing their forecast collaboration for decades, so it would be unwise to rely upon official statements to predict the future in this area. Every new technology was supposed to lead to a new age of collaboration between companies. Anyone interested in a good chuckle can simply go back and read articles from the late 1990s about how XML was going to greatly improve company collaboration. Those same authors, consultants and salespeople who falsely built up XML as a panacea are now off pumping up some other technology. The messaging on XML was so outrageous at one point in the late 1990s that I had to repeatedly explain to clients that XML was a document format, not middleware. Salesmen at my company had convinced these decision makers that XML would take care of all integration, so they should not worry. My salesmen had themselves, no idea what XML actually was.

Collaborative Versus Consensus Forecasting

In this book I have included a section on collaborative forecasting for the following reasons:

- To provide some realistic information as to the frequency with which collaborative forecasting is employed (often lacking in many of the articles on the topic)
- To properly differentiate collaborative forecasting from consensus forecasting

Some of the literature on collaborative forecasting reads as if the companies come together to arrive at a forecast, making collaborative forecasting sound suspiciously like CBF. However, in the vast majority of cases, collaborative forecasting really comes down to one company sharing its forecast with another company. The receiving company then chooses—quite unilaterally—if it will use the forecast. In fact, the term "sharing" is a more accurate description of what happens in reality than "collaboration." Because the forecasts are shared rather than collaborated on, it makes little sense to use CBF software for the collaborative process flow. Secondly, CBF and collaborative forecasting work at two entirely different levels of aggregation.

Types of Forecast Collaboration Software

Forecasts can be shared between supply chain partners using the following two methods:

1. Collaboration based upon an agreed-upon file format

2. Collaboration based upon a collaborative participant logging into an application

EDI-based Forecast Collaboration

The majority of supply chain collaboration between companies still takes place via EDI (electronic data interchange), which is a type of file-based forecast collaboration (forecast collaboration is just one of the objects that can be shared with EDI). The most common forecasting EDI transaction is the 830. Many companies publish how to interact with them via EDI on their web sites. The following was taken from Kroger's document, *Introduction to 830's aka Forecasting*, which I found online and is instructive of the level of detail available right on the web:

> *Kroger/Peyton is currently using a new forecasting tool that will allow the supplier to receive, via EDI, a thirteen-week forecast of item movement for the Kroger Local DCs and a seventeen-week forecast of item movement for the Peyton Regional DCs. This information will be communicated to the supplier in the EDI 830 transaction. This new tool utilizes key historical and promotional plan factors such as display, retail price, advertised, and item seasonality, to create an item forecast. This forecast has proven to be very accurate in forecasting future movement for items shipping from our distribution centers.*

Non-EDI File-based Forecast Collaboration

EDI is only one method of exchanging files. It has a couple of advantages: it's been around for some time and it has a series of defined formats that are universally published. However, decades of EDI use demonstrates that it, in fact, has high overhead. The use of SaaS-based electronic trading solutions is reducing this overhead by a good deal as described in the quote below from the site Finance Director Europe:

> *The SaaS takes care of the message mapping requirements, communications protocols and dialogue with the trading partners. All this is managed with no need for extra hardware or software. SaaS is 'multi-tenanted' so costs are spread over all users. Firms with small volumes of transactions can benefit without large capital outlay.*

XML is another method for electronic data exchange. For some time XML was the toast of the town and a magic tonic and cure to all applications integration ills, but it has not taken off as it was over-promoted. There is simply a much lower up-side than was originally advertised for something that is basically a marked-up HTML document, even if it is self-describing and has extra fields added to it (although XML is also involved in the translation of EDI messages). Both SAP and Oracle accept XML forecast documents in their demand collaboration solutions. However, much of this is simple trendiness. Customers like to hear the word "XML" and it makes applications more marketable that use the document standard, so vendors add XML to their applications.

Many applications can receive forecasts from collaboration partners in the form of spreadsheets or flat files, an advantage for companies that are not interested in having customers log into the application, but would prefer to stay away from EDI or XML. These spreadsheets or flat files can be imported into the application directly. This requires relatively low effort on the part of the collaborative partner. Essentially they need to export the forecast from their system and then format the extract to match the application's file format. This is simple to do with a transformation script. However, because the application file formats are proprietary to the vendors, the partner has to maintain multiple formats and multiple transformation scripts to collaborate with other partners, each of whom might be using a different application. One of the advantages of EDI, even though it is unwieldy and archaic, is that the file formats are published and agreed upon and have been for many years.

Application-based Forecast Collaboration
When the collaborators actually log into the application user interface in order to provide their input, this is called application-based forecast collaboration. Applications such as SAP SNC use a thick client (the normal SAP GUI) for most of the application screens. However, for partner collaboration, the application produces an HMTL interface so that it can be accessed by partners without having to install any software on their computers. Other applications, such as E2Open, offer a SaaS solution so that the entire application is web-based.

My personal view is that companies that maintain SaaS solutions—regardless of the domain of the software—make better collaboration environments. Software vendors like E2Open and Arena Solutions (for bill of material management), or Consensus Point (for CBF) create better collaboration environments than those that do not offer SaaS solutions. Therefore, SaaS applications should always be given top priority during software selections where collaboration is a need.

Facebook is probably the most collaborative application in the world. Essentially, it is an SaaS solution in terms of technology, although we don't refer to it as SaaS as it simply is known as a website. It is difficult to imagine that Facebook would have grown to be the number two website on the Internet after Google if Facebook had required that their users download a "Facebook application" before they could begin collaborating. Social media sites, in general, have shown how powerful web front-ends are for enabling collaboration. In fact, social media sites have done a far superior job of enabling widespread collaboration than any vendor focused on the enterprise market for collaboration. Companies like Facebook and Twitter make their sites very easy and inviting to use. While posting vacation pictures or entering a "tweet" is much less challenging than collaborating on thousands of SKUs, the enterprise software vendors still have a great deal to learn from the social media sites.

Collaboration environments must also be easy to use for the following reasons:

1. A good proportion of those logging into the system do not work for the company that controls the application.

2. Unlike forecasting applications that a company buys for its own use, companies cannot force employees at other companies to use a poor user interface; one that consumes a lot of time to accomplish a task.[14] Executives and large consulting companies have become so used to force-feeding software with poor user interfaces to their internal workers, that when a weak collaboration user interface fails to gain user compliance within their collaboration partners, they are a bit beside themselves as to how that could have happened. And of course unlike with internal IT implementations, excecutives do not have the luxury of blaming their customers or suppliers for being stupid when they don"t use their poorly rolled out application.

Controlling the Collaborative Forecasting Input

A specific group of people is invited to have input; this is one of the core concepts of both consensus and collaborative forecasting. That group should have the domain expertise—as well as the correct incentives—to improve forecast accuracy, the first step toward controlling forecast quality. When obtaining collaborative input, a company will often find that some companies add value to the forecast, while others do not.

As with consensus forecasting, it's necessary to measure the forecast accuracy of individuals (and in this case companies) over time and reduce or eliminate the input from those with a poor forecast accuracy, and increase the input of those who increase forecast accuracy. For a variety of reasons, not every company is a good candidate for collaborative forecasting. And also, as with consensus forecasting, if the owners of the collaborative forecasting application are not willing to adjust the weightings of the input based upon the history of accuracy for each participant, then the collaborative process is unlikely to add very much value to the forecast.

Collaborative forecasting has a distinct advantage over consensus forecasting because those participants who are "adjusted down" in their influence on the

---

[14] Large companies can exert great pressure on smaller companies to comply, which not coincidentally is the environment where many of the successful collaboration projects occur.

forecast are external to the company, which makes reduction of their input or their removal from the process much easier. However, this does not stop individuals inside of the company from siding with an external participant and lobbying against their forecast input being reduced.

Collaborative Forecasting Versus CPFR

Collaborative Planning Forecasting and Replenishment (CPFR) is a particular type of collaborative forecasting that is based upon a high degree of information sharing between the CPFR partners and has found application in retail. CPFR forecasts are over a short-time horizon, so it differs significantly from traditional supply chain forecasting. Some industry experts see CPFR as particularly beneficial for high inventory, turn consumer product items. SAP has a product built around it called SAP APO F&R (forecast & replenishment); however, it is not widely installed and CPFR has found success in only a few companies, the best known being Walmart.

CPFR is chronicled in many articles and several books have been written specifically about the concept. However, there is little doubt that CPFR is petering out as a trend. Lora Cecere at the Altimeter Group talks about what prevented CPFR from reaching its potential:

> *The results are clear. After ten years of active projects, collaborative planning forecasting and replenishment and VMI failed to reach its promise for three reasons:*
>
> ***Too laborious.*** *Just too much work for the benefit. The added costs did not measure up to the benefit.*
>
> ***Retail forecasts not up to the task.*** *For CPFR to work, retail forecast accuracy needs to be high and with sufficient granularity to ensure analysis. The dirty little secret with CPFR is that at most only three retailer forecasts—****Best Buy, Food Lion and Walmart****—were up to the task.*

Lack of integration into enterprise processes. *For most Advanced Planning System (APS)/Enterprise Resource Planning (ERP) deployments, there was no logical connection for the data.*

It should be pointed out that few analysts would write about why a supply chain concept or trend failed to meet expectations; Lora does that here, and should be commended for it.

Conclusion

Collaborative forecasts are technically the only category of forecasting that uses inputs from outside the company. However, there is significant conceptual overlap with consensus-based forecasting (a major distinction being that CBF is often aggregated, while collaborative forecasting has a strong tendency to be disaggregated). As with most supply chain CBF, forecast collaboration is a shallow area in terms of companies performing it in any meaningful way.

There are two basic approaches to forecast collaboration: to collaborate based upon an agreed-upon file format (such as EDI, XML or a spreadsheet) or to log into a collaborative system. Software for collaborative systems where participants log in should be one hundred percent web-based and easy to use; in fact, these points should be considered prerequisites for all collaborative software purchases. Vendors that have a SaaS solution for their collaborative system should be viewed as being in a different category than those that do not. When compared to the price of an SAP or Oracle application, the prices and implementation costs for SaaS-based collaborative software are very reasonable, leaving little reason not to use a specialized vendor for this area. Issues with integrating back to the advanced planning system or to the ERP system are minor, and the larger issue is how to get collaborative participants to actually use the software.

Corporations have been talking about collaboration for decades. However in a few short years, social media sites (which are essentially collaborative systems) have developed into major business models. They demonstrate that easy access in the form of web front-ends and pleasing user interfaces, as well as incentives (people like to collaborate with others in a many-to-many environment) is critical to increased participation. Companies and vendors have yet to master these twin criteria in order to make collaborative forecasting a widespread phenomenon. Secondly, most vendors are not recognizing the lessons regarding the necessity of ease of use of collaboration software. The success of collaboration websites like Facebook has had little to no impact on the products and approach of most forecasting collaboration vendors. The best collaboration application I have ever seen does not do forecast collaboration, and every forecast collaboration vendors is at least a decade behind this vendor. Information from this space is also not being used by consulting companies to adjust collaboration projects to help make them more successful.

For all the discussion about the importance of collaboration across the supply chain and how much opportunity there is to share information by web applications, it is interesting to note how much of a typical company's collaboration is still based upon EDI transactions. However, the fact that EDI information is passed between partners does not necessarily mean the data is used, and while collaboration on objects such as advanced shipment notifications and purchase orders is now commonplace, companies have been slow to move outside of what are essentially transactional objects and into planning objects like forecasts. Information sharing is certainly not limited by technology, and every year the technological barriers fall a bit more. Instead, it is limited, in part, by the relationships between buyers and suppliers, which are as much competitive as collaborative. This fact is left out of many white papers, conference presentations and books on the topic.

There are, and always have been, great opportunities in collaborative forecasting. However, given the problems across all forms of supply chain collaboration, the underperformance of collaborative forecasting should not surprise anyone. It should also be a cautionary tale; a number of actions must be performed in order to have success in this area. However, not many companies are that interested in following the rules of what works. For this and several other reasons I predict a continual high fallure rate for forecast collboration projects.

CHAPTER 9
Bias Removal

Introduction
In Chapter 7: "Consensus-based Forecasting Explained," I discussed the strong bias of the sales forecast. In this chapter, I will broaden out the analysis of bias, drawing upon examples outside of supply chain management. Bias is an uncomfortable area of discussion for many because it describes how people who produce forecasts can be irrational and have subconscious biases, or how people consciously bias their forecast in response to incentives. This discomfort is evident in many forecasting books that limit the discussion of bias to its purely technical measurement. No one likes to be accused of having a bias, which leads to bias being underemphasized. However uncomfortable as it may be, it is one of the most important areas on which to focus in order to improve forecast accuracy.

What is Bias?
Forecast bias is a tendency for a forecast to be consistently higher or lower than the actual value. Forecast bias is distinct from forecast error in that a forecast can have any level of error but still be completely unbiased. For instance, even if a forecast is fifteen percent higher than the actual values half the time, and fifteen percent lower than

the actual values the other half of the time, it has no bias. But forecast which is on average fifteen percent lower than the actual value has both a fifteen percent error and a fifteen percent bias. Bias can exist in statistical forecasting or in judgment methods. However, it is much more common with judgment methods and is in fact one of the major disadvantages with judgment methods.

After bias has been quantified, the next question is the origin of the bias. With statistical methods, bias means that the forecasting model must either be adjusted or switched out for a different model. Grouping similar types of products, and testing for aggregate bias, can be a beneficial exercise for attempting to select more appropriate forecasting models.

For judgment methods, bias can be conscious, in which case it is often driven by the institutional incentives provided to the forecaster. Bias can also be subconscious. A good example of subconscious bias is the optimism bias, which is a natural human characteristic. Forecasting bias can be like any other forecasting error, based upon a statistical model or judgment method that is not sufficiently predictive, or it can be quite different when it is premeditated in response to incentives. Bias is easy to demonstrate but difficult to eliminate, as exemplified by the financial services industry.

Positive Forecast Bias in the Financial Services Industry

Forecast bias exists in every type of forecasting, from supply chain forecasting to medical research to financial services industry forecasting and every type of forecasting in between. Covering financial services forecasting bias is useful for my purposes the following reasons:

1. Of the areas I researched for this book, the financial services industry is at the very end of the bias continuum, and yet considering how outlandish the bias is in this area, it is comparatively little discussed. This is because continuation of the financial services industry in its present from is based upon the projecting an image that there is, in fact, little bias.

2. The financial services industry also happens to be where there exist some of the strongest financial incentives to produce a forecast with a positive bias. These incentives cannot be disputed and are easy to demonstrate.

3. Historical forecasts from the financial services industry are some of the most publicly available forecasts. Financial services companies produce forecasts both for internal consumption and for external consumption. Their internal forecasts are, of course, hidden (and often do not match their published forecasts, which we know from the court documents of financial industry lawsuits), but their public forecasts are part of the historical record. Therefore, we know much more about their accuracy and bias than the forecasts of supply chain departments that do not publish their forecasts for external consumption.

4. The reason for each actor's conscious bias (we don't spend time discussing subconscious bias in the financial services industry) is well known and is based upon easy to trace compensation. Connecting the dots in financial services industry bias is child's play.

5. The long history of obvious forecast bias in the financial services industry, with so little changing in terms of institutional incentives or government regulation, provides an excellent example of how difficult it is to remove even the most obvious bias from a system.

A good example of the forecast bias, which is produced by institutional financial incentives, is described below:

> *Sell-side analysts are pressured to issue optimistic forecasts and recommendations for several reasons. First, their compensation is tied to the amount of trade they generate for their brokerage firms. Given widespread unwillingness or inability to sell short, more trade will result from a "buy" than from a "sell" recommendation. Second, a positive outlook improves the chances of analysts' employers winning investment banking deals. Third, being optimistic has historically helped analysts <u>obtain inside information from the firms they cover (underline added)</u>. While all these pressures introduce an optimistic bias to analysts' views, the magnitude of the bias is held in check by reputational concerns. Ultimately, an analyst's livelihood—the ability to generate trades and attract investment banking business—depends on her credibility.*
> — Anna Scherbina

This should be reminiscent of an earlier example of forecast bias: the sales forecast. While a salesperson can provide a deliberately low forecast, there is also a minimum level which the salesperson can forecast and still maintain their credibility. Obviously a salesperson cannot (at least normally) create a forecast of half of what they actually think will sell. In this way we can see that setting a forecast that matches the consumer's perception of the forecast occurs in many spheres. Anna Scherbina makes this point explicitly in the next quotation:

> *Analysts will set the optimistic bias at an optimal point that balances the benefit of being upbeat against the cost to their reputation.*
> — Anna Scherbina

Here the case is made that financial forecasters must trade off pressures to create optimistic forecasts with their reputational concerns. In this way, the forecast of financial analysts can be seen as less of a forecast and more of a *balancing act;* they attempt to develop numbers that garner favor with the powerful companies from whom the analysts' investment banks gain business while keeping some semblance of credibility with investors. This "credibility" also determines whether "information channels" are kept open or closed and highlights how political factors can influence a financial analyst's forecast.

> *If, in addition to being penalized for their forecast errors, analysts face an additional penalty (e.g., being cut off from the sources of inside information) for being too pessimistic relative to others, those with sufficiently low private estimates may decide to drop coverage altogether.*
> — Anna Scherbina

This is, in fact, a bias that affects all journalists as well. They are required to offer opinions on powerful institutions, but their ability to write about the institutions depends upon access to these institutions, which can be cut off if the journalist does not provide the type of spin that the institutions desire. Her research also alludes to the timing of when more biased forecasts can be expected. Institutions know this and use the control of access to reward those who disseminate information about them that they like and punish those who do not. I know this as a person who writes on supply chain planning software. The way to make the most money in writing is to write positively-biased articles that promote products and do not advise readers as to problems they may face. This is why most the information on the Internet regarding enterprise software conforms to this model. It is also an excellent way to attract and retain advertisers.

> *The tradeoff between career concerns and the pressure to be optimistic generates predictable patterns of forecast bias. In particular, optimistic forecast bias is increasing in the uncertainty of the underlying earning. This bias has two components, one that analysts deliberately add to their private estimates, another that arises when sufficiently negative views are kept quiet. Feeling less accountable in uncertain environments, analysts are inclined to issue more optimistic forecasts.*
> — Anna Scherbina

What this means is that financial analysts wait for certain times to create positively-biased forecasts. There are times when a positively-biased forecast will have less of a negative effect on one's reputation. Certainly the dot com stock bubble of the late 1990s was a perfect example. However, similar examples can be found during any period where there is a financial bubble. If we analyze the dot com bubble, we can find multiple layers of bias at work. Reported corporate earnings had a strong upward bias, or were rigged by compliant internal accounting departments and major auditing firms at the direction of senior executives who were over stimulated by stock option incentives. Analysts then added another layer of bias with their projections. After the stock bubble deflated, an enormous number of companies released earnings revisions, which means that the previous earnings during the stock bubble had been falsified. Very few company accountants, executives or external auditors were prosecuted for creating fake earnings, and few analysts were punished for creating clearly biased forecasts.

In terms of the final outcome, individuals in multiple areas made enormous amounts of money from these behaviors. The lesson for these individuals was to continue their behavior. The lesson for others, who observed these financial windfalls, was to produce their own biased financial forecasts. In this way, positively-biased forecasts were actively **promoted** by the overall market for projections and the regulatory environment. Many of the people who work in the regulatory bodies that oversee financial services also have a bias, as they often come from the financial services industry and return to industry positions when they leave their posts.

All of these biases continued after the dot com bubble and were instrumental in the 2008 US financial meltdown, and the same biases exist even as this book is published. The internal financial incentives remain in place, and any regulatory change has been primarily cosmetic, which is why future financial bubbles and meltdowns are in our future, even though it is entirely within our power to stop them. An evaluation of what factors lead to the great depression show a strong relationship to bias as well. With respect to bias in the financial services industry and other fields, very little changes from year to year. This brings up an important point for supply chain forecast bias: the question every organization should ask is what incentives have been created to perpetuate bias in the forecasts of those that work in the company. Once you begin to look for bias, it is easy to find.

Bias Accounted for at the UK Department of Transportation

In addition to financial incentives that lead to bias, there is a proven observation about human nature: we overestimate our ability to forecast future events. We also have a positive bias—we project that events that we find desirable will be more prevalent in the future than they were in the past. This is one of the many well-documented human cognitive biases. Cognitive biases are part of our biological makeup and are influenced by evolution and natural selection. This human bias combines with institutional incentives to give good news and to provide positively-biased forecasts.

The UK Department of Transportation is keenly aware of bias, and has developed cost uplifts that their project planners must use depending upon the type of project that is being estimated. An uplift is an increase over the initial estimate. Different project types receive different cost uplift percentages based upon the historical underestimation of each category of project. For instance, rail projects receive on average a forty percent uplift, building projects between four and fifty-one percent, and IT projects between ten and two hundred percent—the highest uplift and also the widest range of uplifts. A quotation from the official UK Department of Transportation document on this topic is telling:

Bias Removal

Our analysis indicates that political-institutional factors in the past have created a climate where only few actors have had a direct interest in avoiding optimism bias.

However, once an individual knows that their forecast will be revised, they will tend to adjust their forecast accordingly. Therefore, it is important that adjustments to a forecast be performed without the forecaster's knowledge. The UK Department of Transportation has taken active steps to both identify the source and magnitude of bias within their organization. They have documented their project estimation bias for others to read and to learn from. However, most companies refuse to address the existence of bias, much less actively remove bias. Several reasons why the most companies tend shy away from addressing bias are listed in the graphics below:

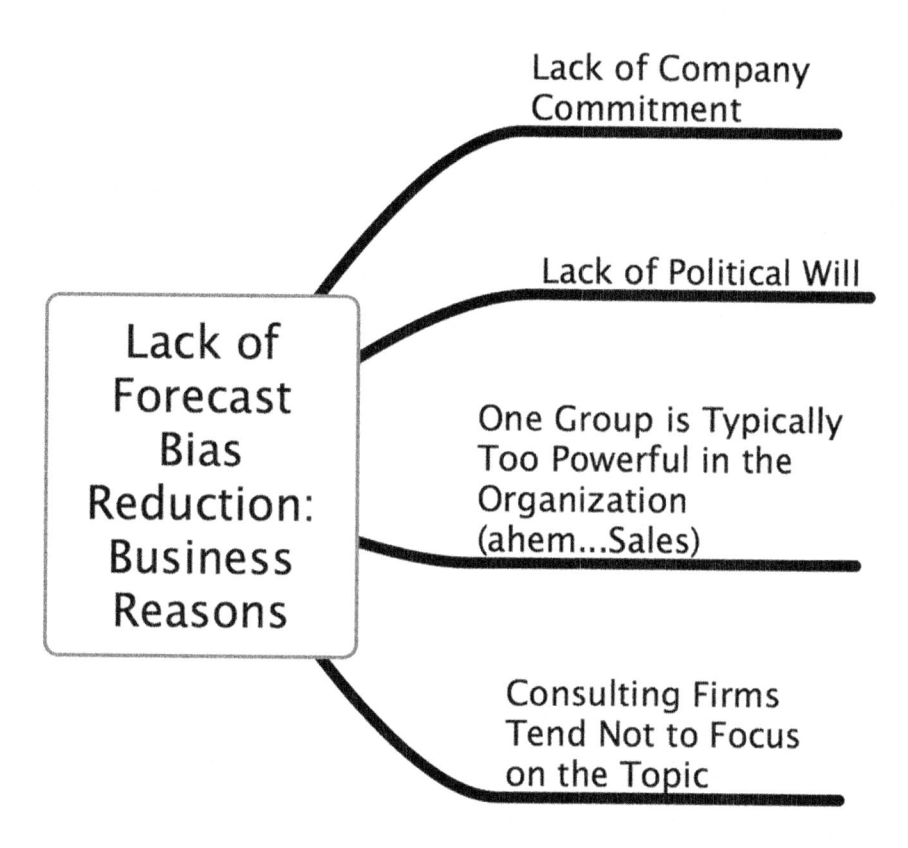

Lack of Forecast Bias Reduction: Business Reasons
- Lack of Company Commitment
- Lack of Political Will
- One Group is Typically Too Powerful in the Organization (ahem...Sales)
- Consulting Firms Tend Not to Focus on the Topic

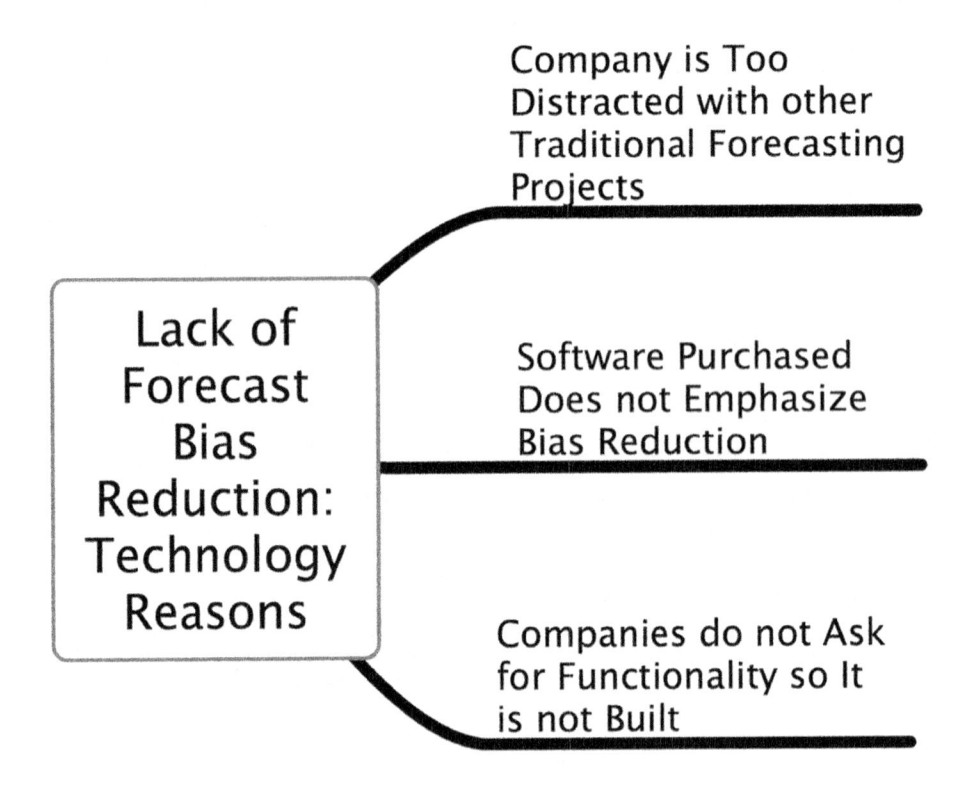

Lack of Forecast Bias Reduction: Technology Reasons

- Company is Too Distracted with other Traditional Forecasting Projects
- Software Purchased Does not Emphasize Bias Reduction
- Companies do not Ask for Functionality so It is not Built

How Large Can Bias Be in Supply Chain Planning?

A number of research studies point out the issue with forecast bias in supply chain planning. According to research by Shuster, Unahobhokha and Allen, forecast bias averaged roughly thirty-five percent in the consumer goods industry. They point to research by Kakouros, Kuettner, and Cargille (2002) in their case study of the impact of forecast bias on a product line produced by HP. They state: "Eliminating bias from forecasts resulted in a twenty to thirty percent reduction in inventory."

Bias Identification Within the Application

All of this information is publicly available, and can also be tracked inside of companies by developing analytics from past forecasts. Yet companies often do not track the forecast bias from their different areas (and, therefore, cannot compare the variance) and they also do next to nothing to reduce this bias. More on this is described at the following post:

http://www.scmfocus.com/demandplanning/2010/02/managing-the-politics-of-forecasting-bias/

Forecast bias can always be determined regardless of the forecasting application used by creating a report. However, it is preferable if the bias is calculated and easily obtainable from within the forecasting application. Bias tracking should be simple to do, and should be quickly observed within the application without performing an export. Of the many demand planning vendors I have evaluated over the years, one vendor stands out in their focus on actively tracking bias: Right90. The application's simple bias indicator, shown below, shows a forty percent positive bias, which is an historical analysis of the forecast.

Trust Worksheet		Return to Dashboard	Show Tr Details
Personnel	My Target Q4 ' 10	LTG Q3'09	Trust Factor
Alex Tyson	$150,000.00	$120,500.00	2.5
Brian Mandarich	$150,000.00	$125,000.00	3.1
Mia Utley	$150,000.00	$70,000.00	9.9
Serena Sanders	$150,000.00	$85,000.00	8.5
Michael Spitz	$150,000.00	$53,000.00	9.7
Total	$750,000.00	$453,500.00	7.4

Right90 explicitly measures and displays bias in the interface. The first step to addressing and removing bias is the ability to easily identify where it exists.

The Importance of Distinct Bias Removal Workflow and Functionality

Most forecasting applications I have come across do not have forecast bias adjustment workflow built into them. This workflow is important because the software must provide an easy and systematic way of reducing bias. As with most things, the more difficult something is to do, the less likely it is to get done.

Supply Chain Forecasting Software

So what is "forecast bias adjustment workflow?" Essentially, this is a dashboard or screen that allows both an easy review and adjustment of different forecasts. The dashboard is only available to forecast administrators. An example of this is shown below:

Personnel	Sales	QTD Actuals Q4 '10	My Target Q4 '10	LTG Q3'09	Trust Factor	Ac	Bi	Cp	Cn
Jason Dryer	$55,000.00	$29,500.00	$150,000.00	$120,500.00	2.5	3.7	-60%	2.0	3.0
Sandy Lewis	$200,000.00	$25,000.00	$150,000.00	$125,000.00	2.1	2.7	60%	4.0	2.0
Reggie Davidson	$150,000.00	$80,000.00	$150,000.00	$70,000.00	1.3	3.7	-55%	1.0	2.8
Bob Torrence	$160,000.00	$65,000.00	$150,000.00	$85,000.00	1.5	2.7	50%	2.0	4.0
Angela Rial	$190,000.00	$97,000.00	$150,000.00	$53,000.00	2.9	3.5	32%	1.0	2.5
Total	$775,000.00	$296,500.00	$750,000.00	$453,500.00	2.1	2.2	4.0%	2.0	3.2

Trust Worksheet — Elements of Trust

This screenshot compares the different forecast contributors. The supervisor of these contributors can then adjust their forecasts based upon each person's trust factor. It allows the forecast to be adjusted based upon previous bias of the individual making the contribution. See the graphic on the next page, which shows that the overall Trust Factor for the forecast being viewed is actually a combined value, with bias as just one component of the Trust Factor calculation.

Trust Factor		8.4
Total		
Ac Accuracy		8.2 out of 10
Bi Bias		20%
Cp Completeness		7.0 out of 10
Cn Consistency		7.2 out of 10

Being able to track a person or forecasting group is not limited to bias, but is also useful for accuracy. For instance, the screenshot on the following page is from Consensus Point and shows the forecasters and groups with the highest "net worth." This network is earned over time by providing accurate forecasting input.

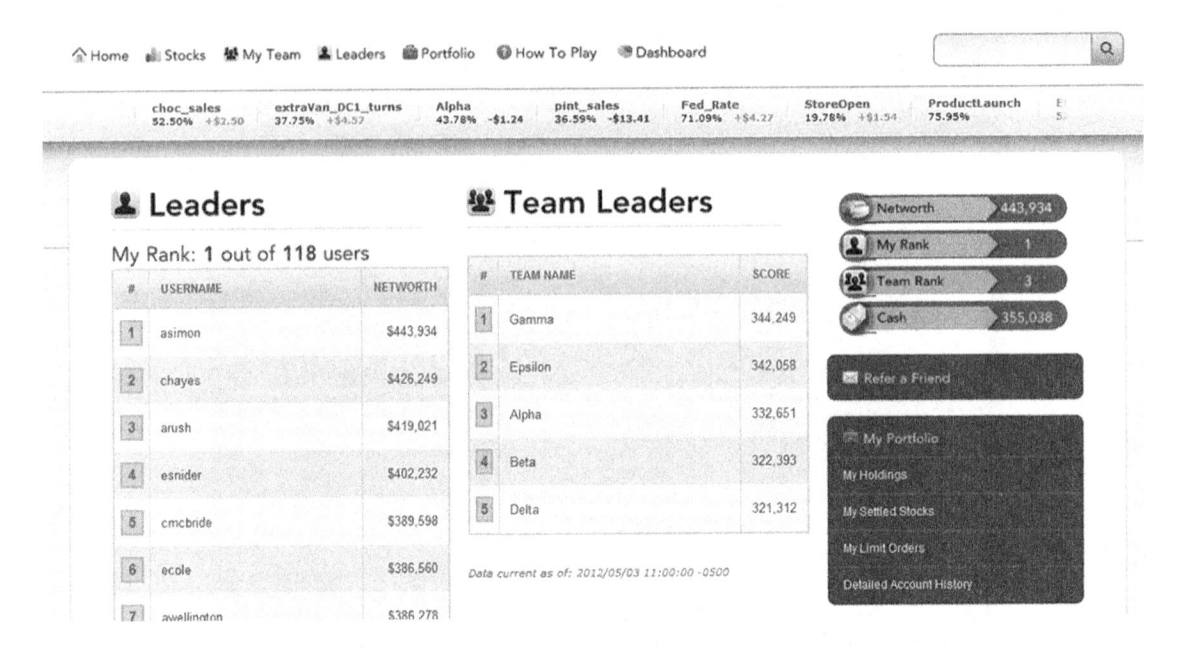

This provides a quantitative and less political way of reducing input from lower quality sources. It also promotes less participation from weak forecasters, as they can see that their input has less of an impact on the forecast. These types of performance dashboards exist in a few vendors, but forecasting accuracy could be greatly improved if they were universal. In all forms of forecasting, an easy way to compare the performance of forecasters is a necessity. Forecast inputs must be tracked and reviewed, and adjustments must eventually be made because there are wide quality differences between forecasters. These type of dashboards should be considered a best practice in forecasting software design.

The consensus-based vendors, Inkling Markets, Consensus Point and Right90, have the greatest focus on bias removal that I have seen. Why the statistical vendors lag in this area is an interesting question, and in my view can be rationally explained by the fact that judgment methods are known to have more bias than statistical methods.

Using Bias Removal as a Forecast Improvement Strategy

It's very difficult to find a company that is satisfied with its forecast. I have yet to consult with a company that has a forecast accuracy anywhere close to the level that it really could be. Everything from the use of promotions, to the incentives they have set up internally, to poorly selected or configured forecasting applications, stand in the way of accurate forecasts. I often arrive at companies and have to deliver the bad news about how their forecast systems are mismanaged and I am sometimes asked by a director, who is worn out by funding successive improvement initiatives for forecasting "but why have our results not improved." My answer is often that they are very simply violating the rules established in scholarly sources for forecast management, and therefore they have poor outcomes.

However, it is also rare to find a company that has a well thought-out plan for improving its forecast accuracy. When I listen to the plans from executives to improve their forecast, they almost always focus in the wrong areas and miss out on some of the most straightforward ways to obtain forecast improvement. New software is usually seen as the magic bullet but can only be part of the solution. Secondly, as described in Chapter 13: "Why Companies Select the Wrong Forecasting Software," commonly employed strategies such as using more sophisticated forecasting methods or changing the interval of the forecast error measurement are typically dead ends. One of the simplest (although not the easiest) ways of improving the forecast—removing the bias—is right under almost every company's nose, but they often have little interest in exploring this option.

Conclusion

Forecast bias is quite well documented inside and outside of supply chain forecasting. Bias is based upon both external factors such as incentives provided by institutions, as well as being a basic part of human nature. How much forecast bias is influenced by institutional demands for bias is an interesting field of study, made even more interesting and perplexing in that so little is done to minimize incentives for bias. Properly timed biased forecasts are part of the business model for many investment banks that release positive forecasts on investments that they already own. The so called "pump and dump" is an ancient money making technique. Investment banks promote the positive biases for their analysts, just as supply chain sales departments promote negative biases by continuing to use a salesperson's forecast as their quota. These institutional incentives have changed little in many decades, even though there is never ending talk of changing them and even though it is well known how incentives lower forecast quality, they persist even though they conflict with all of the research in the area of bias. The easiest way to remove bias is to remove the institutional incentives for it. However, as many companies have a strong preference against doing so, it falls to the actual forecast process, where adjustments are taken in the demand planning software after biased forecasts have been entered.

Software designed around the mitigation of forecast bias can help highlight bias and can provide mechanisms to adjust it within the application. Within the application, there should be the ability to identify bias and the ability to adjust bias quickly and easily. Companies by and large do not ask for this, so software companies do not develop bias identification in their software (and do not build bias identification as a main component of the user interface). Bias identification is important enough that it should have its own dashboard, or view, within all demand planning applications, not only for general ease-of-use but because adjusting for bias is about more than identification and adjustment; it is also about making the case. The case for bias can best made in a presentation format, to demonstrate to others that the bias exists and action should be taken to minimize its effect on the final forecast. When bias is demonstrated in this way, it's more difficult to dispute. If conversations in bias are kept at a high level and not demonstrated with a visual aid, which shows the bias clearly, all types of excuses will be offered by the groups that produced the biased forecast as to why there was, in fact, no bias. The application's bias dashboard should support that presentation by showing bias from many products and from different vantage points in real time.

Bias can be identified by many criteria including bias by individual, bias by an overall department, bias by-products and geography, etc. Bias information must be detailed because those with a biased forecast will most often push back by saying there was a good reason for the forecast at the time, or that the person tabulating the bias does not have sufficient detail to make the claim of bias. Therefore, its not sufficient if the dashboard allows an expert to determine the existence of bias, the application should present well enough to make the case to people who are not experts in forecasting. The software should have the ability to provide decision support, but ultimately, there must be the institutional will to eliminate bias, and that cannot be obtained from a software application.

CHAPTER 10

Effective Forecast Error Management

Forecast Error Measurement Methods

When I was developing the outline for this book, I knew I wanted to get the forecasting error measurement method out of the way quickly in this chapter. It's the least important and least interesting feature of forecast error, and the forecast error measurement method is covered extensively in other information sources.

Forecast error measurement is very simple. Only a few measurements are in use, and these measurements are pre-calculated inside all of the forecasting applications. These measurements are listed below:

- MAD – Mean Absolute Deviation
- MAPE – Mean Absolute Percentage Error
- RMSE – Root Mean Squared Error

Which error measurement method to use for demand planning (which as I will describe is different than supply planning's use of forecast error) comes down to what the company wants to measure. Each measurement method has advantages and disadvantages, and each is better at measuring a different aspect of forecast error.

- MAD is useful for understanding the *size* of the error.
- MAPE is good for understanding the *percentage* of the error.
- RMSE is useful if you think that larger errors should be *weighed more heavily* (errors are squared in this method).

Each method has a different way of dealing with zeros in demand history, and this is an important distinction. MAD is the best for dealing with zeros because it uses no division in its formula, unlike MAPE, that can produce an error value when there are periods of zero demand history. Dealing with zeros in the forecast history is an interesting topic and is described in the following post:

http://www.scmfocus.com/demandplanning/2010/07/zero-demand-periods-and-forecast-error-measurement/

The interesting part about forecast error measurements is that that even after a company standardizes on one, forecast error measurements are generally treated as if there is some known accuracy level that the company should expect. There is a way of determining a baseline accuracy expectation, but few companies go through the process to set this baseline, even though it is so easy to do. Michael Gilliland at SAS in his paper, "Forecast Value Added Analysis", recommends using a naïve model to set this baseline:

> *MAPE is probably the most popular forecasting performance metric, but by itself, is not legitimate for comparing forecasting performance. MAPE tells you the magnitude of your error, but MAPE does not tell you what error you should be able to achieve. By itself, MAPE gives no indication of the efficiency of your forecasting process. To understand these things, you need to use FVA analysis.*
>
> *An organization must understand what forecasting can achieve and what it cannot. An organization must focus its efforts on generating usable forecasts; forecasts as accurate as the nature of the demand*

patterns allow us to be, and to focus on achieving this level of accuracy as efficiently as possible. Waste and worst practices occur when an organization pursues the unachievable – the perfect forecast, or accuracy that simply cannot be achieved due to the nature of the demand.

I believe the "unachievable" nature of many forecasting accuracy expectations is why it is so difficult to get a solid number about forecast accuracy from companies, and why forecast accuracy quotations are so often devoid of context. This is a good point at which to describe some of the most important contextual factors to forecast accuracy.

Understanding the Contextual Factors of Forecast Error

There are many forecasting books with lengthy chapters on forecast error measurement. Forecast error measurement is a major issue but not, as many presume, because of the calculation methods over which most of the discussion on forecast error centers. Paradoxically, many of these books focus on the *mathematics* of forecast error measurement without focusing on the equally, if not more important *contextual issues,* of forecast error measurement, including questions such as the following:

1. How difficult is the product type in question to forecast (easy as with a high-volume consumer product, or difficult as with a service part)?

2. Where in the forecasting process is the error being measured? Is it the forecast error generated by the system or the manually adjusted final forecast? (If it's the latter, does the company have clean history that was systematically generated versus manually adjusted?)

3. Where in the forecast hierarchy is the error being measured?

4. At what geographic aggregation is the forecast error being measured?

5. Over what duration is the error is being measured?

These questions are a few of the reasons there is really no such thing as a *"seventy-five percent forecast error,"* without the forecast error being stated or understood within context. Interestingly, when you ask people "where" the forecast is measured or the duration of measurement, they will often say that they are not sure.

I usually have to cycle through several people within a company to get answers to all of the contextual questions. This means a large cross section of people think that a forecast value is a single value rather than one made up of multiple values based upon different contexts that change depending upon the factors I have listed previously. Another thing I find interesting is that the forecast error often quoted seems too similar between companies. For some reason it is very common to think that one's forecast error is "around seventy-five percent."

The Forecast Error Context of Aggregation

Some of the ways that companies measure forecast error defy logic, and aggregation of the error is a major area of self-delusion. For instance, I once consulted at a company that measured their forecast error as a ***monthly-dollarized*** value. So, for example, if they sold $1,000,000 in one month when the forecast was $800,000, their forecast error would be twenty percent. This was the forecast error measurement that was used by the demand planning department within the supply chain organization. Strangely, this is actually more the way an S&OP forecasting process would measure forecast error. A forecast error at this level of aggregation is simply not useful for supply planning. The following quotation from a Right90 white paper, "7 Secrets of Sales Forecasting", is related to this point:

> *Aggregate forecast accuracy is NOT meaningful. Some companies congratulate themselves on having high overall sales forecast accuracy and do indeed have very good sales forecasts. Other companies, have high aggregate forecast accuracy (I said I would do $100M this quarter and I did), but get the details of the forecast wrong, which causes a lot of pain. Yet other companies do not even measure forecast accuracy and do not know how well they are doing at all. Three examples of cases where total accuracy was good but the outcome was not:*
>
> *My bookings accuracy is 100% (except we could not ship the items ordered because they were not built).*
>
> *My pricing accuracy is 100% (except that the prices went down on the low margin items so we had a loss).*

My unit shipment accuracy is 100% (except that I shipped my winter boots in June so they came back).

— Right90

Customers demand specific products, and typically at a product-location combination. Some companies have more leeway in aggregation than others based upon their business. For instance, one of my clients—a paint company—could mix its white paint with a color to create a variety of colors at the point of sale. There are also examples of highly substitutable products, where a customer is quite willing to accept a different SKU for the initial SKU. Companies that have "fungible" products of this type can aggregate their forecast error by product, but the customers of most companies demand a specific product at a specific location. Companies that meet demand from a location other than the one where they initially forecasted the demand to be (and where they placed the stock), normally still count this as forecast error as there is a cost to reship the stock to a new location. The forecast is designed to place stock at the correct location, and therefore, it's important to measure the location error.

The Forecast Error Context of Product Type

Forecast accuracy is significantly affected by the demand history of the product in question. Products with high and consistent volumes, such as popular consumer products, are easy to forecast and a low forecast error is no reason for celebration. There still may be opportunities for improvement. On the other end of the spectrum are slow-moving products, for which a high forecast error is no reason for concern and may not present opportunities for improvement. Nothing illustrates the importance of determining a meaningful forecast better than observing the forecast error of service parts. Service parts have very low and irregular demand. The historical pattern listed below is illustrative:

	Jan	Feb	Mar	Apr	May	June	July	Aug	Sept	Oct	Nov	Dec	January Forecast
Demand History	0	0	0	1	0	0	4	0	1	0	0	0	
12 Month Moving Average													0.5
Crostons													0.4
Exponential Smoothing													0

The twelve-month moving average is .5. Let's take this as the forecast. Because the demand in most months is zero, the forecast is difficult to compute. Even for the months where there is demand, the forecast error ranges from fifty percent to eight hundred percent. However, should this forecast be considered ineffective and worthy of significant effort to improve? The answer is no. It happens to be an item that is very difficult to forecast, and while different time series techniques can be employed, few will provide much improvement to the result you see here. While a forecast error of this type would be completely unacceptable for a higher-volume finished goods product, it is acceptable for this type of demand pattern.

Therefore, forecast error measurement cannot be evaluated the same way for different products. Instead, all forecast error values are conditional, and must be considered within the context of the challenges faced by the forecast. An excellent example of this is provided by weather forecasting. ForecastWatch evaluated weather forecast accuracy nationally (in the US) and found the following differences in forecast accuracy:

> *Forecasts were most reliable in the South and the Southwest, on the West Coast, and in Hawaii, where temperatures vary little, and forecasts were least reliable in the northern Great Plains, where temperatures vary the most due to the influences of warm, moist air from the Gulf of Mexico and cold, dry air from the Arctic.*

Should weather forecasters in the South, Southwest, West Coast and Hawaii be graded on the same scale as the northern Great Plains? Of course not.

The Forecast Error Context of the System-generated Versus the Final Forecast

It's important to measure both the system-generated forecast as well as the final forecast, which has often been adjusted manually. There are several reasons for this. Primarily, it's important to measure the effectiveness of the system in isolation. Secondly, it's important to measure how much forecast accuracy is changed both by manual intervention or judgment methods versus the statistical forecast. Never assume that forecast accuracy is improved simply because forecast adjustments are being made.

For these reasons, companies that are serious about improving their forecast accuracy will maintain forecast accuracy for both the system and for every individual that makes adjustments to the forecast. Many statistical applications do not support this in the user interface, which is why it is often necessary to create a report from the forecasting system.

The Forecast Error Context of Location

Forecast error has many purposes in demand planning, and if we were only concerned with demand planning, we could have a great deal of flexibility in forecast error measurement. However, as the supply planning system is the ultimate customer of the demand plan, and the forecast error is used to determine how much extra stock to carry in order to make up for variability in demand, there is much less flexibility in forecast accuracy measurement than generally thought. Actually, the issue that is often lost in translation during discussions about forecast error measurement has to do with the main purpose of the forecast error, which is to feed to the supply planning system to adjust safety stock so that the correct quantities and dates can be assigned to procurement, production, stock transfer, and in the case of service parts, repair. Supply planning applications can only use a forecast error at a product-location combination, as this is where the material is actually stocked. This is shown with SAP APO SNP in the screen shot on the next page:

Supply Chain Forecasting Software

Create Product SNA-1 for Location 0000001000

Product	SNA-1	Base Unit	EA
Prod. Descript.	SCM Focus White Wine		
Location	0000001000	Becker Berlin	

Tabs: Pkg Data | Storage | ATP | SNP 1 | SNP 2 | Demand | **Lot Size** | PP/DS

Lot Size Profile and Days' Supply Profile
Lot Size/DS Profile [ ] [ ]   Lot Size Unit [ ]

Procedure | Quantity and Date Determination

Procedure
- ● Lot-for-Lot
- ○ Fixed Lot Size [ ]
- ○ Periodic — Period Type [ ]
- ○ Reorder Point — Lot Size Strategy [ ] / Reord. Pnt Mthd [ ]

☐ Lot Size Always
☐ Last Lot Exact
Number of Periods [ ]
Planning Calendar [ ]
☐ Start of Lot Size Grouping
Reorder Days' Supply [ ]

☐ Underdel. Tol.

The forecast error is entered here, or the system can calculate the value.

Stock Data

Safety Stock		Safety Stock Method		Min. SFT	
Reorder Point		Service Level (%)		Max. SFT	
Max. Stock Level		Demand Fcast Err.(%)			
Stock	0	RLT Fcast Error (%)		Replen. Lead Time	

This value can be directly entered, or can be automatically calculated by the system. However, very few companies dynamically calculate safety stock within the supply planning system in this manner.

As this is where the rubber meets the road with respect to the forecast error: consideration should be given to whether this is how the forecast error should be measured in the demand planning department and if this should be how the rest of the company (aside from finance, which measures its error in dollars and uses entirely different duration measurements) should also think of the error.

The Forecast Error Context of Duration
Forecast errors are commonly measured with a monthly duration, most likely due to the fact that forecasts are usually created in monthly buckets. The forecast horizon differs greatly by company, but the forecast bucket tends to be much more consistent, resulting in a January forecast, February forecast, etc., or twelve forecast buckets per year. The relationship between the duration of error measurement and the error magnitude is a simple one: the longer the duration of the forecast error measurement, the smaller the forecast error, and vice versa.

The important question to ask at this juncture is: Why is a forecast necessary in the first place? I discussed this briefly in Chapter 2: "Where Forecasting Fits within the Supply Chain Planning Footprint." However, a detailed walkthrough of why a forecast is created will lead us to select the most relevant duration for the forecast error measurement. To do so, we must get into the topic of lead-time demand.

The Lead Time Demand
Imagine a company that has no supply constraints and no supply or production lead time on its products. A company in this enviable position would not need to forecast, because any demand could be satisfied from an imaginary infinite bucket. Now let's change the assumptions a bit so that this same company still has no supply constraints but has a lead time of two weeks. In this case, what should we choose as the duration over which the forecast error is measured? Think about this for a moment before reading the answer in the footnote.[15]

If the forecast were one hundred units over the two-week lead time, and the forecast error was consistently never more than twenty-five percent over lead time in the past, then an inventory of one hundred and twenty-five units should enable the company to meet all demand. If the forecast error was never more than forty percent over lead time, then an inventory of one hundred and forty units should be carried (if the intent is to meet all demand—this is not always the intent but we will make that assumption here).

---
[15] The answer is two weeks.

The amount of extra inventory to carry over predicted demand is based in part upon this forecast error. ***Calculating extra inventory is, in fact, the primary use of forecast error in supply planning.***

This logic shows itself in the standard safety stock formula. As we read through it, let us look at what it includes:

$$\text{Safety stock: } \{Z*\text{SQRT}(\text{Avg. Lead Time } * \text{ Standard Deviation of Demand}^2 + \text{Avg. Demand}^2 * \text{ Standard Deviation of Lead Time}^2)\}$$

Notice from the formula above that lead time is multiplied by demand, and that the standard deviation of the lead time is multiplied by the demand (in our example we assumed zero lead-time variance). This is because safety stock attempts to calculate, and quite rightly, the extra stock required to be safe over the lead time (i.e., safety stock). This is referred to as the "lead-time demand." Lead-time demand error is the most relevant measurement for forecast error, which leads to the following statement:

> *From the supply planning perspective, the most important qualification is the forecast error over the lead time of the product-location combination.*

Therefore, while it's useful for the demand planning department to maintain a variety of internal forecast error measurements, the **lead-time demand forecast error at a product location** should be published by demand planning to the rest of the company, and should be the most commonly used—and most commonly quoted—forecast error. It is the most accurate representation of the forecast error that is relevant for supply chain planning.

Using the Naïve Forecast for Baselining

A powerful method of contextualizing a forecast is to create a naïve—or unsophisticated—forecast. A naive forecast is not a specific forecasting model, although it is sometimes defined as simply the last period's demand. However, several models can be used for a naïve forecast, all of which are simple in their design. A naive forecast can be the sales from the last period, a moving average, or for seasonal items, sales from the same period last year.

Some use the term "naïve forecast" with disdain, as if it were not usable for forecast creation. However, naïve forecasts can be surprisingly effective. After all, if a naïve forecast is so unsophisticated, why would it be used? The answer is that naïve forecasts can often beat forecasting models that are much more sophisticated and cost more to implement. Michael Gilliland at SAS is a proponent of creating a naïve forecast for every product and comparing it to the company's forecast in order to estimate the added value of the forecast process.

Somewhat surprisingly, naïve forecasts are underused due to political barriers; it is difficult to sell the use of naïve forecasts due to the general and unfounded assumption that simple forecasts can always be beaten by more complex methods. It is embarrassing for many people in leadership positions to admit to their reliance on naïve forecasts, and this is one reason we don't often hear companies talk about them. This extends across different forecasting areas, and in every area, naïve methods tend to be rejected in favor of more complex methods, as is evidenced conclusively when one studies the history of complex versus simple methods. However, many people use naïve methods without being aware of doing so. For instance, an index mutual fund is essentially a naïve forecast strategy and is the opposite of active stock selection. The index fund holds a grouping of stocks or other financial instruments in one area instead of forecasting which in that group will beat the average. The concept states that active selection cannot beat averaging.

The naïve forecast is so valuable because it sets the stage for what forecast accuracy expectations should be. If a naïve forecast is used, and the result is a thirty-five percent accuracy at product location over replenishment lead time, this then sets a different expectation than if the forecast accuracy under the same circumstances were eighty-five percent. This is called baselining. Without baselining, a company is left unsure as to how effective their forecast efforts are. For instance, if in the first case an accuracy level of forty percent is achieved, and in the second case a forecast accuracy of eighty percent is achieved, a company may still come away confused as to which forecast performance they should be satisfied with (often they are dissatisfied with the forty percent accuracy because it just "seems low"). However, when a baseline exists, a company can know what the added value is of their active forecasting efforts.

In addition, naïve-forecasting baselining can help a company determine where forecasting resources should be invested. Active forecasting will not beat naïve methods for some products, and so resources applied to these products is a misallocation of limited resources. Other products may be improved by active forecasting, but not by enough to justify the improvement. This is also a misallocation of limited forecasting resources. One of the most valuable pieces of information a company can have is which portions of their product database are improved by active forecasting and which are not.

How to Perform a Naïve Forecast Comparison
In order to be able to perform a naïve forecast, the application must be able to create a forecast and store it in a location that does not interact with the final forecast. For instance, in Demand Works Smoothie, any forecast can be created and stored in a measure/row that is not the final forecast. This naïve forecast is, therefore, kept separate from the final forecast that is sent to the supply planning system.

Performing the naïve forecast in the same system as is used for production is not necessarily the best approach if that system is not a good prototype environment. It simply depends upon the system that is being used. More on what makes a good prototype environment is listed in the link below:

> http://www.scmfocus.com/demandplanning/2010/07/prototype-environment-and-background/

The demand history and the previous forecasts can be exported from the production system to the prototype system, and the prototype system can then produce the naïve forecast for every product location going back say six months in time (this is not an automatic process, but must be set up in the application). The naïve forecast can then be compared against the actual forecast. If the active/current forecast cannot beat the naïve forecast, then an active forecast should not be performed and instead substituted with the naïve forecast.

This is essentially a forecast simulation, a term that is used rarely with forecasting. (We have an entire sub-blog at SCM Focus dedicated to supply chain simulation.)

http://www.scmfocus.com/supplychainsimulation/

There are several forms that a forecast simulation can take. They include the following:

1. In the example provided above, a naïve forecast is compared against an active forecast within the same application. This is a manual activity.

2. Forecasts can be compared between different applications, and Appendix A describes how to import one forecast into another forecasting system in order to produce an apples-to-apples comparison.

3. A simulation can be performed by an automated procedure within the forecasting application that results in one final forecast, but which was derived through the iterative comparison on multiple forecasts. This is described in Appendix C.

It is increasingly apparent that, to gain more knowledge of how to improve forecasting, companies must begin to perform forecasting simulations where the results are placed into some type of content management system and archived for future use. Forecasting simulations must include documentation. Many demand planning departments are not comfortable doing forecasting simulations. However, supply planning has a good body of work on simulation, which can be leveraged to ensure forecasting simulation is undertaken properly. I discuss supply chain simulation in detail in the book, *Supply Planning with MRP/DRP and APS Software*.

Conclusion

The easy part of forecast error measurement is selecting the method, and as was discussed, it is important to focus on the multiple contexts in which forecast error can be measured.

The most important lesson I would like people to take from this chapter is that when stripped of its context, forecast error value is meaningless. Unfortunately, stripping a forecast of its context is a very frequent practice. Just because the forecast accuracy on some easy-to-forecast finished goods product is eighty-five percent does not mean that there is little to no opportunity to improve the forecast. Likewise, a forty percent forecast error on a very low demand item does not mean that there are significant opportunities to improve the forecast. The context of the forecast error is the key to identifying opportunities for improvement.

The most important question to ask when standardizing on an error measurement is why supply chain organizations create forecasts in the first place. The correct answer is that while many forecast error measurements are useful within the demand planning department, the most relevant forecast error measurement to use is the ***lead-time demand forecast error at a product location.*** However, this means breaking out of the narrow confines of demand planning to a fuller understanding of how the forecast is used by the system that receives the demand plan: the supply planning system. One also needs to consider how forecast error directly impacts the safety stock value, half of which is designed to account for the forecast error and half of which is designed to account for the variability in lead time.

CHAPTER 11
Lifecycle Planning

Background

Lifecycle planning is also known by the term Product Lifecycle Management (PLM). At this time, PLM is still presented by some software vendors as a specific application. SAP, Agile, Siemens and several other vendors still use PLM to describe their applications. However, it is not reasonable to do so because there are many aspects to lifecycle planning that are distributed throughout a wide variety of enterprise applications, and not only in the applications that are marketed as "PLM." For instance, lifecycle functionality exists in demand planning, supply planning and also production planning, as well as ERP and bill of material management systems (BMS). Simply put, no PLM application can contain all lifecycle functionality required by companies.

Within demand planning, there are two ends of the continuum of lifecycle planning. At one end, new products are added and forecasts are created for them. At the other end of the continuum products are removed, meaning they must be removed from the forecasting database as well. In between these two extremes, a product may trend upward or downward based upon its phase of life in a way that is not predicted by its demand history.

The way that lifecycle planning trending is applied to products is an important differentiator between the various demand planning applications. In this chapter, we will look at how lifecycle planning is performed in four demand planning applications.

Lifecycle Planning in SAP DP

SAP DP uses something called phase-in and phase-out profiles for lifecycle planning. These profiles are used to increase or decrease the forecast. An increase of two percent would constitute one profile, while an increase of 2.2 percent would be another profile. I worked at one client that had over 6,000 profiles, and another with 11,000 profiles. Maintaining and keeping all of these profiles straight is a tall order. I describe this in more detail below:

> http://www.scmfocus.com/demandplanning/2010/09/the-problem-using-dp-for-lifecycle-planning/

SAP essentially acknowledged the heavy maintenance load imposed by phase-in phase-out profiles when they introduced the APO Lifecycle Assistant, which provides far more functionality with respect to making lifecycle changes. The date when the product will be phased out can be entered. Weights can be used to apply a historical demand from one product (the predecessor) to another (the successor), allowing a product to be assigned the forecast of a similar product, which can then be used in both the ramp-up and ramp-down stages of a product's lifecycle. However, the APO Lifecycle Assistant is not part of DP's standard product, but is an extension and must be paid for separately. As no client of mine has ever used it, I have never personally tested this add-in. SAP add-ins are discussed further in this post:

> http://www.scmfocus.com/sapplanning/2011/03/21/understanding-apo-add-ins/

Lifecycle Planning in ToolsGroup

Supersession is the substitution of one product for another product. In lifecycle planning, this often takes the form of phasing out one product and replacing it with a newer version. Seeing the demand of both products in an integrated way is one of the challenges. ToolsGroup has made this very clear in their user interface, which is why I wanted to include them in this section.

ToolGroup can show both the phase-out product and the phase-in product on the same screen. See below, and notice the transparent portion of the block graphs.

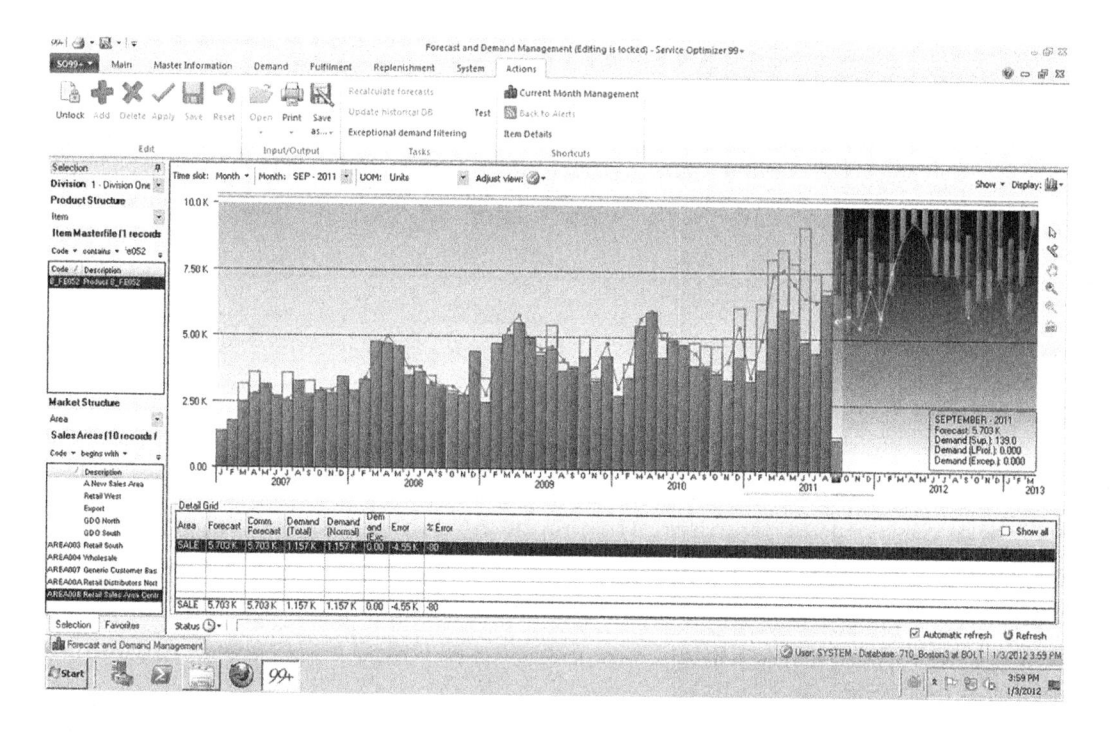

If the selected item supersedes another item (i.e., it assumes the demand of the superseded item in addition to its own), the demand bar on the graph displays both the original demand for the selected item (solid green bar) and the acquired demand associated with the superseded item (green perimeter with no fill): the superseded demand.
— Kristen Nordstrom, ToolsGroup

Lifecycle Planning in JDA Demand Management

Lifecycle planning is managed very specifically with respect to dates in JDA Demand Management. The dates include:

- *History Start Date:* The earliest demand history date that the system uses in producing a forecast.

- *Demand Post Date:* Date up to which demand has been posted (DFU:DmdPostDate). The period into which the demand post date falls is the first forecast period.[16]

- *Effective Date:* The date when the system begins producing forecasts.

- *Discontinue Date:* The date after which the systems stops producing forecasts.

The user can specify all of these dates very easily in the JDA interface. These dates, shown on the screenshot below, are then applied at the product level.

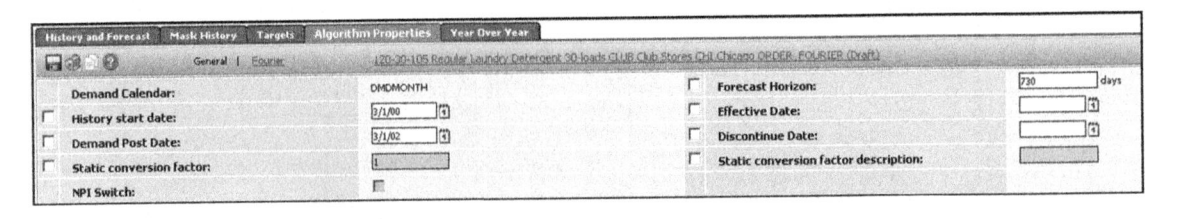

Using these dates, JDA Demand Management can easily control the important lifecycle dates for a product. The dates can be applied within the user interface by a planner, or can be adjusted for a large number of products by performing an upload, with the dates adjusted as desired, to the JDA Demand Management application database.

Copying Demand History Between Like Products

One way of performing lifecycle planning is by copying one product's demand history over to another product. This is particularly useful during a new product

---

[16] *Demand Post Date refers to the last date that demand was posted to the system. It separates out the "history" from the "forecast" and serves as the basis for defining the first forecast period. For example, if I am forecasting in weekly buckets on a Sunday start, and my demand post date is set to Feb 5, 2012, this date represents that the last posted history was on Feb. 5, 2012 encapsulating the sales from the prior week. Therefore, the first bucket of future forecast is for the week of February 5, 2012. — Paula Natoli, JDA*

Lifecycle Planning

introduction, where a company believes there to be a high degree of similarity between the new product and an existing product. Copying demand is an alternative to providing a product with uplift commensurate with how another product performed. While a company can use a variety of approaches to predict the demand of a new product, one cannot do much better than to find a like product that has already been introduced and has a demand history.

JDA Demand Management provides an easy and detailed way to copy the demand history as well as other factors such as the tuning parameters, forecasting method, etc.

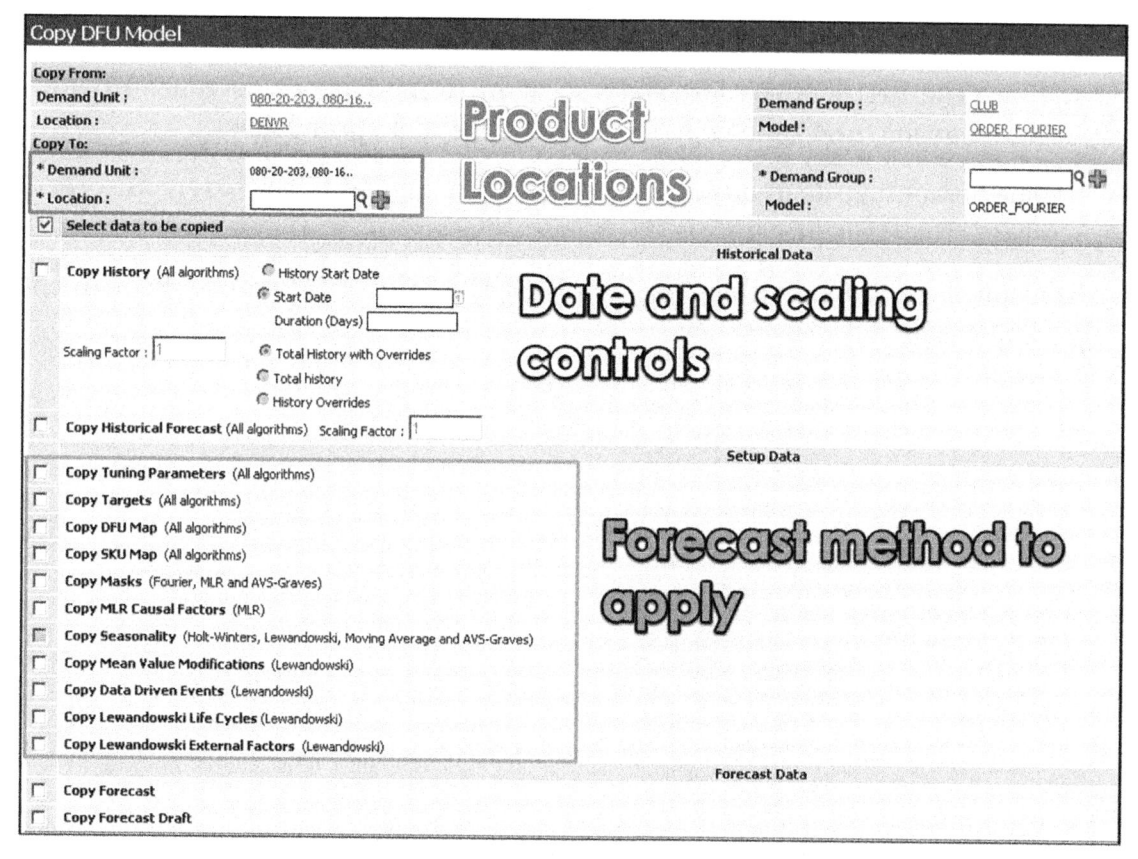

Copy DFU Model

Copy From:
- Demand Unit: 080-20-203, 080-16...
- Location: DENVR
- Demand Group: CLUB
- Model: ORDER_FOURIER

Product Locations

Copy To:
- * Demand Unit: 080-20-203, 080-16...
- * Location:
- * Demand Group:
- Model: ORDER_FOURIER

☑ Select data to be copied

Historical Data

☐ Copy History (All algorithms)
- ○ History Start Date
- ● Start Date
- Duration (Days)

Scaling Factor: 1
- ● Total History with Overrides
- ○ Total history
- ○ History Overrides

Date and scaling controls

☐ Copy Historical Forecast (All algorithms) Scaling Factor: 1

Setup Data

☐ Copy Tuning Parameters (All algorithms)
☐ Copy Targets (All algorithms)
☐ Copy DFU Map (All algorithms)
☐ Copy SKU Map (All algorithms)
☐ Copy Masks (Fourier, MLR and AVS-Graves)
☐ Copy MLR Causal Factors (MLR)
☐ Copy Seasonality (Holt-Winters, Lewandowski, Moving Average and AVS-Graves)
☐ Copy Mean Value Modifications (Lewandowski)
☐ Copy Data Driven Events (Lewandowski)
☐ Copy Lewandowski Life Cycles (Lewandowski)
☐ Copy Lewandowski External Factors (Lewandowski)

Forecast method to apply

Forecast Data

☐ Copy Forecast
☐ Copy Forecast Draft

*The ability to mix and match different features of a product in the forecasting system, as seen above, makes JDA's functionality quite flexible. Notice also that the demand history can be copied for **specific portions of the overall demand history**. Secondly,* *there is a great deal of flexibility in terms of what can be copied as the lower settings demonstrate. I consider this type of flexibility with respect to lifecycle planning a best-practice design.*

Lifecycle Planning (and Other Adjustments) in Demand Works Smoothie

There are several ways to manage lifecycle planning in Smoothie. The first is more of a "one off" approach, while the second is a systematic way of applying lifecycle changes to groups of products. Both methods are explained below:

Method 1: Copy and Paste Spreadsheet Functionality in Smoothie for Lifecycle Planning

The steps for this method are:

1. Place the SKUs of the forecast you want to increase or decrease in value into a group, and then copy the time series to a spreadsheet.

2. The percentage decrease or increase is then applied in the external spreadsheet (Excel, for instance).

3. Copy the changed values back to Smoothie's internal spreadsheet in the application data sheet view.

Lifecycle Planning 183

An example of this is shown in the screen shot below:

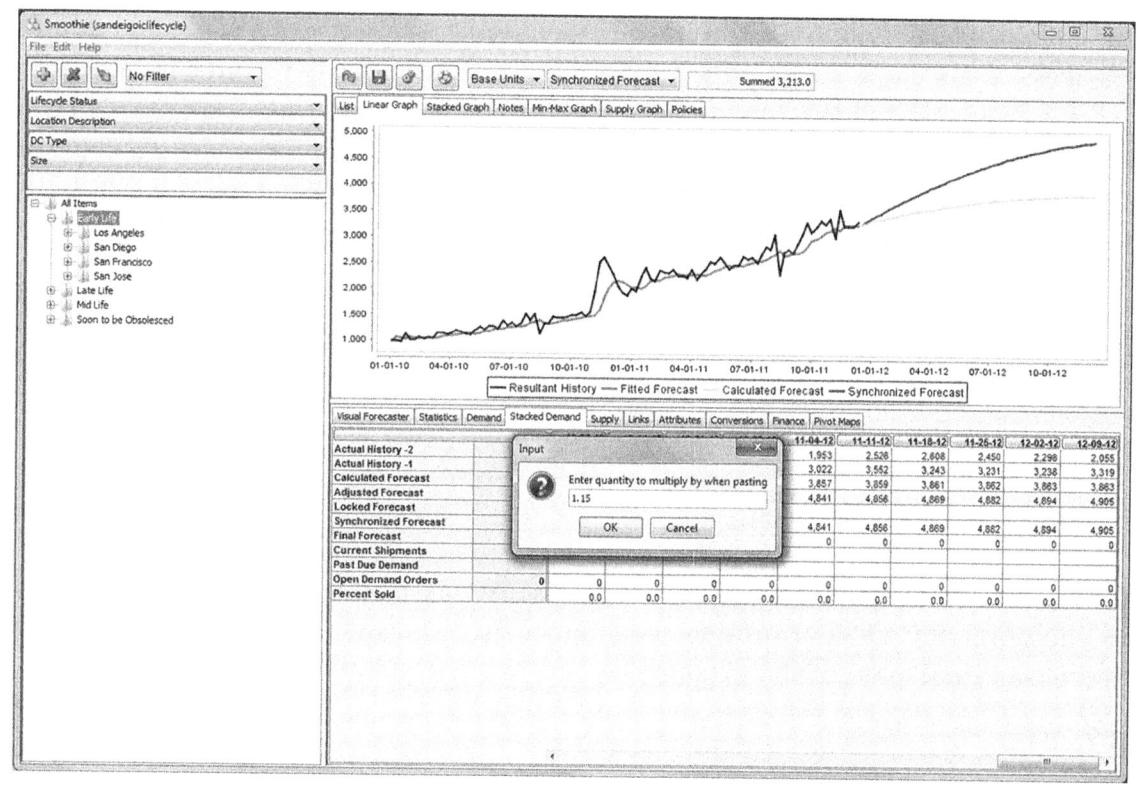

In Smoothie, values in a single field or an entire row can be adjusted and imported from a spreadsheet. Data can be copied back as adjusted, or can be increased by a certain value with the "Paste Multiply" function. Smoothie then asks for a value by which to multiply the copied values. To increase the values by fifteen percent, one would type in 1.15 (for 115 percent) in this entry box. This is just one of the options available for performing a paste to forecast measure in Smoothie.

Method 2: Setting Lifecycle as an Attribute

Smoothie's flexible attribute-based forecasting capabilities can be used for multiple purposes. Attributes are a flexible mechanism for any type of grouping, and lifecycle planning is really just another form of grouping—you are choosing to treat a group of products in a *different way* from the rest of the product database. An attribute can be created very easily in Smoothie by simply adding a column to the import file and titling it something like "Lifecycle." Then, populate it with the different lifecycle categories that the company wants to apply to the product. The examples I have created below could be set up as attributes:

1. Early-life
2. Mid-life
3. Late-life
4. Soon to be obsolesced

However, any number of lifecycle categories are possible. These could be assigned to each product. Once a product is grouped in this way, it can be increased or decreased in as part of the group.

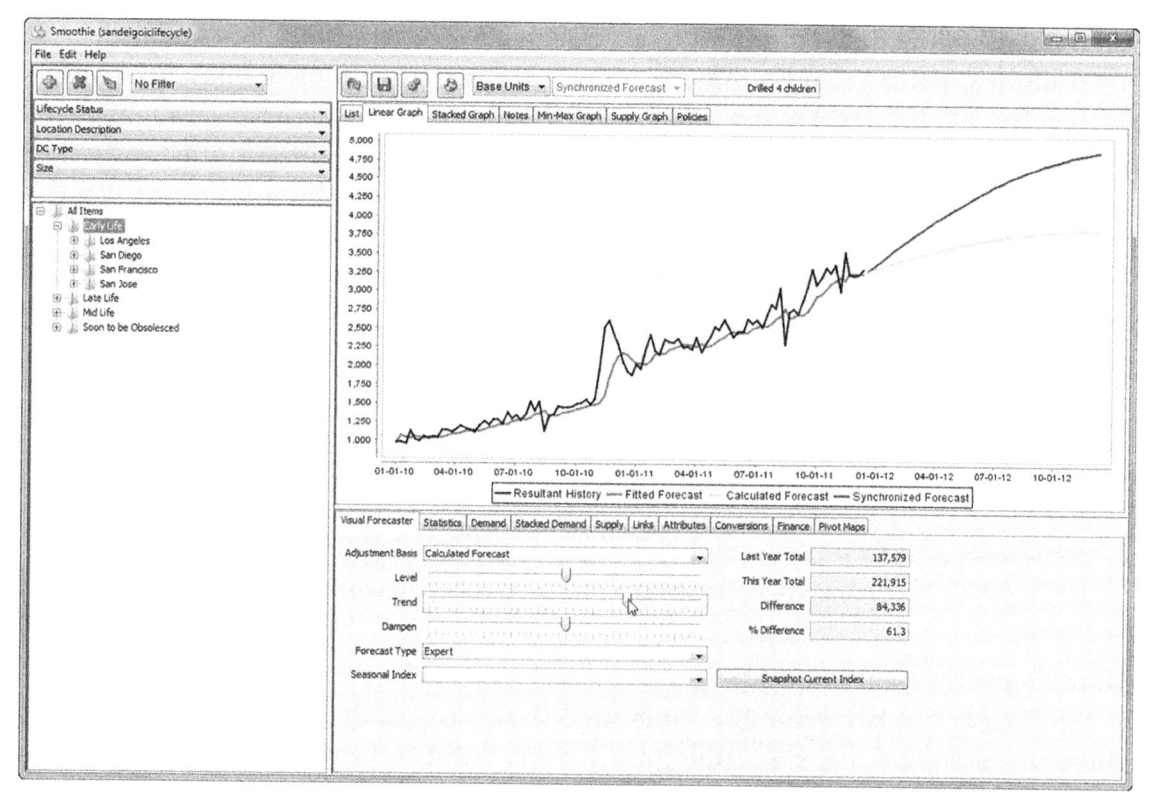

Once placed into a group or attribute, the groupings of products can be increased or decreased by moving the sliders at the bottom of the screen. This can be done interactively without affecting the final forecast. When the change to be made has been agreed upon, the forecast can be saved. The forecast will have then been adjusted.

Conclusion

Lifecycle planning can be relatively simple to manage or a major maintenance headache, depending upon the functionality provided by the application. In this chapter, several major ways of performing lifecycle planning were compared and contrasted:

1. The application of phase-in and phase-out profiles
2. Supersession between one product and another
3. Very specific controls for dates of lifecycle changes
4. Attributes

Even if a company has committed to an expensive solution that offers weak lifecycle functionality, software with effective lifecycle function can easily pay for itself as the benefits of efficiently performing lifecycle planning outweigh the costs, and this can allow for what I refer to as a "blended solution." More user training or further investments in configuration are often presented by IT as the solution and by the person who selected the software who prefers to defend a bad selection, but in my experience are not answers to a solution that has consistently failed to provide lifecycle capabilities. While these factors will universally be offered up as reasons why an application has failed to make the desired impact, in many instances the answer is to get another application. The cost benefit of this approach versus all other approaches is very high, and is easy for me to demonstrate. More on blended solutions can be read at the link below:

http://www.scmfocus.com/supplychaininnovation/2010/08/the-benefit-of-blended-solutions-based-upon-component-based-software/

Many companies consistently expend a lot of effort on lifecycle planning. Regardless of the long-term direction of a company, there is simply no excuse for making planners use poor lifecycle functionality when there are excellent alternatives in the market that can be combined with other demand planning applications.

CHAPTER 12

Forecastable Versus Unforecastable Products

I have analyzed a good deal of product databases over the years, and many of the products that I have analyzed from different companies are clearly unforecastable. There is a simple reason for this. Many products that are difficult to forecast have no discernible pattern in their demand history, and without a discernible pattern, no mathematical algorithm can create a good forecast. This is not generally understood. Part of the reason that too much effort is spent on very hard-to-forecast products is due to a misimpression about when statistical forecasting can add value, and when it can't. This is well said by Michael Gilliland in *The Lean Approach to Forecasting*:

> *The best a forecaster ever can do is discover the underlying structure or rule guiding the behavior that is being forecast, finding a model that accurately represents the underlying behavior—and then hoping that the underlying behavior doesn't change. Unfortunately, there is an element of randomness that surrounds virtually all behavior, and the degree of randomness will limit the accuracy you can achieve.*

One of the first questions to ask is whether there is value to actively generating a forecast. In some cases the answer is no. However, instead of recognizing that a product is not forecastable and adjusting to this reality, more sophisticated mathematics are often employed in a vain attempt to improve the forecast. Clients I have worked for in the past have adopted this philosophy, as have the majority of consultants and vendors I have worked with, and this philosophy is also reflected in forecasting academic papers I have read. Since so many well-educated people agree on this thinking, it must be correct—right? Well actually they don't all agree. A number of academics have written on the concept of unforecastable products, but for some reason their research does not seem to get sampled and disseminated. However, the scholarly literature is not objectively sampled. In fact, most consultants in don't read it at all. Proven approaches like turning off forecasating for unforecastable products leads to short, and insufficiently lucrative consulting engagements.

However, there is little evidence that sophisticated mathematics can improve the forecast of difficult-to-forecast products, and this is a problem. Some studies do not show improvement from more advanced methods. But first, the improvement is never very large, and secondly other studies come by later to contradict the original studies. In addition, complex methods should have to exceed a higher bar. Academics can apply complex methods in a laboratory environment over a few products far more easily than can be done by industry. This fact, along with the point that sophisticated methods are much more expensive for industry to implement than simple methods, is rarely mentioned. This point is made very well by J. Scott Armstrong:

> *Use simple methods unless a strong case can be made for complexity. One of the most enduring and useful conclusions from research on forecasting is that simple methods are generally as accurate as complex methods. Evidence relevant to the issue of simplicity comes from studies of judgment (Armstrong 1985), extrapolation (Armstrong 1984, Makridakis et al. 1982, and Schnaars 1984), and econometric methods (Allen and Fildes 2001). Simplicity also aids decision makers' understanding and implementation, reduces the likelihood of mistakes, and is less expensive.*

The Inconvenient Truth About Statistical Forecasting

For statistical forecasting, the only products that can be forecasted are those that have a discernible pattern to their demand history, and not all products have this pattern. Forecastability can usually be determined—or at least indicated—without any math by simply observing a line graph of a product's three-year demand history. If there is no discernible pattern, it is unlikely that the product is forecastable with mathematical methods. (Products that are using just the last few periods to create a forecast are the exception to this rule.) An algorithm that can appear to be predictive can be built for unforecastable products, but more often than not this is an illusion created by the forecaster who over-fitted the forecast. As is pointed out by Michael Gilliland, just because a model can be built to match the past, does not mean it should be used to perform forecasting:

> *The statistical approach is based on the assumption that there is a structure or pattern in the behavior we are trying to forecast. As human beings, we are very good at finding structure and pattern in the world around us—even when none exists. Clouds look like poodles, a burnt cheese sandwich reveals the Virgin Mary, and an ant's innocent meandering in the sand caricatures Winston Churchill. We readily come up with lucid explanations of the ups and downs of the stock market and of demand for our products and services. Unfortunately, the patterns we see may not be real, and even if they are, we have no assurance they will continue into the future.*

Products that have a very stable history exist at the other end of the continuum of forecast difficulty. Typically, it is very easy to forecast for products with a stable demand history; however, if this is the case, actively forecasting the product does not add very much value to supply planning (the ultimate consumer of the demand plan) because a product with stable demand history does not *need* to be forecasted. Products with stable demand can be managed effectively and efficiently with reorder point logic, where orders are based upon a reorder point or a reorder period.

Very stable and very unstable products converge in their forecasting approach, as is evidenced by the fact that a many-period moving average is equally useful for products with both a stable demand history and products with an unstable demand history. When both stable and unstable demand history products are run through a best-fit forecasting procedure, the normal result is that both will be fitted with a stable or level forecast. Companies have a very strong tendency to actively forecast all items in their product database without first asking the following question:

What is the value added by forecasting for the different product categories?

However, the rule of thumb is simple:

A forecast adds value to the supply planning process when the demand planning system is creating a forecast for a product for which there is a discernible pattern for demand and if the forecast is not simply a constant or relatively constant value.

Creating forecasts for the entire product database for S&OP forecasting or for other purposes may be important and necessary. However, the forecasting process that results in a demand plan being sent to supply planning can be segregated based on the rule of the value added to supply planning.

Intermittent or Lumpy Demand

Intermittent—or "lumpy"—demand is one of the most common features of a product's demand history that makes a product unforecastable. Services parts are the best-known example of a product with lumpy demand. However, I have come across intermittent demand in many different types of companies. For instance, one of my clients was a textbooks publisher. A large percentage of their product database had an intermittent demand history which would normally not be expected of this type of product. However, due to the fact that different US states buy textbooks in large volumes whenever funding comes through, the demand ends up being quite unpredictable for many books. A school system will not make any purchase for some time, and then will buy many textbooks all at once. For example, California is on a seven-year procurement cycle, which means they wait seven years between purchases.

And this is a very important distinction that explains why demand, which one would expect to be forecastable, is much less forecastable in reality. This is because many products have significant lags and batching between procurement and consumption, unrelated to EOQ-driven ordering. In the case of this textbook publisher, the intermittency was related to when state funding was approved for textbook purchases.

"Demand shaping" is the term used to describe how companies influence purchasing behavior so that demand is less intermittent and more predictable (typically through offering incentives). Demand shaping is a popular concept and is a very good idea in principle. Unfortunately, a term has not been coined to describe the opposite of demand shaping (demand wrecking?), but it is common practice among the majority of companies. Most companies actively increase the intermittency of demand (thus reducing the product's forecastability) by doing things like creating promotions and instituting end-of-quarter sales "pushes." Customers respond to these behaviors by further batching their demand. It is well known that eventually customers become habituated to end-of-quarter price reductions and postpone their buying in anticipation of the end of the quarter. There are a host of other programs often initiated by companies that make demand less forecastable than it ordinarily would be if natural or true demand were received. Michael Gilliland reinforces exactly what I have seen inside of companies.

> *Many organizational practices (such as promotional activities, sales contests, and quarter-end push) only serve to increase volatility. Typical practices are designed to produce record sales weeks rather than promote smooth, consistent and profitable growth...Rather than creating costly incentives to spike demand, it may make more sense to design incentives that smooth demand.*

> *Management has control over the often-misguided policies and practices that serve to increase volatility, and management can change them.*

> *One of the surest and cheapest ways to get better forecasts is to simply make the demand forecastable.*

It's important to understand how much demand shaping would change the business landscape. Demand shaping would mean removing the policies that increase intermittency and offering incentives to smooth demand beyond the customer's natural purchasing frequency, to better match the company's supply capability. This is a tall order, and it must be understood that normally demand planning cannot do anything about the company's sales incentive policies as these are controlled by the sales or marketing departments. These departments have historically been insensitive to problems they impose upon operations. Secondly, in the US at least, sales and marketing have been much more powerful than operations for decades. This point is brought up in the book, *Factory Physics*:

> *The influences of the golden era on the current condition of American manufacturing are subtle and complex. Besides promoting a de-emphasis on manufacturing details, the emphasis on marketing and finance in the 1950s and 1960s profoundly influenced today's American manufacturing firms. Recognizing these areas as having the greatest career potential, more and more of the "best and brightest" chose careers in marketing and finance. These became the glamour functions, while manufacturing and operations were increasingly viewed as "career breakers."*

The erosion of operations' influence has steadily continued, with sales, marketing and finance setting policy, and operations being forced to execute this policy with very little in the way of input. Management books talk about how the world should be, with a company's departments coming together to make joint decisions that are highly rational and integrative. However, the reality is that the politically powerful departments get their way regardless of how the policy affects other departments. Sales, marketing and finance see themselves as the departments within the company that add value, while operations is essentially viewed as commodity.

Many companies have already made outsourcing the manufacturing function. If it could be done feasibly, companies would like to outsource all nonmanufacturing supply chain functions as well! However, outsourcing other supply chain functions is not really feasible, as third party logistics never came close to its promise of integrating these capabilities. This topic is covered on the SCM Focus sub-site "fourth party logistics":

http://www.scmfocus.com/fourthpartylogistics/

This is why it is hard to see demand shaping as having much of a future. Any real enthusiasm on this topic would come at the expense of incentives and recognizing how they are structured within companies. Moving to demand shaping would mean sales and marketing completely changing the way they do business to be in line with the long term interests of the company. It would also mean giving up the power they currently enjoy to destroy value. This is clear also from the airline industry. In the US for decades now one airline has lead all others in on-time performance, customer service and profitability. This is an operationally driven company which invests little in marketing. This airline is called Southwest, and although they could easily be copied, none of the major airlines do so, preferring their old sales and marketing and customer dissatisfaction approach. Why? I would argue that while all the major airlines could improve all of their performance metrics by moving to the Southwest model, they haven't because sales and marketing would have their power eroded. And because the airline business is monopolistic, they can afford to continue to operate in this fashion.

ToolsGroup and Lumpy Demand

Of the vendors I have analyzed, probably the one (that does not specialize in service parts) with the greatest focus on demand intermittency is ToolsGroup. This is consistent with ToolsGroup's orientation toward planning, as is demonstrated in the screen shot below:

Supply Chain Forecasting Software

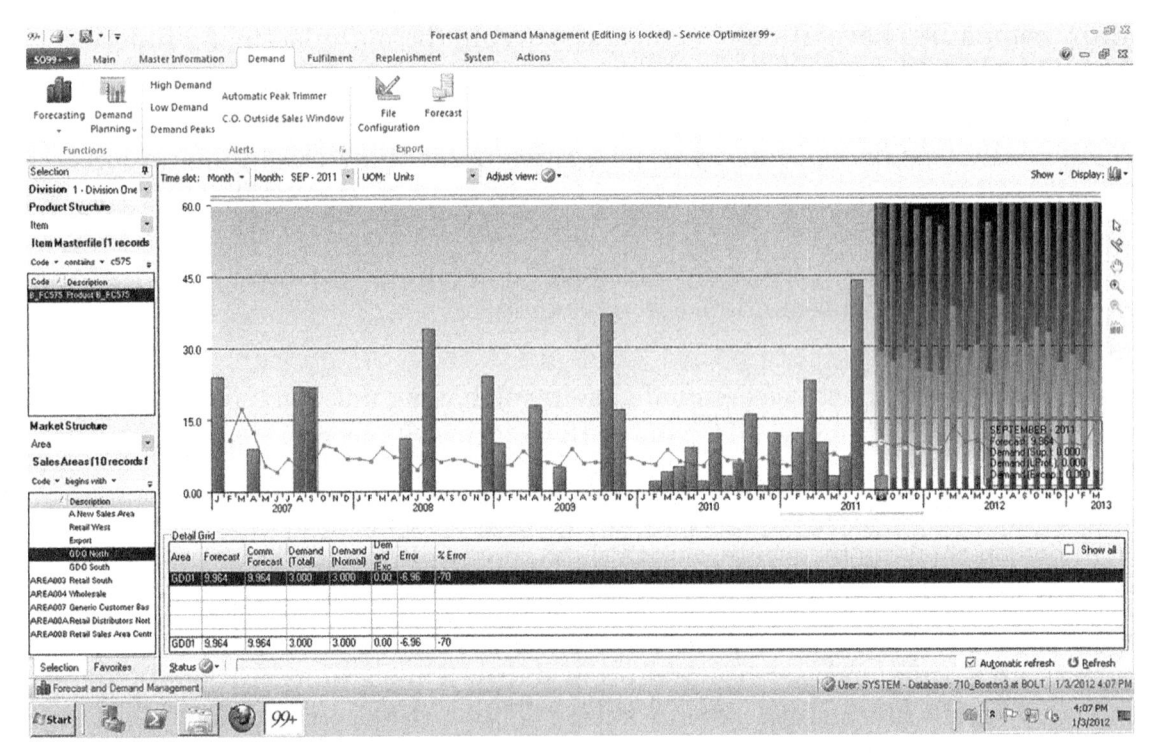

Notice that with ToolsGroup, the lumpiness shows in the demand history. However, the future lines on the dark background are very long. This is called the prediction interval, which is the range over which a forecast is likely to fall. On a lumpy product like this one, notice how large the range is when compared to the more predictable demand pattern below:

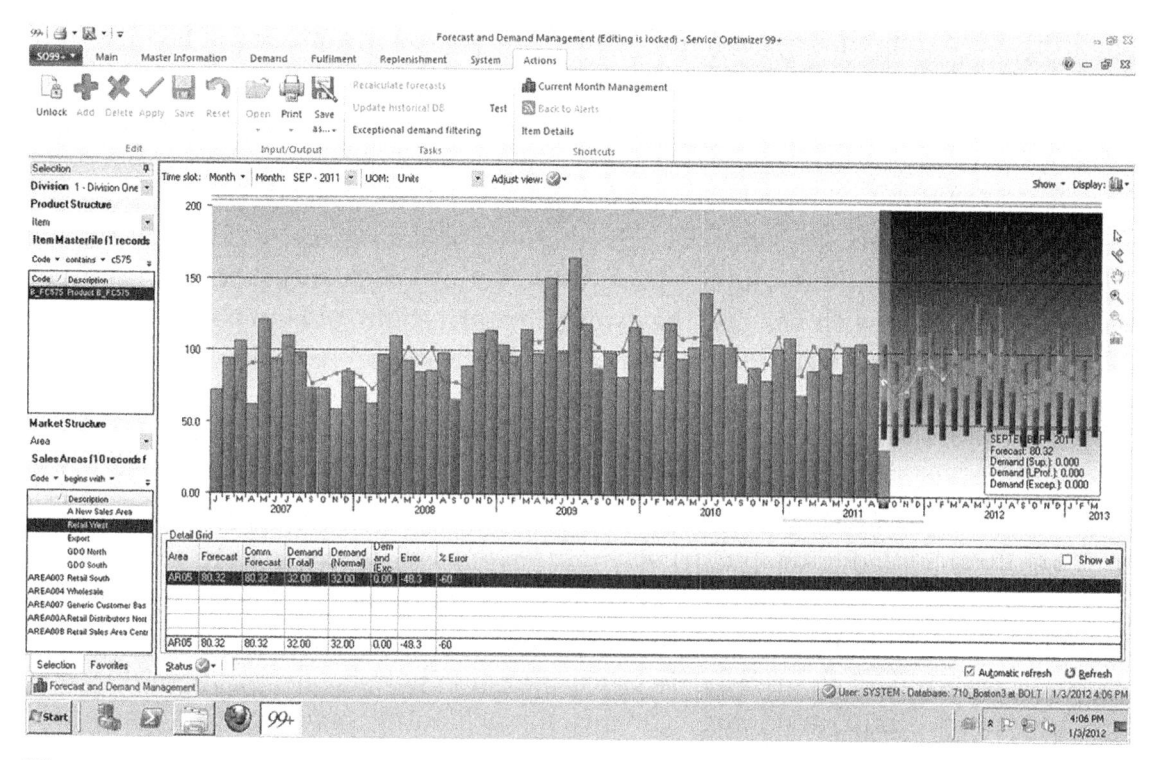

The more predictable item has a smaller range of values. It is inherently more forecastable. ToolsGroup's interface allows to me to demonstrate a basic concept about forecasting, which is what a good user interface should be able to do.

Trends in Lumpiness Case Study 1: Trader Joe's Versus Normal Supermarkets

Across different industries, lumpy or erratic demand histories are becoming more common. ToolsGroup has also observed this phenomenon and wrote about it in their white paper, "Mastering Lumpy Demand". One reason for the increased prevalence of lumpy demand histories is that the number of products that must be planned keeps increasing. This would not be a problem if the growth in the number of products matched the growth in demand, but it doesn't; the number of products easily outpaces the growth in demand. This is referred to as product proliferation, and is driven by the introduction of new products without the removal of low volume items from the product database. Product proliferation is described in many articles and research papers, although strangely the phenomenon is not usually tied back to forecasting. Product proliferation reduces forecastability, meaning, of course, that the company must carry more inventories. The increased costs imposed on the supply chain because of product proliferation are generally not estimated.

The increased number of SKUs maintained by companies can be used to quantify product proliferation. Simply comparing pictures of older grocery stores to present day supermarkets can also make it obvious. Today's supermarkets are so much larger and so filled with variety, they would be unrecognizable to people from previous eras. According to the Food Marketing Institute, present-day supermarkets carry between 15,000 and 60,000 SKUs, with the average being around 45,000.[17]

Trader Joe's, still in operation today, is representative of grocery stores that maintained fewer SKUs in the past. Trader Joe's is a specialty food retailer (they can't really be called a supermarket) and they carry approximately 4,000 SKUs per store. Unlike supermarkets that have a high number of low-turning SKUs, Trader Joe's eliminates poor selling items. This strategy allows them to have a sales per square foot figure that is twice that of Whole Foods, another very successful grocery chain, and places them in a much better position from a forecasting and overall supply chain planning perspective. With fewer SKUs and fewer lower-turning SKUs as a percentage of the database, Trader Joe's is in a better position to have a lower forecast error, and therefore, more efficient management of their inventory than would a typical supermarket. This also translates into a lower cost supply chain. Many strategy consultants and software salesmen like to tell their clients that any complexity added to the supply chain can be managed with advanced tools and advanced techniques. This is incorrect, and most of the people making these claims do not know enough about supply chain management or software to make these proposals. Part of a supply chain's efficiency and resulting costs is a function of the discipline that is employed to limit the number of products. One step in this direction is to reduce product proliferation. However, Trader Joe's rational approach to SKU management is an anomaly; the fact is, product proliferation is here to stay.

---

[17] Something that is not frequently discussed is that this proliferation is only possible because products are now shipped from such vast distances, meaning grocery items can be produced in one location and shipped thousands of miles away. The average produce in a supermarket travels 1,500 miles between the farm and the retail location.

Trends in Lumpiness Case Study 2: Netflix and the Long Tail

A second example of increasing lumpy demand history is found in the movement toward online retailing. The Internet has provided some companies[18] with the ability to sell online, satisfy demand from fewer distribution points, and still hold and offer a much wider number of SKUs. Companies like Netflix leverage online storefronts and national distribution networks to offer more selection than ever before. To immediately grasp this development, consider the demand history of a single Blockbuster Video store (back when Blockbuster dominated the video rental space) versus the present day Netflix distribution point. Netflix carries roughly 100,000 unique titles and ships out roughly 35,000 titles, or a third of its title variety, every day. Netflix is differentiated in the video rental market by its selection of titles—the broadest available. All of Netflix's national demand is distributed over fifty-eight distribution points (as of 2011). At its height in 2009, Blockbuster Video had 4,500 stores in the US and carried roughly 6,500 unique titles per store.[19]

Netflix currently operates roughly (58/6,500) or 1/112th as many distribution points as Blockbuster Video did at its zenith, and carries roughly (100,000/4,500) twenty-two times as many unique titles. This means that even with twenty-two times the number of unique titles, Netflix is in a position to manage its inventory more efficiently than a Blockbuster Video store. A Blockbuster Video store could hold only a fraction of the titles that Netflix can, and therefore, could only carry high-demand items. In the video market, title selection is a very important factor in customer satisfaction, and Netflix's intelligently designed network of warehouses provides this selection. Therefore, Netflix's added value over Blockbuster Video, even when Netflix was just starting out, was tremendous, and their distribution network gave them such a price advantage and greater convenience, that once Netflix became widely known, the store-based rental market, including Blockbuster Video, went into rapid decline. Blockbuster Video had an enormous head start, much better brand recognition, greater financial resources, etc., than did Netflix.

---

[18] Not all products are a good fit for being sold online as the online grocery store WebVan learned.
[19] Actually, one way that Blockbuster Video became so popular was by offering more titles and better inventory management capabilities over many smaller, independently operated stores. However, even with that number of titles, Blockbuster Video stores concentrated their inventory in recently released titles. Blockbuster Video was the leader in DVD inventory management, but no physical store-based inventory model can compete with what is essentially a direct-from-warehouse inventory model.

However, Netflix had the better design. Netflix is known as an Internet phenomenon and while their website is, in fact, excellent, they are equally a supply chain management phenomenon.

Netflix carries roughly 93,500 more titles than each Blockbuster Video store did.[20] Clearly, with so many titles, some of which are "specialty" titles, Netflix happens to have more lumpy demand for their less popular items. Netflix is one example of a company that is exploiting hyper selection to attract and retain customers, and Amazon.com is another. The fact is that Internet storefronts allow companies to carry more items than they ever could in physical storefronts. However, this also means increased numbers of lower or lumpy demand products in the mix which must be managed by demand planning systems.

Now that we have described some of the factors driving the increase in lumpy demand history, we will describe one of the major myths related to dealing with difficult-to-forecast products.

Dealing with Lumpy Demand with Complex Methods

Lumpy or intermittent demand is the bane of effective forecasting. One of the major approaches to dealing with difficult-to-forecast products has been to apply increasingly sophisticated forecasting methods, the results of which have generally not been positive. However, this has not changed the belief that using more complex forecasting methods is an effective strategy. Executives often see complex forecasting methods as a magic bullet. In fact, it seems that the more indecipherable the forecasting method, the higher its status, as exemplified by one of the major intermittent forecasting methods called Croston's. Croston's has been a source of hope for executive decision makers to improve the forecasting of lumpy demand items since it was first incorporated in enterprise demand planning software. It's difficult to see where all of this confidence and enthusiasm is coming from, as various research papers on Croston's are inconclusive regarding its benefits.

---

[20] An exact approximation is not possible as some stores carried different titles, so the number of total unique titles in the system was higher. However, every title was not available at every Blockbuster Video store, whereas every Netflix title is available to every Netflix customer.

Wayne Fu, at Servigistics[21] and myself analyzed Croston's and determined that it would only improve the forecast over much more simple methods in a very small number of situations. This article is available at the link below:

http://www.scmfocus.com/demandplanning/2010/07/crostons-vs-smoothie-methods/

Therefore, forecast methods that are too complex to be easily understood, backward engineered and placed into Excel, are not particularly beneficial as they are frequently emulated by simpler methods. In fact, the forecasting methods that are actually being used at most companies tend to be quite simple, and the obsession with the complex methods is mostly talk. Complex methods seem to hold the continual promise of improved forecast accuracy, but are much less frequently implemented than simple methods.

Croston's is one of the most complex forecasting algorithms used in demand planning, and few people understand the exact mathematics for what it does. This is, in my view, why it continues to be popular regardless of its value in improving forecast accuracy. In fact, it's not difficult to predict that Croston's will continue to be popular because of the general and entirely unfounded belief that difficult-to-forecast products benefit from more sophisticated mathematical forecasting models. Commercial incentives and pressures are at play in both what vendors offer in their applications and what is written about forecasting. New forecast methodologies are not necessarily developed because they are superior to simpler and easier-to-implement techniques, but because they help get research papers published and help sell software and obtain consulting contracts. Some complex forecasting methods are incorporated into applications simply because clients demand them. One software vendor I am familiar with added Croston's to their product, not because they thought it was going to be beneficial to customers, but because executives kept asking for it. Adding Croson's made their applications seem more "leading edge." The lack of benefit from more complex methods is described in J. Scott Armstrong's research paper "Conclusions of 25 Years of Research", quotes from which I have listed below:

---

[21] A service parts planning vendor. Because they work in the service space, they are of course, very experienced with forecasting lumpy demand history.

> *More important, Table 1 provides little evidence to suggest that sophistication beyond the methods available in the 1960s has had any payoff. Relatively simple methods seem to offer comparable accuracy; twenty-one studies concluded that there were negligible differences, and for the eighteen studies showing differences, eleven favored sophistication, and seven favored simplicity. However, of the eleven cases favoring sophistication, three have since been challenged, and three cases were based on the superiority of exponential smoothing (available prior to 1960). We are left with five comparisons favoring sophistication and seven favoring simplicity.*
>
> *In general, the findings on sophisticated methods are puzzling, and it is unlikely that they could have been anticipated in 1960. Many of the sophisticated methods made good sense. For example, it seemed reasonable to expect that models in which the parameters are automatically revised as new information comes in should be more accurate.*

However, more complex methods can produce the illusion of producing a more accurate forecast because they often fit better with demand history. This is called "over-fitting" and was pointed out by Michael Gilliland earlier in this chapter.

> *Highly complex models may reduce accuracy. While these complex models provide better fits to historical data, this superiority does not hold for forecasting. The danger is especially serious when limited historical data are available.*

J. Scott Armstrong's research is a meta-analysis—it combines the results of multiple studies that address a specific hypothesis. The breakdown is as follows:

1. Eleven studies showed that complex methods outperformed simple methods
2. Twenty-one studies showed no improvement by using more complex methods
3. Seven studies showed that simple methods outperformed complex methods

Even though, on average, complex methods did not improve forecast accuracy, in fact, the performance of a more complex method in a tightly controlled research study gives an unfair and unmentioned advantage to that complex method. That is, the more complex methods perform better in a controlled research study than in a real life environment where they require more forecasting effort and maintenance.

Now that we have discussed the myth of increased model sophistication for difficult-to-forecast products, we will move into the topic of how to identify unforecastable products.

Examples of Unforecastable Demand

The central premise of this chapter is that many products are inherently unforecastable. As was stated earlier, a lack of forecastability can be determined mathematically and it can also be determined visually. I find that displaying the graphics of unforecastable products is a very educational exercise, and I have used this technique with clients to get the point across. A visual representation of unforecastability is better, in my view, than representing the same thing with a series of numbers in columns.

The following graphics are examples of unforecastable demand history. An analysis of each is provided below the screen shot.

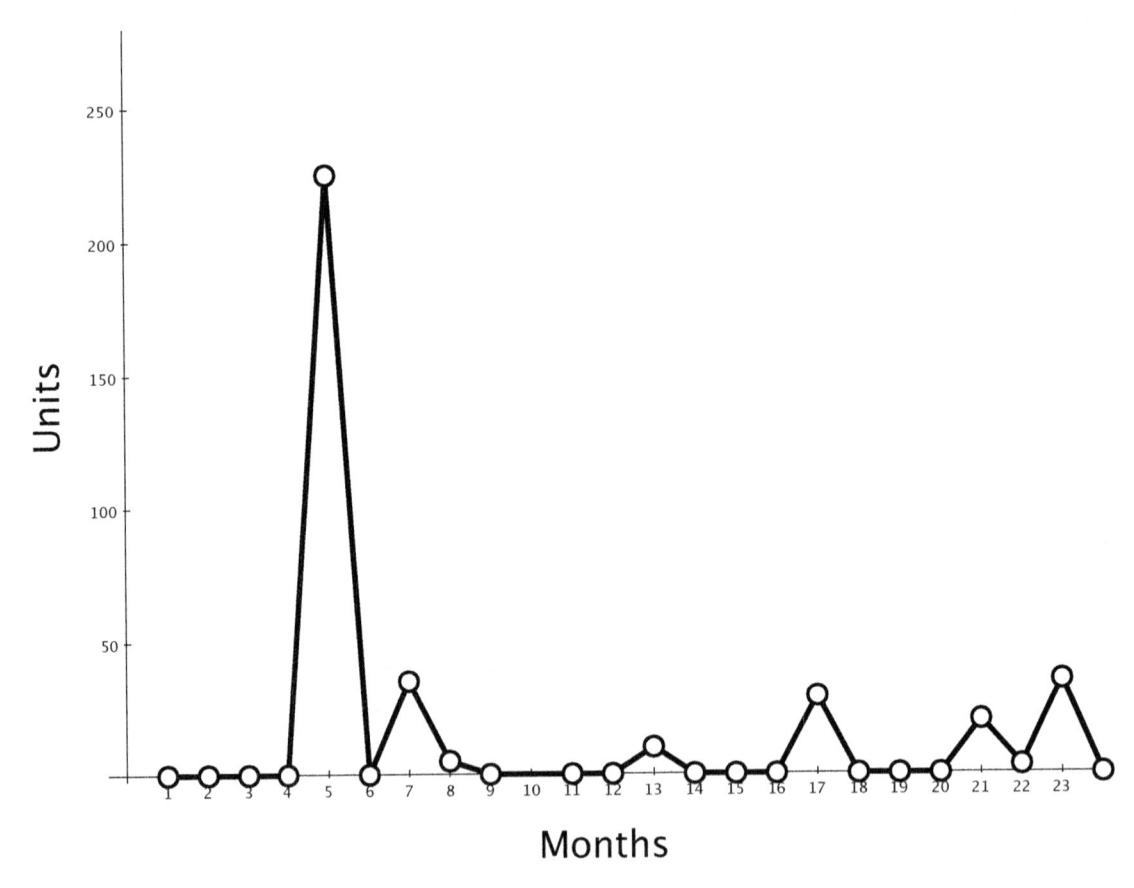

This product is clearly statistically unforecastable as there is no discernible pattern. This product has one demand peak in month seven (July), and several other smaller demand points, but simply not enough to forecast another demand point. This is a fairly obvious unforecastable demand pattern. The next example is a bit more complicated.

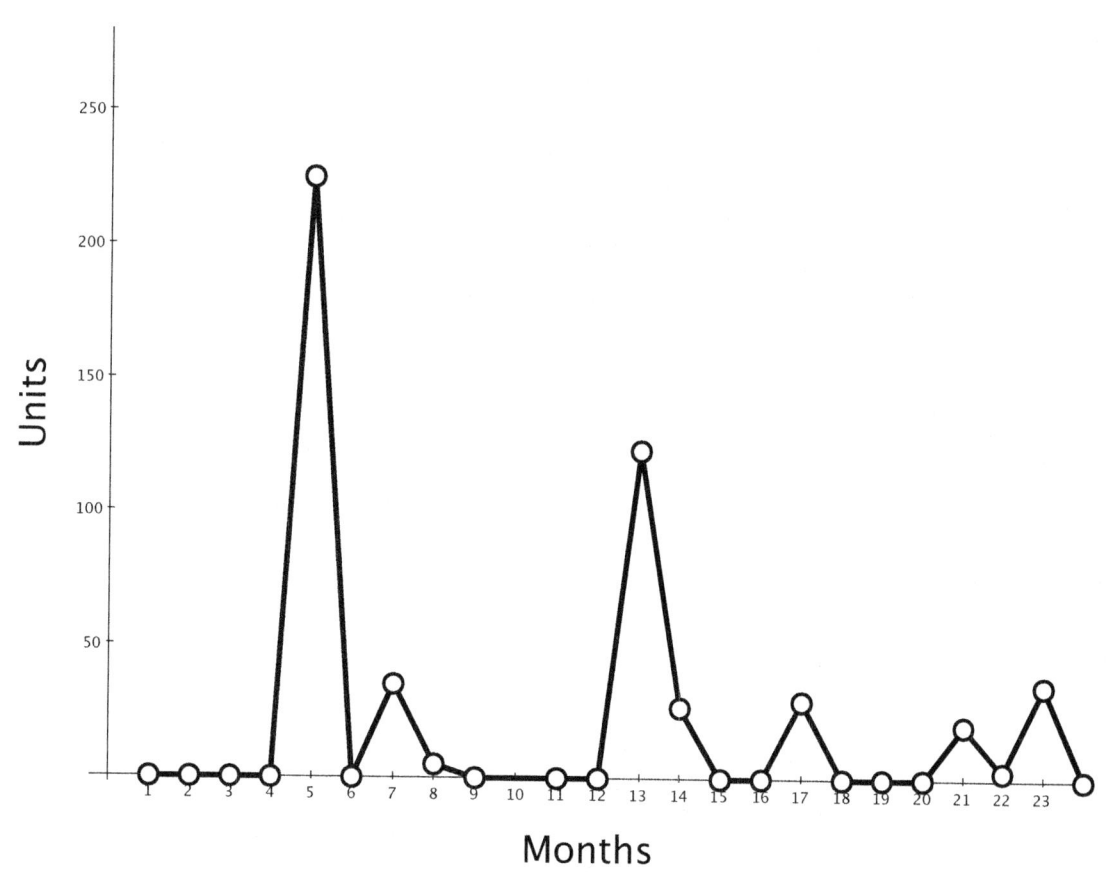

In this case there are two demand peaks, and it might appear to be a good bet that the demand peak will repeat a third time...except it is not a good bet, because the first peak is in month five (May) of the first year, and the second peak is in month one, (January) in the second year. Where this product is going next is anyone's guess. This product is also unforecastable.

Lumpy Demand in JDA

While graphical analysis of forecastability is a great educational tool, it's not useful for evaluating an entire product database. For this task, usually mathematics must be performed on an extract from the system. Some vendors provide the functionality of evaluating forecastability within the application. One of these vendors is JDA.

JDA DM has an automated approach for lumpy demand identification. JDA DM flags demand that it considers too lumpy. Within their application an exception will be posted. This is called a "1013 – Irregular Demand History" exception, and can be seen in the screen shot below.

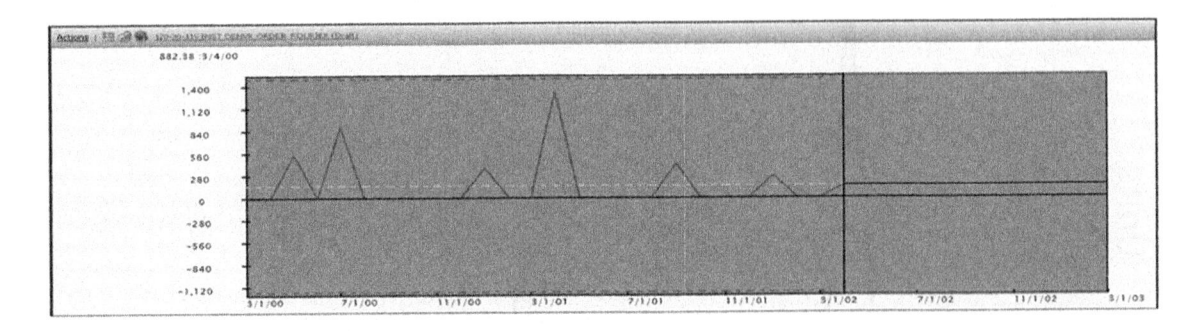

In fact, JDA DM has the concept of unforecastability built into its software, although it is not explicitly called this. The result that is produced by JDA DM is a many-period average, as is described in the quotation from JDA DM's training manual below:

> *Lumpy demand occurs when demand for a DFU is so varied that **no pattern is distinguished**. When the system detects lumpy demand, it will produce a one-term model with the level equal to average history.*

There are a large number of products for which no forecast can be developed that is superior to a many-period moving average or a modified many-period moving average. That is true of a purely statistical means, although judgment methods also rely at least partially upon historical pattern recognition, even if the patterns that are recognized are in the history of similar products.

Research into Methods for Dealing with Lumpy Demand

Lumpy demand is an area that has been extensively researched and for which there are many specialized forecasting algorithms. Common methods used for lumpy demand forecasting include:

1. Simple Moving Average
2. Single Exponential Smoothing

3. Croston's Method

4. SBA (Syntetos and Boylan) Method

We have already discussed the (many period) simple moving average, which is extremely simple to implement. The methods become more complex as they move from numbers one to four.

Problems with the Common Approaches for Dealing with Difficult-to-Forecast Products

The most common approach to managing difficult-to-forecast products is to put more effort into forecasting them and to attempt to forecast them with more complex algorithms. It's not as if this common approach hasn't had sufficient time to prove itself. The problems with forecasting these products are not related to limitations in mathematics or to limitations in hardware or software design that will be rectified in the future. In fact, decades ago, the hope was that more powerful computer systems would enable the automated use of more complex forecasting methods. This, of course, has not come about.

Is It Necessary to Actively Forecast the Entire Product Database?

There is no reason to hold this belief, yet it is frequently assumed to be true. More often than not, the question simply is not asked and companies forecast the entire database. Instead of taking this approach, the product database should be segmented into those product-location combinations for which active forecasting will improve the forecast, and those that will not.

How to Identify Unforecastable Products

Bill Tonetti at Demand Works has the following to say on forecastability measurement:

> The most common estimates of "forecastability" are the coefficient of variation, which is the ratio of standard deviation divided by the series mean, and MAD-Mean ratio, which is the ration of Mean Absolute Deviation, divided by the series mean. Both of these statistics essentially do the same thing; however, the MAD-Mean ratio is superior in that it removes forecastable trends and seasonalities from the estimate by

> *using MAD instead of SD. Smoothie, and several other applications, provide these output statistics to help companies to gauge forecastability.*

In the past I have used a formula to identify unforecastable products. The formula is placed into a spreadsheet. It can work with variables which are exported from a demand planning system. For instance, Smoothie generates a series of values that can be used as inputs to a formula that determines if products are forecastable. These values, output by the statistics file in Smoothie, include the following:

1. Series mean
2. Series Standard Deviation
3. Mean Absolute Deviation
4. Mean Absolute Percentage Error
5. R Squared
6. Model Selected (Seasonal, Level-Seasonal, Trend, etc.)

Most statistical enterprise demand planning systems can produce the identical output.

> http://www.scmfocus.com/demandplanning/2010/06/forecastable-non-forecastable-formula/

Once this analysis is complete, any company can neatly divide their product database into forecastable and unforecastable products, which can help them better manage their forecasting efforts.

Excluding Dependent Demand Products from the Analysis

In the past, when I have discussed with clients the percentage of a product database that is forecastable, the issue of dependent demand products naturally comes up. When performing the forecastability analysis, it's *unnecessary to include dependent demand products.*[22] This is because the dependent demand is easily

---

[22] For those who are unfamiliar with this term, "dependent demand" means the products that depend on the demand of another product.

calculated during the supply planning process. However, when a forecastability percentage is presented after the analysis is complete, it's important to explain that removing dependent demand products makes the database look much less forecastable than it actually is. All dependent demand products for the forecastable products are of course also forecastable.

Managing Products with No Forecast with Supply Planning

One might think that it's not really possible to simply stop forecasting products. In fact, it is quite possible and easy to implement, although there can be a fair amount of complexity in the methods designed to calculate reorder points (something that is not commonly understood by those that oppose reorder point planning on the grounds that it is too simple). In the book, *Supply Planning with MRP/DRP and APS Software,* I cover reorder point planning differently than it is covered in a number of supply planning books, so I won't repeat the information here. Suffice it to say that there are many cases where it is better not to send a forecast to the supply planning system, and the supply planning system will still manage quite well. Therefore, a simple moving average forecast can be sent for unforecastable products, or no forecast at all.

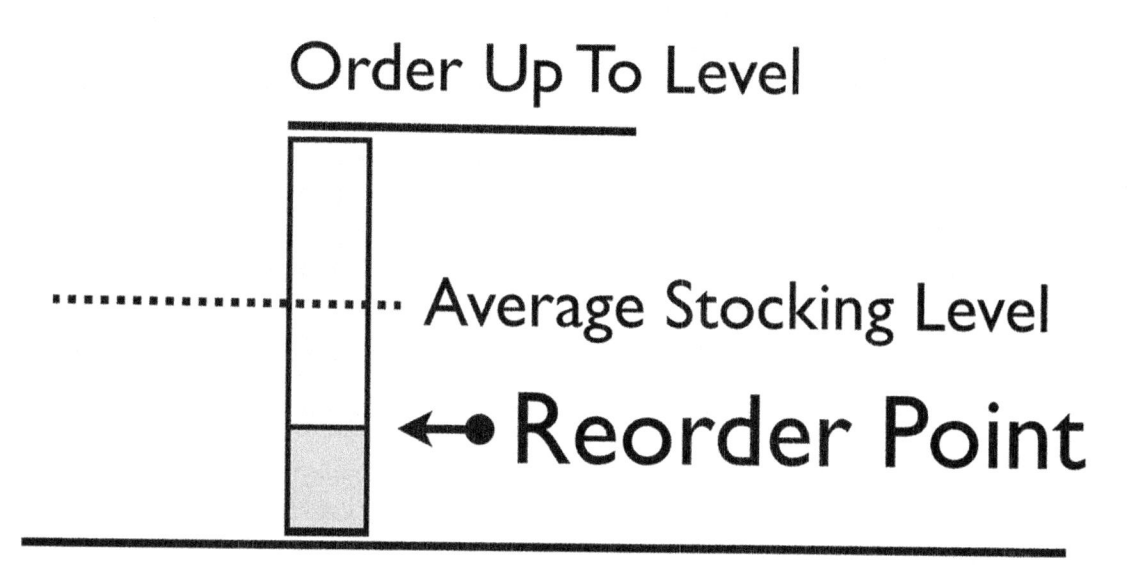

Order Up To Level

·········· Average Stocking Level

← Reorder Point

Reorder point setting does not require a forecast because the order is placed when the inventory drops to a certain level. However, there is not "one right way" of doing this. Regardless, the company gets away from continuing to invest effort in forecasting unforecastable products.

Conclusion

Analyzing the forecastability of the product database is one of the important steps to moving toward a more effective way of managing the forecasting process. For some products, a more advanced forecasting method cannot reasonably be expected to be an improvement over a simple, long duration moving average forecast. A number of trends are reducing forecastability of the product database, including actions by marketing (such as promotions) and SKU proliferation (spreading the same demand over more products). Interestingly, the connection is not frequently made between these trends and forecastability. The more erratic demand becomes, the less forecasting can add value, and increased amounts of inventory must be carried to ensure that sufficient inventory exists when demand does arrive. This fact is lost on people who are unfamiliar with forecasting.

Forecastability of the entire product database can be determined by a formula. Viewing a line graph of demand history and searching for a discernible pattern can determine forecastability of a single product or product grouping. If a pattern cannot be found visually, it is unlikely that a statistical system will be able to produce a forecast better than a level, also known as a multi-period moving average. A second category of products for which there is similarly little benefit to forecasting are those with extremely stable demand histories. Both demand histories can be set up with reorder point planning in the supply planning system.

CHAPTER 13

Why Companies Select the Wrong Forecasting Software

Background

A specialty forecasting software vendor once explained to me that many of the companies they deal with often try to use inappropriate forecasting solutions before finally deciding to use this vendor's software. According to this vendor, companies first attempt to perform the forecasting using their existing CRM systems and then, when that doesn't work, their ERP systems. Both the vendor and I know that these systems are not suitable or designed for consensus-based forecasting, and the vendor makes a product that is specifically designed for CBF.

In my own personal consulting experience, I find companies frequently use the wrong software to manage forecasting processes. There are a couple of reasons for this. Many decision makers do not know that specialized solutions have been designed for the different types of forecasting. Secondly, they are also unaware that it is quite difficult, if not impossible, to get a forecasting system designed to manage one process to handle a completely different process.

When forecasting applications were first developed external to the ERP system, a narrow spectrum of applications was developed for demand planning and these were primarily designed for the statistical forecasting process. However, statistical forecasting is only one of several forecasting processes, and over the years the variety of demand planning applications has increased significantly. Therefore, attempting to force all of a company's forecasting needs through a single application is no longer necessary or desirable. The diagram below represents the various forecasting processes:

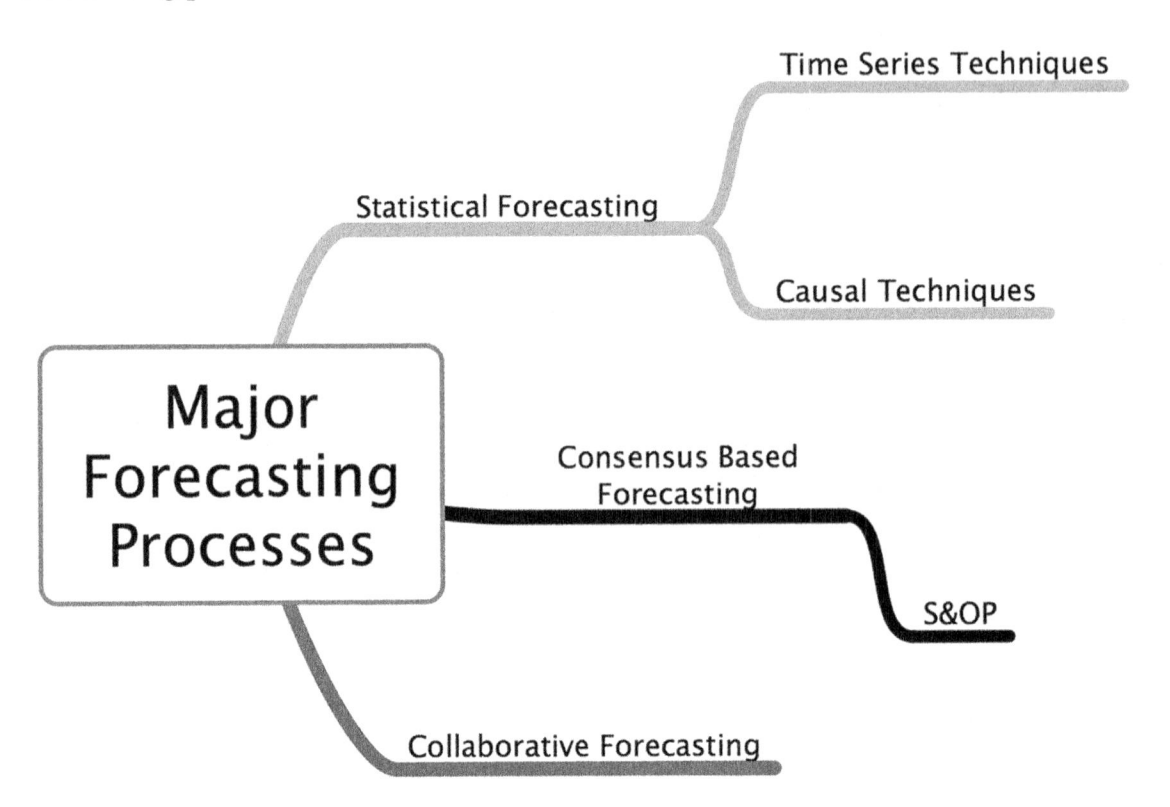

Major Forecasting Processes
- Statistical Forecasting
  - Time Series Techniques
  - Causal Techniques
- Consensus Based Forecasting
  - S&OP
- Collaborative Forecasting

A common mistake companies seem to make is trying to use statistical forecasting packages to manage the other forecasting processes. Part of the reason that companies do this is because both the major vendors (who tend to only offer statistical packages) and the major consulting companies (IBM, Accenture, Deloitte, etc.) incorrectly advise companies that statistical demand planning software can be used to manage non-statistical process forecasting. I have discussed this topic with several best-of-breed vendors in different demand planning niches and have on several occasions been told that the major consulting companies either don't understand or don't care to understand that using statistical demand planning software for all of a company's forecasting needs is extremely inefficient.

The largest software vendors generally lag the best-of-breed vendors in the area of forecasting software, but this lag does not stop them from selling their software. They take a portfolio management approach to software, and can sit and wait while smaller and more pioneering vendors innovate. Many companies looking for the best software on the market fall into the trap of selecting their software by brand. Tom Reilly at Autobox, a best-of-breed forecast application vendor, describes the problems that he sees with good forecast software selection:

> *Companies choose integrated systems that provide full ERP solutions based on the old "you won't get fired for buying IBM" herd mentality. These large ERP "womb to tomb" solutions are the market leaders, but do each of their components lead the market? We think not. IT drives a lot of the decision making and they have a perfunctory view. The "one size fits all" garments never really do fit quite perfectly. The road less traveled can be rocky, but can also be rewarding.*
>
> *The forecasting systems found in the major ERP systems use simple and flawed models that don't question the data and end up with silly baseline forecasts. They ignore the concept of level shifts, seasonal pulses and changes in trend. The way they handle outliers is far too simple. If you give them a time series like 1,9,1,9,1,9,1,5 they won't be able to find the outlier, or in this case, inlier.*
>
> *You need to consider why the large ERP vendors don't participate in forecasting competitions. Why should they risk their market position? Why should they be exposed when they are fat and happy? You should consider reviewing results from independent competitions to see who is delivering quality-forecasting tools http://www.neural-forecasting-competition.com/ Many who participate are not software houses, but there are a few that did.*

If one best-of-breed vendor becomes very popular in the enterprise software space, the large vendors have so many resources that they simply purchase that vendor (at which point innovation tends to decline). However, some of the applications provided by the smaller vendors are exciting and have a great potential to improve forecast accuracy. This topic is covered in the post below:

http://www.scmfocus.com/enterprisesoftwarepolicy/2012/03/11/why-the-largest-enterprise-software-companies-have-no-reason-to-innovate/

Even within one demand planning software category, the major consulting companies do a poor job of advising their clients. Instead, they select the vendors that maximize the revenues of the consulting companies rather than actually comparing the business requirements against all the vendors in a category. Because companies across the country have relied upon large consulting companies for their demand planning software selection, many demand planning departments cannot perform forecasting operations that are basic in best-of-breed applications. The big winners in all of this are the major software vendors and Microsoft, because the less planners can get out of a forecasting system, the more they will use Excel.

Obtaining Quality Information on Demand Planning Software

It is hard for companies to access unbiased information on demand planning software. I have already discussed the biased information that is available from the major consulting companies, and how the major vendors buy off the editorial viewpoints of major media outlets with advertising, access control, and sometimes direct financial contributions in the cases of analysts. If you will recall, in Chapter 1: "Introduction", I discussed the shortage of books on enterprise demand planning software. Books on demand planning either do not address software, or tend to provide a rather biased coverage of the application in which that writer is an expert. However, the problems are not limited to these issues.

For instance, there is currently only one analyst firm prominent in supply chain software, and that is Gartner. However, Gartner tends to offer high-level advice and it is well known that they tend to favor the large vendors over all others. They also receive a lot of income from the biggest vendors. I discussed the issues with incentives and forecast bias in Chapter 9: "Bias Removal", incentives result in biased reviews the same way they result in forecast bias. And when it comes to the Internet, much of the information available about demand planning is quite commercial in nature.

Therefore, you can see how problematic it is for companies to access quality unbiased information on demand planning applications. Accurate information on software can be difficult to obtain even when companies spend time doing research and reach out to other companies that have implemented the software. Vendors put companies that are evaluating their software in touch with companies that have implemented the same software; however, vendors tend not to use companies that have had significant problems with the software as reference accounts.

Thus, it is important to get hands-on experience with software. In particular, the planners—the eventual users of the system—should get firsthand experience with the software, and their input should be included in the decision-making process. Executives, who do not forecast for a living and are not demand planners (furthermore very few executives are ex-demand planners), cannot independently evaluate forecasting software with the same insight as planners. Executives have the authority to choose software and to give budgetary approval, but this should not be confused with domain expertise—they need support from their planners to make good choices.

The False Dichotomy of Consensus Versus Statistical Methods

Currently, many companies are reading articles like the one that I critique below that describes a false dichotomy between consensus and statistical methods in terms of what the company should focus on.

> http://www.scmfocus.com/demandplanning/2010/02/incorrect-forecasting-article-by-cio-on-nike/

This article uses a quote from AMR Research to describe how Nike is moving toward consensus methods:

> *"There's been a change in the technology for demand planning,"*
> *says AMR Research Vice President Bill Swanton, who declined to*

address the Nike case specifically. "In the late '90s, companies said all we need is the data and we can plan everything perfectly. Today, companies are trying to do consensus planning rather than demand planning."

— CIO

The reason that the article in CIO is unhelpful is that Nike will always have a statistical forecasting process and a consensus forecasting process regardless of what forecasting category is "trending" or "hot" at the time. Software must be designed specifically for the process in question. Statements such as, "Eighty-five percent or sixty percent of forecast improvement opportunities lie in statistical or consensus forecasting," are not useful as a rule of thumb to direct effort. All of the forecasting processes must be addressed, and solutions exist to most effectively address every type of forecasting process. In addition, a thoughtfully selected solution that is matched appropriately to the forecast process in question can easily pay for itself in improved forecast error and lower supply chain costs.

Performing Quality Software Selections

Companies have little support in performing quality software selections. A thorough and unbiased software selection means the following:

1. Do not allow the consulting firm assisting in the selection to base the selection on relationships with software vendors.

2. Do not allow the consulting revenues that will benefit the advisory firm if a certain package is implemented drive the selection of the software. (Large consulting companies tend to have resources trained in certain applications, and they would like to staff implementations of these applications. Take a guess what software they will select for your company!)

3. As a general statement, never let a consulting firm take control of, or skew or stack the deck in the selection process. Consulting companies have different incentives than do implementation companies. The company ultimately has to live with the application long term. The consulting company is just there to make money off of the implementation. Secondly, the historical record of software recommended by consulting companies has been quite poor in terms of matching requirements to applications. There is no reason

to give their recommendations more than passing acknowledgement. Also, consulting companies are not filled with conscientious individuals who will care if they stick their clients with high maintenance and poorly performing forecasting application, and the higher one goes up in a consulting company the more focused the individuals are on making their consulting service sales quotas.

4. Don't allow people who either have no or very little software implementation experience very much influence in software selection. Software selections must be staffed with individuals with actual software experience. Most large consulting companies provide strategy consultants rather than consultants with a software background. For consultants with no software background, software selection projects are simply box checking exercises.[23]

5. Perform a thorough analysis of the business requirements. Rank each application by how it actually performs in real usage with the requirement. Do not rely on only literature or statements made by vendors.

6. Understand the demand planning software offered by the marketplace.

7. Perform detailed research, and create a write up of this research and the logic behind the selection. (The type of explanation required to back up the selection decision is far too detailed to be placed in PowerPoint or other presentation software.) You can read about the problems in attempting to document and made decisions on complex topics in Edward Tuffe's article on PowerPoint and the Columbia disaster at the link below:

http://www.edwardtufte.com/bboard/q-and-a-fetch-msg?msg_id=0001yB&topic_id=1

8. Involve those who will actually use the system in the selection process. (Usability is a critical area usually overlooked in most software selections.)

---

[23] This reminds me of a software selection or comparison from IBM where Steelwedge was compared to SAP BW for S&OP forecasting. IBM had the two listed as very close even though SAP BW is a data warehouse and Steelwedge is an actual S&OP application. Choosing to use BW for S&OP is essentially the same as choosing a development environment in which an S&OP solution could be created. Comparing an application to a development environment is ridiculous. However, a real software selection is impossible when the most important box to check for the consulting company is the box of which vendor they have the better relationship with and which vendor can maximize the consulting company's revenues.

Extend demos into multi-hours affairs with many of the demand planners in the presentation for the entire duration. Provide some type of structured rating approach and forms, which requires that planners write down their observations so that these notes can be referenced in later discussions.

9. Ensure that any information sources that provide opinions on the software are unbiased. This means that the source should not take direct contributions or advertising from vendors.

10. Perform a comparative total cost of ownership (TCO) analysis. I have done this for a number of applications, often with surprising results. The process of developing the TCO can help in evaluating the project assumptions. At the link below, I have a demand planning TCO which you can use as a template:

   http://www.scmfocus.com/demandplanning/2011/09/what-if-you-paid-nothing-for-sap-software-how-saps-tco-compares-for-demand-planning/

Many companies live in a continual state of denial regarding their forecasting problems. They tend to think, "if only the demand planners would change the way they do XYZ, then things will be better." However, the basic issue of whether the company has the right forecasting applications for their needs seems to be far less frequently discussed. Demand planning is different than supply planning or production planning in that unlike these areas—where it is quite feasible (although even here, often not optimal) to use a single solution—there are too many forecasting needs to meet all of them realistically with a single solution.

Conclusion

There are lots of reasons that companies select the wrong forecasting software. The reasons extended from excluding the members of the company with forecasting domain expertise from the decision making process to being deliberately misled by consulting companies that don't have their interests at heart. Poor software selection greatly restricts companies from improving their forecasting. Forecast improvement is very difficult if you have selected a bad application. The software selection process is the most important part of forecast improvement because it determines what the ceiling will be for the company's forecast accuracy.

There are many easy things that can be done to improve software selection. They do require a far more methodical approach than the rather half-baked approach to software selection, which is more of the norm, but they are completely worth it. Once a bad forecasting application is selected, there becomes as very strong tendency to try to justify the solution no matter how poor its performance. Companies usually stick with bad software for at least six years before considering switching to a new application. Planners are often the first to be blamed. "Why do the keep using Excel so much after we bought this expensive solution?" The next to be blamed is training. "The planners just need to be retrained." No one wants to own up to the fact that they made poor decisions and did not manage the software selection properly. I have a better idea, follow the rules in this chapter, do not make software selections based upon brand and get the right solution right out of the gate. It's really not that difficult, but does require a disciplined approach. Then take all the mental energy that is used to deflect blame and come up with various excuses for the application, and instead use it to improve the use of a well-selected system and achieve better forecast accuracy.

CHAPTER 14

Conclusion

Introduction

A central premise of this book is that there are many opportunities to improve forecast accuracy. Within the book, a number of ways to make improvements have been described, none of which are hypothetical and all of which can be implemented as of the time of this book's publication. However, I am a realist. Even though the approaches and technologies are available, not many companies will be able to implement them. Many of the ideas presented in this book are conceptually simple yet difficult to implement in practice because companies often develop a mindset around demand planning that makes it very difficult for them to change and improve. Some of the major problems faced by demand planning organizations that stand in the way of improvement are:

1. An inability to allocate demand planning resources to focus on the right things.

2. Not baselining the statistical forecast models that are used against naïve models.

3. Poor demand planning software selection (typically led by a major consulting company with partnerships with a very large software vendor).

4. Overall, poor consulting in forecasting, with companies relying upon systems consultants for forecasting advice, many of whom are primarily applications specialists (unfortunately, there does not seem to be much of a market for pure forecasting specialists, unless they are connected to some application).

5. Attempting to perform one category of forecasting using an application that was designed for a different category of forecasting (i.e., attempting consensus forecasting in a statistical forecasting application).

6. A myopic focus on getting all demand planning needs met by a single application.

7. An overemphasis on the wrong issues, such as forecast error measurement type, rather than focusing on the context of the forecast error.

8. An inability to access the best forecasting software available.

9. Refusing to admit to and address forecast bias.

10. Using best-fit forecasting incorrectly.

11. Relying upon static hierarchy demand planning applications, combined with an inability to find more appropriate applications to leverage attribute-based forecasting in many different forecasting dimensions.

12. Receiving little support from other areas of the company, such as marketing, which could make it easier for the demand planning department to produce better forecasts.

In fact, forecasting is so poorly managed at most companies that forecasting would be a prime candidate for outsourcing if companies felt they could trust a third party with their data and were able to commit to a high level of communication and let the third party know of important information, such as future promotions, in a timely manner. This topic is covered in more detail in the post below:

http://www.scmfocus.com/demandplanning/2012/03/outsourced-forecasting/

Overall, the biggest impediment is simply being open minded enough to take a different approach to what is the norm and to what one is used to. Adhering to how things are usually done in companies with respect to forecasting does not make a lot of sense, because common practice misses so many easy areas of improvement.

Attribute-based Forecasting

A second premise of this book is that forecasting by attributes is the future of forecasting. In fact, the future should be here already, but industry implementations frequently lags what is available in software. Attribute-based forecasting greatly improves the functionality of the demand planning application and also reduces the amount of maintenance required, the time to implement the application and improves the overall sustainability of demand planning solutions. With the right attribute-based forecasting system (and there are enormous differences between applications that claim attribute capabilities), the static hierarchy, which requires external reference tables or realignment to provide flexibility, can be a thing of the past. This allows the virtual hierarchy (or attribute sequence) to be flexibly altered and customized per user. This is an important advance in the history of forecasting software. Many of the associated benefits of attributes were described in this book and extend from efficient top-down forecasting to being able to flexibly group products for anything from lifecycle planning to volume manual adjustments.

An important consideration when comparing and selecting demand planning software is the competency of the software's data layer. To a great degree, the data layer determines what can be accomplished in the application, as well as the effort required to maintain the application. Software vendors that offer applications with a static hierarchy (with some attribute capabilities after the fact) are typically not the answer. Once a company has become convinced of the benefit of forecasting by attributes, it can be a challenge for them to select the right software, as they will face vendors who say their system can forecast by attributes when, in fact, this functionality in their software is weak. Fooled by the vendors, companies often end up with weak attribute-based forecasting systems, which is why I am being so specific about warning companies on this topic.

Here is one of the most important things I have learned from my experiences in enterprise software: The existence in the release notes of a description of functionality, or of a statement that an application "can do" something, says nothing about how easily that "thing" can be done in actual practice. The ease of controlling a system is instrumental in whether the desired functionality can be implemented and maintained. This may be one of the most misunderstood truisms about enterprise software, and is something I will continue to write about even if many others choose not to. This is also why software selection should never be based upon a simple comparison of functionality between various applications—an actual checking off of a list without any in-depth research into the implications of an application having or not having a particular function except to reduce the dimensions of the analysis.

Simply put, not all attribute capabilities and ROLAP technology are created equal, as the post below describes:

> http://www.scmfocus.com/demandplanning/2012/03/why-not-all-attribute-and-rolap-solutions-are-equal/

Different Forecasting Software for Different Forecasting Processes

A third premise of this book is that different software is designed for different software processes, and no forecasting application is the best at incorporating all the different processes. Currently, one of the biggest mistakes companies make is attempting to implement consensus-based forecasting processes in an application designed for statistical forecasting.

There are both significant design differences within any one forecasting category (the user interface, the functionality, the data layer, etc.) as well as in the different categories of enterprise demand planning software. There is no way of getting around the fact that companies have multiple forecasting processes, and while in books and on the conference circuit the pendulum may swing in favor of one category of forecasting over another, the different types of forecasting must be accommodated and companies should be able to do all the categories of forecasting well. Consensus-based forecasting cannot substitute for statistical forecasting any more than statistical forecasting can substitute for collaborative forecasting. By showing a number of different forecasting software categories and emphasizing design differences with the categories I have attempted to increase awareness about the available options. Companies are missing out by not broadening the scope of their forecasting application holdings.

Bias Removal

A fourth premise of the book is that bias removal is extremely important for improving forecast accuracy. Bias is one of the easiest things to evaluate technically. Conversely, removing bias is one of the most difficult things to do politically. In fact, as much as companies declare their interest in improving forecast accuracy, they are positively timid in their efforts to address—much less reduce—forecast bias. For many companies, it is as if the large body of work on forecasting bias simply does not exist.

Bias rears its ugly head in every type of forecasting that I have researched. Bias is so prevalent and unquestioned that it's really quite an interesting field of study, and if bias were more openly acknowledged, many people with quite prominent positions would cease to be relevant as prognosticators. For instance, when Goldman Sachs releases a "buy" recommendation, media outlets often repeat their recommendation. However, the media does not point out or ask if Goldman Sachs holds a position in the asset they recommending as a "buy." Does the ability to make money bias their recommendations? It's curious these questions are not asked more frequently.

Excellent record keeping is necessary for bias removal to be effective. One of the reasons people are unable to see bias more broadly is because they lack the collective memory of past predictions. However, record keeping is a huge challenge for companies that are not familiar with doing this. Many parts of the business are managed without an extensive archival of anything but financial records. A short-term approach will never work for forecasting, because forecasting is by its nature dependent upon the quality of historical data. Many companies are just doing the bare minimum by keeping historical sales and measuring a single forecast error. Most companies don't even segment their system-generated forecast error from their manually-adjusted error, as is described in this post below:

> http://www.scmfocus.com/demandplanning/2012/02/how-much-can-your-forecasting-accuracy-be-improved/

Considering today's level of technological sophistication, it is baffling that most companies don't know the effect of the bias of different areas of their company on their forecast, much less the effect of the bias of different individuals. On the other hand, many vendors don't emphasize bias detection in their applications, so in many cases companies are required to build custom reports to determine forecast bias. It is rare for software vendors to make bias identification a focal point (although consensus forecasting vendors seem to be ahead of the curve on this topic). Therefore, most companies lack software with an internal dashboard that allows the company to adjust for bias. This is where custom report building comes into play.

Forecastablility

A fifth premise of this book is that not all demand histories are forecastable. Companies can and do consider all of their products as being applicable to forecasting, when, in fact, this is not true. Statistical forecasting is based upon being able to detect and replicate a discernible historical pattern. Some products inherently lack a discernible pattern, but many of the activities performed by companies actively and significantly increase the lumpiness of the "natural" demand pattern far beyond what the normal differential between ordering and consumption would be. A lumpy demand history decreases the forecastability of the product database. Most marketing activities, particularly over the past three decades, have added to this lumpiness and have done nothing but increase the number of unforecastable products in the database.

Operations does not have an equal place at the table, so decisions that are quite bad for a company from a supply chain perspective are the norm. Trader Joe's is an example of a company that takes a disciplined approach to new product introductions and rationally puts themselves in an excellent position for good forecast accuracy and efficient distribution. However, Trader Joe's is so unusual in this respect that they are considered a quirky anomaly.

Products without a discernible historical pattern do not benefit from forecasting, and forecasts that are produced for these products do not help supply planning make better ordering and stocking decisions. Many people—even those with experience—lose sight of the fact that making better ordering and stocking decisions is the main purpose of forecasting. Forecasting is performed to provide value to other planning components of the company. Unfortunately, those vendors who promise to apply sophisticated techniques to products with lumpy demand histories are mostly selling companies an illusion.

Products that lack a discernible demand history can be placed on reorder point planning in the supply planning system. A forecast is not required for products on reorder point planning. The lesson to take away is: Don't assume that a forecast needs to be created for every product-location combination.

The Future

As with other areas of supply chain planning, companies now have more options for their demand planning than ever before. The offerings have moved beyond statistical forecasting applications, to those customized for consensus and collaborative forecasting and even S&OP forecasting. All of this diversity and choice also means that more analysis is required to pick the best solution, which is something that many companies—many of whom have only ever purchased and implemented statistical forecasting applications, and who even in just that limited exposure to software selection currently have the wrong applications for their needs—are simply not used to doing. This is why implementation of forecasting solutions significantly lag the best that is available currently and will for some time to come. This means that forecast accuracy will greatly lag it potential within companies. Within each forecasting category, significant innovations have taken place. While these innovations have yet to be broadly leveraged, they can make forecasting far more accurate than it has been in the past. As one example, for the first time we are seeing SaaS forecasting solutions, which are important for obtaining inputs from multiple sources (both inside an organization and among multiple organizations), which reduces one of the major barriers to increasing the forecasting inputs. Right now these solutions tend to be focused on consensus or collaborative forecasting processes. However, SaaS applications can offer significant benefits for statistical forecasting as well. SaaS applications allow for more remote assistance, which is particularly beneficial for statistical forecasting applications as frankly speaking, companies have a problem mastering statistical forecasting applications. It also opens the door for outsourced forecasting, something that was not technologically feasible in the past, but is already feasible, and will be increasingly feasible in the future.

Taking Full Advantage of The Recommendations This Book

There are quite a few suggestions in this book, all of which can help improve forecast accuracy. These suggestions can be overwhelming, especially if one is new to many of the ideas in this book. Very few companies practice the approaches that are listed in the book.

A common question I asked is where to start. Only an analysis of your operations can provide the answer to that in specific detail. Furthermore, a company can tolerate only so much change at once. Success with more complicated or significant changes usually requires, or at least benefits from, a track record of success with smaller and simpler changes.

One of my favorite places to start is by adding a relatively inexpensive forecasting application to the current mix, which is very good at doing something which the current forecasting application has great difficulty doing. This can save a great deal of planner time, which is both appreciated and allows them to spend more time doing things that add more value to the forecast. Another great place to start is the evaluation of how much manual adjustments are improving or degrading the forecast. Many executive decision makers tend to arrive at what area to focus on intuitively. I would recommend against this, as there are simply too many areas in forecasting that require improvement to make the decision this way. One of the most important factors is how planners will receive the change. This of course must be researched. The most constructive approach I have seen is to democratize the process by listing all of the possible changes to be made and jointly ranking them with the planners. Describe everything that would be entailed with each of the improvements and then consider starting with those that are most highly ranked. By completing this process, you have a good likelihood of having buy-in and people will tend to make more effort, when they feel as if they had input to into the decision.

Appendix A:

Saving the Prior Forecast for Forecast Adjustment
Being able to save the previous forecast for use in the next planning cycle's forecast is important. Smoothie has a way of doing this, which I want to highlight here. It is a very valuable function that has multiple uses, particularly for testing and forecast adjustment.

Using Measures to Store Different Forecasts
Measures are rows that can be imported into Smoothie. There are six measures in Smoothie. The advantage of maintaining the previous forecast into a measures row is that the previous forecast would contain all changes up to the previous planning period.

Comparative Measures for Testing
During testing, it is important to compare a forecast created in an external system to that created by Smoothie.

There are several ways to compare a forecast in Smoothie. Measures (rows of numerical data) are entered in Smoothie by adding tabs to the import file. For measure importation, the tabs for demand planning include the following:

- imported_forecast

- reference_1
- reference_2
- reference_3
- adjusted_history
- promotion

All that is necessary to create the sheets in the workbook, which are represented by tabs at the bottom row of the spreadsheet. Then name the tab/sheets in a workbook to exactly as listed above. Of course, Smoothie offers templates of multi-tabbed spreadsheets that are pre-named to its customers. It should also be noted that all of these measures are optional. There are only two required tabs-sheets for demand planning in Smoothie and these are:

- attributes
- actual_history

An example of all of these tabs is in a spreadsheet is shown below:

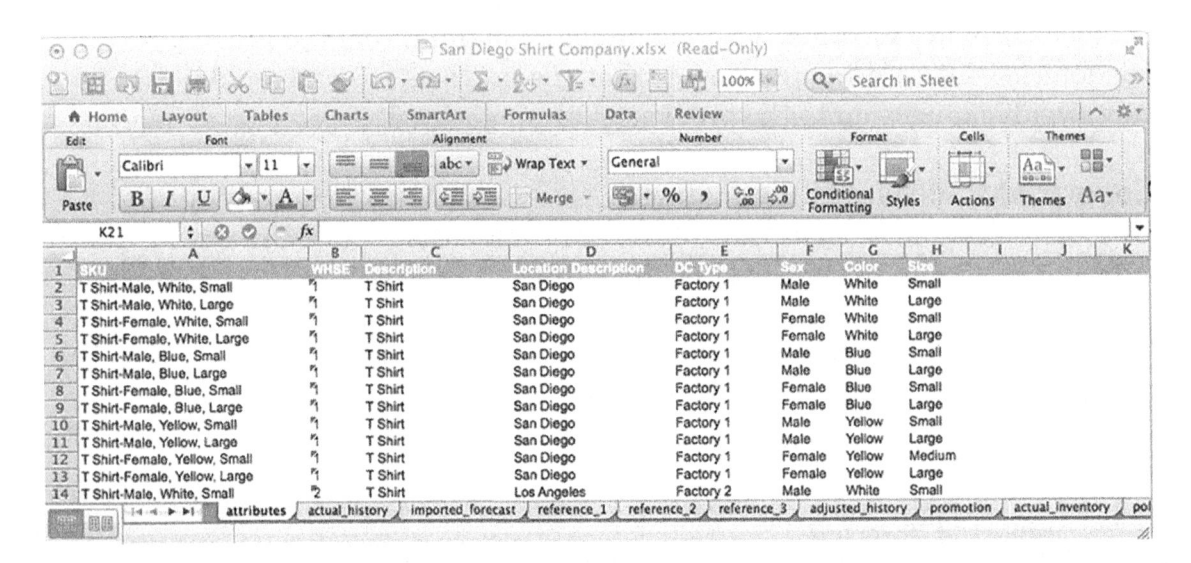

Smoothie allows any forecast to be adjusted by any measure. This adjustment is performed in the visual forecasting tab in Smoothie. The entire future forecast can be adjusted by the previous forecast, which is stored in a measure or imported forecast row. Planners can make manual adjustments, and then the forecast can be finalized. The new forecast would equal the following:

Previous Forecast (as saved as a measure or imported forecast row) + Manual Changes = New Finalized Forecast

JDA Demand Management allows bulk manual adjustments through their Forecast Override screen, enabling very specific control over the periods that receive the override. JDA DM allows this override to be applied to a single product or to groups of products.

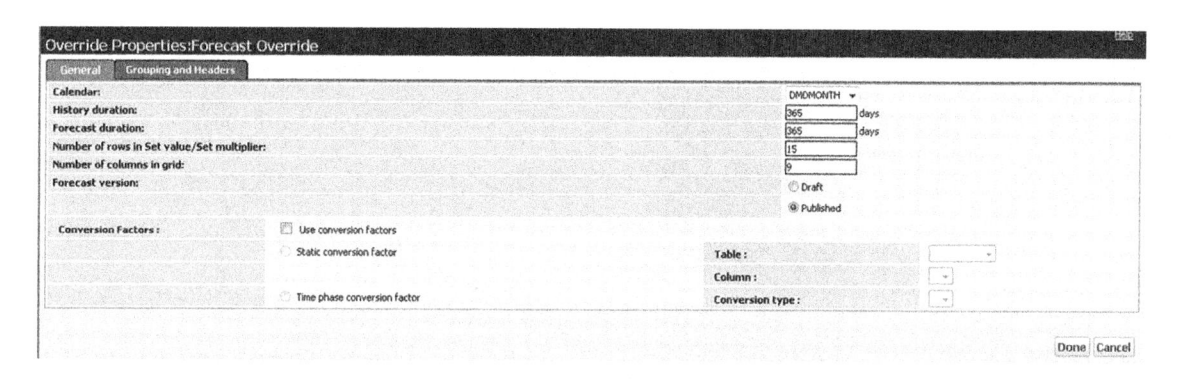

JDA DM allows for quite comprehensive control over manual adjustments; this is one of the strengths of JDA. High degrees of control as exhibited above lead to lower maintenance.

Appendix B: Forecast Locking

Forecast locks, which are not frequently discussed, are used differently depending upon the application. In JDA DM they are the following:

Forecast locks are fixed forecast quantities that override all other forecast types. Locks are typically applied when you know the forecast quantity for a particular time period or periods, for example, if you know that a customer is going to order a specific quantity at a specific time. One use of a forecast lock is for a promotion, where all the items to be manufactured are expected to be sold.

Selecting the drop-down menu in JDA DM can easily lock any forecast. The locked forecast shows as a black dotted line to differentiate from other lines in the graphical portion of the user interface.

232 *Supply Chain Forecasting Software*

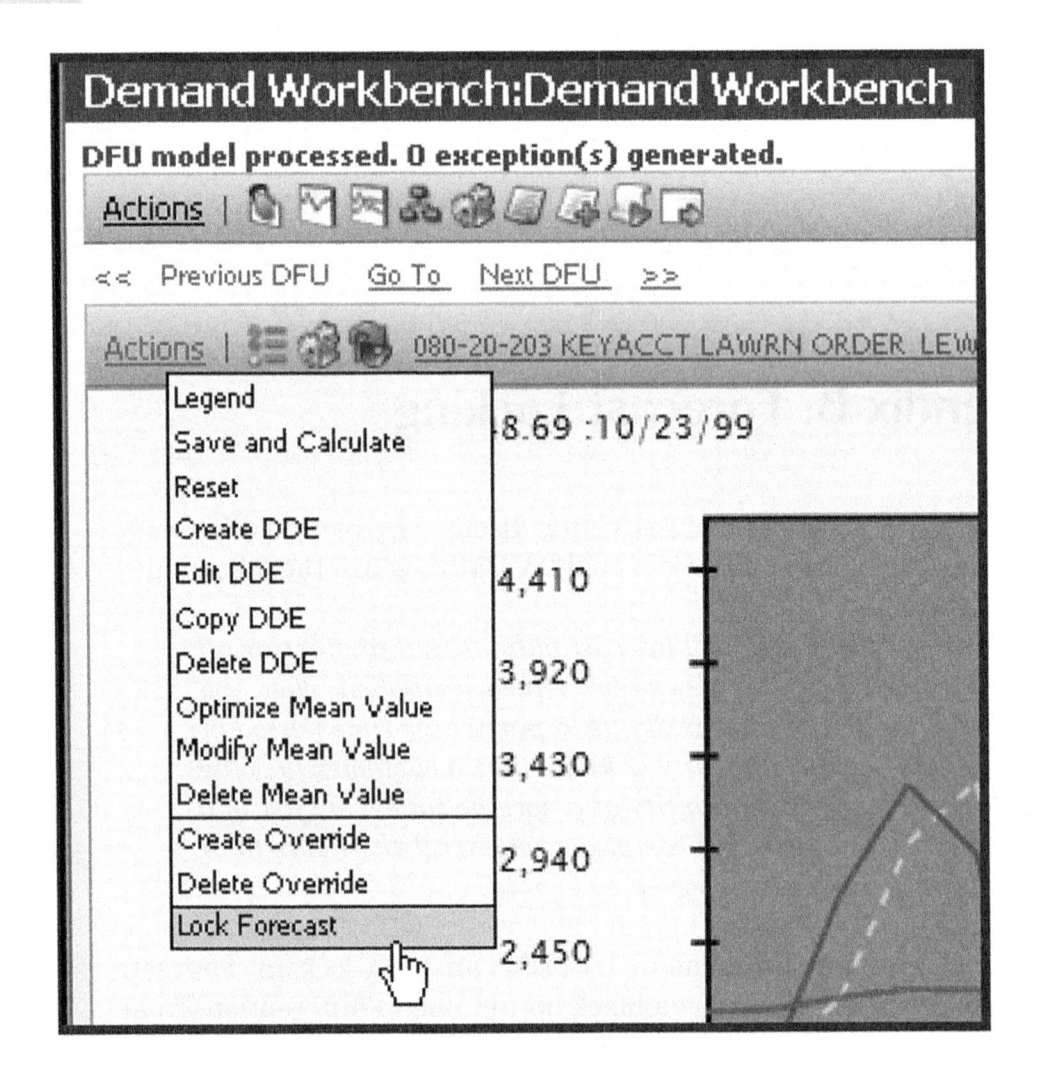

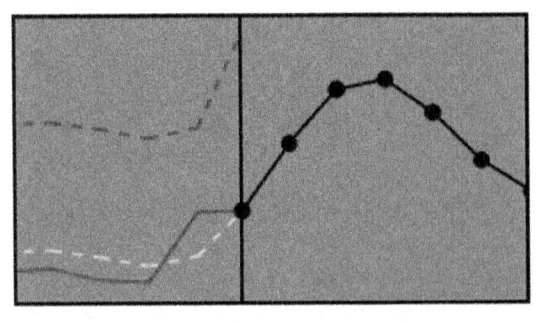

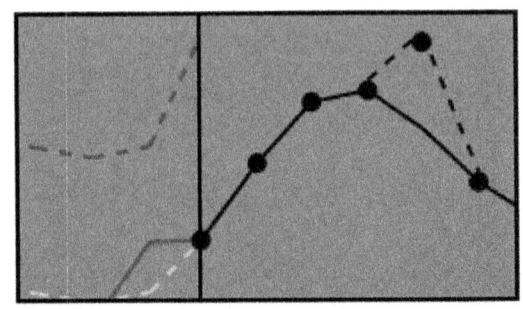

Appendix C: The Lewandowski Algorithm

In Chapter 10: "Effective Forecast Error Management," I discussed the importance of forecast simulation, which in some cases is performed with a second forecasting application, the results of which are compared to the production forecasting application. In Chapter 7: "Consensus-based Forecasting Explained," I discussed the importance of supply planning simulation in order to develop knowledge around the costs of various constraints. I also talked about how forecasting is only one part of the S&OP process. In both of these cases, I bring up the benefits of performing simulation in an external application. However, "simulation" is a broad term. A look at a portion of Wikipedia's entry is informative.

> ***Simulation*** *is the imitation of the operation of a real-world process or system over time. The act of simulating something first requires that a model be developed; this model represents the key characteristics or behaviors of the selected physical or abstract system or process. The model represents the system itself, whereas the simulation represents the operation of the system over time.*

Wikipedia's entry may be a bit too limited, as it refers to simulation as the imitation of a real-world process. However, in several of my examples I use the term "simulation" or "prototyping" to describe the use of one system to triangulate against the results of another system.

Another form of forecast simulation is incorporated into JDA DM with the use of the Lewandowski algorithm. Lewandowski is a form of adaptive smoothing. Similarly, a best-fit procedure will often adjust forecast parameters over time as conditions change. The Lewandowski algorithm, as implemented in JDA DM, is not a black box but allows the user to control how the algorithm works, as can be seen in the screen shot below:

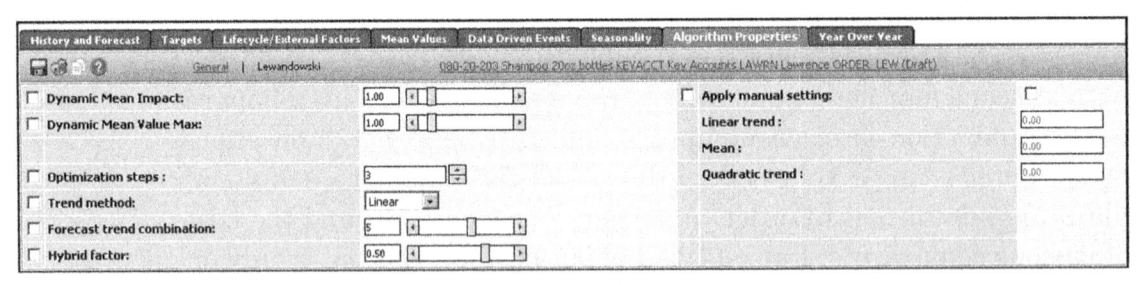

As illustrated above, the Lewandowski algorithm has a number of settings including optimization steps, which control how many times the algorithm iterates before it settles on a result.

And in the JDA DM training manual we find the following quotation:

> *First a linear regression is performed on the history. The value of the linear regression during the first period of history is taken as the initial mean value. From the initial mean value, the initial dynamic mean line (spanning all historical periods) is calculated.*

The screen shot above shows how the user can control the algorithm, including the ability to control the optimization steps. The Lewandowski algorithm does not simply apply a forecast model to a demand pattern, but adjusts the parameters to come up with the best result. Best-fit algorithms also perform similar types of adjustments, receiving feedback from error results and trying other iterations. In this way, these procedures can be seen as part of forecast simulation. However, these procedures are quite a bit different than when one forecast application is used to simulate or compare against the results in another forecasting application. The main point of this appendix is simply to explain that the term "simulation" can be used in a number of different ways, not only in forecast applications, but other applications as well.

Vendor Acknowledgements and Profiles

Below are brief profiles of the vendors whose application screen shots I have included in this book.

Profiles:

SAP
SAP does not need much of an introduction. They are the largest vendor of enterprise software applications for supply chain management. Showcased in this book are multiple SAP products. These include SAP ERP and the SNP and SPP, which reside in the APO-SCM suite.

http://www.sap.com

Demand Works
Demand Works is a best-of-breed demand and supply planning vendor that emphasizes flexible and easy-to-configure solutions. This book only focuses on the supply planning functionality within their Smoothie product, which includes MRP and DRP.

http://www.demandworks.com

JDA
JDA was started in 1978 and offers a wide variety of supply chain applications. JDA has thirty-seven offices with 3,000 employees and is a combination of brands including i2 Technologies, Manugistics, E3, Intactix and Arthur Retail.

http://www.jda.com

ToolsGroup
ToolsGroup offers unique probability-based supply chain planning (SCP) and inventory optimization solutions that allow companies to master even large, heterogeneous, or demanding supply chains. On the demand side, they incorporate best-of-breed demand modeling, order frequency forecasting, and demand-sensing technology. On the supply side, they offer multi-echelon inventory optimization and replenishment planning.

http://www.toolsgroup.com

Consensus Point
Consensus Point is the leading provider of enterprise prediction markets, and serves corporations and government. Consensus Point is one of the pioneers in implementing its software as an SaaS solution. The company helps customers reduce the risk of uncertainty and improve revenue through accurate forecasts of products and services.

http://www.consensuspoint.com

Right90
Right90 powers the most accurate forecasts for large complex enterprises from the perspective of sales, regions, finance, shipments over time, product, channel and global accounts. Right90 is very focused on sales forecasting and on bias removal.

http://www.right90.com

Inkling Markets

Inkling offers collective intelligence solutions to help organizations decrease operational and strategic risk. Inkling's solutions, anchored by its collaborative predictions platform Inkling Markets, have been implemented by industry-leading corporations and government agencies worldwide.

http://www.inklingmarkets.com

Author Profile

Shaun Snapp is the managing editor of SCM Focus. SCM Focus is one of the largest independent supply chain software analysis and educational sites on the Internet.

After working at several of the largest consulting companies and at i2 Technologies, he became an independent consultant and later started SCM Focus. He maintains a strong interest in comparative software design, and works both in SAP APO, as well as with a variety of best-of-breed supply chain planning vendors. His ongoing relationships with these vendors keep him on the cutting edge of emerging technology.

Primary Sources of Information and Writing Topics

Shaun writes about topics with which he has first-hand experience. These topics range from recovering problematic implementations, to system configuration, to socializing complex software and supply chain concepts in the areas of demand planning, supply planning and production planning.

More broadly, he writes on topics supportive of these applications, which include master data parameter management, integration, analytics, simulation and bill of material management systems. He covers management aspects of enterprise software ranging from software policy to handling consulting partners on SAP projects.

Shaun writes from an implementer's perspective and as a result, he focuses on how software is actually used in practice rather than its hypothetical or "pure release note capabilities." Unlike many authors in enterprise software who keep their distance from discussing the realities of software implementation, he writes both on the problems as well as the successes of his software use. This gives him a distinctive voice in the field.

Secondary Sources of Information
In addition to project experience, Shaun's interest in academic literature is a secondary source of information for his books and articles. Intrigued with the historical perspective of supply chain software, much of his writing is influenced by his readings and research into how different categories of supply chain software developed, evolved and finally became broadly used over time.

Covering the Latest Software Developments
Shaun is focused on supply chain software selections and implementation improvement through writing and consulting, bringing companies some of the newest technologies and methods. Some of the software developments that Shaun showcases at SCM Focus and in books at SCM Focus Press have yet to reach widespread adoption.

Education
Shaun has an undergraduate degree in business from the University of Hawaii, a Masters of Science in Maritime Management from the Maine Maritime Academy and a Masters of Science in Business Logistics from Penn State University. He has taught both logistics and SAP software.

Software Certifications

Shaun has been trained and/or certified in products from i2 Technologies, Servigistics, ToolsGroup and SAP (SD, DP, SNP, SPP, EWM).

Contact

Shaun can be contacted at:
shaunsnapp@scmfocus.com
www.scmfocus.com

Abbreviations

API – Application Program Interface

APS – Advanced Planning and Scheduling

BMS – Bill of Material Management Systems

CBF – Consensus-based Forecasting

CEPR – Center for Economic Policy Research

CM – Contract Manufacturer

CPFR – Collaborative Planning Forecasting and Replenishment

CVC – Characteristic Value Combinations

ERP – Enterprise Resource Planning

FVA – Forecast Value Added

JDA DM – JDA Demand Management

MAD – Mean Absolute Deviation

MAPE – Mean Absolute Percentage Error

MLR – Multiple Linear Regression

MOLAP – Multi Dimensional Online Analytical Processing

MRP – Material Requirements Planning

NBR – National Board of Realtors

OEM – Original Equipment Manufacturer

OLAP – Online Analytical Processing

RMSE – Root Mean Squared Deviation

SaaS – Software as a Service

SAP BI – SAP Business Intelligence

SAP BW – SAP Business Warehouse (synonymous with SAP BI)

SAP DP – SAP Demand Planning

SAP SNC – SAP Supply Network Collaboration

SAP SNP – SAP Supply Network Planning

SLA – Service Level Agreement

SQL – Structured Query Language

S&OP – Sales and Operations Planning

Definitions

Attribute Sequence: Also known as a virtual hierarchy. The reason for this additional term is that it describes the fact that the virtual hierarchy is in reality a sequence of attributes. Attribute-based forecasting systems can represent a virtual hierarchy in a user interface, which is only interpreted as a series of attributes that are related to a product. From the application's viewpoint there is no hierarchy. In contrast, static hierarchies are "true hierarchies" in that they are hard-coded into the data layer and cannot be reordered (See Virtual Hierarchy).

Forecasting Method: The category of forecasting being applied. Time series forecasting is a forecasting method, as is consensus-based forecasting. However, the more specific categories within time series forecasting (such as exponential smoothing and moving average) and within consensus-based forecasting (the Delphi Method, and prediction markets) are also methods. Therefore, the term "method" is specific enough to differentiate between "levels." Categories that are parents or children are both referred to as methods.

Forecasting Model: The specific or exact procedure that was used to create the forecast. A three-period moving average is a model, while a two-period moving average is another model, both of which are within the time series forecasting method. Forecasting models are subordinate to, or children of, parent forecasting methods. Forecasting models are strongly associated with statistical forecasting, and not consensus-based forecasting or collaborative forecasting.

Historical Adjustment: The movement of demand history from the place it was incurred to a place where it was not incurred. This functionality provides the ability to reflect alterations to the supply network in the demand planning system. For instance, if a product is to be stocked in a new location, it is important that the demand history be reflected at this new location (or else, without a reorder point, the supply planning system will not bring in stock) by removing the demand history from the actual location it was incurred and moving it to a new location. Without historical adjustment, the burden is placed upon supply planning to make manual adjustments, which tend to be error prone. Historical adjustment, in the application that has this functionality, does not affect or change the data file. Instead, the historical adjustment is managed within the application. (An application that lacks historical adjustment can have its database directly changed, but this is not desirable.)

Historical Removal: Removes demand history in order to improve forecast accuracy, typically beginning from the earliest period and then working up the sequence of demand history periods. Historical removal works in environments where the older demand history is not reflective of future demand. A historical removal algorithm can remove one period at a time; perform a forecast comparison, or more than one period at a time. Not widely taught, and not generally thought a best practice, historical removal is experimental. Historical removal must be compared to forecasting without historical removal before it is included as a strategy for the company.

Navigational Attribute: An attribute that is not an agreed-upon attribute of a product, but is simply added by a user in order to assist them in making sense of the data. Navigational attributes show up in virtual hierarchy-capable application the same way that a real attribute does, and in fact a hierarchy can be made up of both real and navigational attributes. A navigational attribute can be something as simple as favorites. A user adds a column called "favorites" to a product data file, and codes the column as "Favorites," and "Non-Favorites." This would then appear in the virtual hierarchy in the user interface and could help the user focus on some products that are particularly pertinent to them. Every user could have different favorites. A favorites column could be coded as "Tom's Favorites," "Sally's Favorites," providing multiple user favorites all with just the addition of a single column.

Real Attribute: An attribute that describes an agreed-upon and commonly-used characteristic of a product. Examples of real attributes are things like the color or size of an item. Attributes can be strung together in a forecasting application user interface to create an attribute sequence. This is then a virtual hierarchy. The attributes can be "real" or "navigational."

Static hierarchy: A hierarchy that is built in a database that allows only one sequence of levels. For instance, if the hierarchy is Region – Flavor – Size, the hierarchy could not be reordered to be Region – Size – Flavor in the user interface. Static hierarchies are hard-coded and the levels in the hierarchy can only be reordered through reconfiguration performed by IT.

Top-down Forecasting: This creates a forecast for a grouping of products, and eventually disaggregates down to the SKU based upon some disaggregation/allocation logic (which can be adjusted in some applications). Forecasts based upon aggregations tend to be more accurate, demonstrate seasonality and trends more clearly, and possess less bias. Different groups of products or channels will be optimally forecasted at different aggregation levels and/or using different hierarchies.

In attribute-based forecasting, there is either top-down or bottom-up (SKU level) forecasting, but no middle-out forecasting, as attribute-based forecasting systems have no "middle." This is described in the post below:

> http://www.scmfocus.com/demandplanning/2011/12/why-middle-out-forecasting-does-not-apply-to-attribute-based-forecasting-systems/

There are two basic ways to perform top-down forecasting with attribute-based forecasting systems. One is single attribute and the other is multi-attribute top-down forecasting.

1. Single-attribute Top-down Forecasting: This is where an attribute is used to group products in order to perform a top-down forecast. This is the most common way of performing top-down forecasting in an attribute-based forecasting system. This provides far more flexibility in top-down forecasting than when a level in a static hierarchy is used because attributes can be flexibly assigned to products. Single attribute top-down forecasting is the simplest way to begin using an attribute forecasting system for top-down forecasting. Therefore, it is a good place to start.

2. Multi-attribute Top-down Forecasting: The use of more than one attribute for top-down forecasting. This can be applied with two different approaches. Different segments of the product database have a top-down forecast applied with different attributes. For instance, color may work best for some SKUs, while the packaging size may work better for other SKUs. The second approach is to create a blended attribute, which is then applied to a group of products. This allows two attributes that have been shown to improve forecast accuracy to be used in one top-down forecast.

Virtual Hierarchy: A data layer allows infinite online reordering of the levels or attributes in the hierarchy. For instance, if the hierarchy is Region – Flavor –Size, the hierarchy could be easily reordered to be Region – Size – Flavor in the user interface. This requires no alteration to the data layer. Virtual hierarchies are not hard-coded into the applications data layer. Virtual hierarchies can use the same ROLAP database technology as static hierarchy systems, but configure them in a more sophisticated manner (See Attribute Sequence).

Links in the Book

Chapter 1

http://www.scmfocus.com/writing-rules/

http://www.scmfocus.com/demandplanning/

Chapter 3

http://www.scmfocus.com/demandplanning/2010/02/why-are-forecasting-interfaces-so-hard-to-design/

http://www.scmfocus.com/demandplanning/2011/12/getting-around-the-us-governments-fake-economic-statistics/

Chapter 4

http://www.scmfocus.com/demandplanning/2010/07/pivot-forecasting-renders-forecast-hierarchies-obsolete/

http://www.scmfocus.com/demandplanning/2011/05/flexible-attribute-selection-in-smoothie/

http://www.scmfocus.com/demandplanning/2011/05/a-better-way-of-importing-data-into-forecasting-and-analytic-systems/

http://www.scmfocus.com/demandplanning/2011/05/flexible-attribute-selection-in-smoothie/

http://www.scmfocus.com/demandplanning/2011/03/forecast-disaggregation-in-smoothie-vs-sap-dp/

http://www.scmfocus.com/demandplanning/2011/12/why-middle-out-forecasting-does-not-apply-to-attribute-based-forecasting-systems/

Chapter 5

http://www.scmfocus.com/scmbusinessintelligence/2011/11/is-gartner-now-distributing-sap-press-releases-as-analysis/

http://www.scmfocus.com/demandplanning/2011/05/a-better-way-of-importing-data-into-forecasting-and-analytic-systems/

http://www.scmfocus.com/enterprisesoftwarepolicy/2011/11/29/how-efficient-is-the-market-for-enterprise-software/

http://www.scmfocus.com/demandplanning/2012/02/how-well-are-forecasting-principles-applied-to-software/

http://www.scmfocus.com/demandplanning/2011/05/a-better-way-of-importing-data-into-forecasting-and-analytic-systems/

http://www.scmfocus.com/supplychainmasterdata/2011/04/master-data-management-using-excel-and-powerpivot/

Chapter 6

http://www.scmfocus.com/demandplanning/2010/07/outlier-removal/

Chapter 7

http://www.scmfocus.com/supplychaininnovation/2009/11/why-is-cloud-computing-taking-so-long/

http://www.scmfocus.com/demandplanning/2012/02/combining-the-hierarchies-of-two-different-demand-planning-systems/

http://www.cio.com/article/32334/Nike_Rebounds_How_and_Why_Nike_Recovered_from_Its_Supply_Chain_Disaster

http://www.scmfocus.com/demandplanning/2012/02/what-is-demand-planning/

http://www.scmfocus.com/sapplanning/2011/06/18/why-mps-is-misnamed-in-sap-erp/

http://www.scmfocus.com/supplychainsimulation/2011/10/25/a-sensitivity-analysis-approach-for-supply-chain-optimization/

http://www.scmfocus.com/supplychainsimulation/2011/11/08/the-shadow-price/

http://www.scmfocus.com/sapplanning/2010/03/27/how-sap-dp-should-not-be-used-for-consensus-based-forecasting/

Chapter 8

http://www.scmfocus.com/demandplanning/2010/03/creating-a-predictive-market-demo-with-inkling-markets/

http://www.cio.com/article/32334/Nike_Rebounds_How_and_Why_Nike_Recovered_from_Its_Supply_Chain_Disaster

http://www.scmfocus.com/demandplanning/2012/02/combining-the-hierarchies-of-two-different-demand-planning-systems/

http://www.scmfocus.com/supplychaininnovation/2009/11/why-is-cloud-computing-taking-so-long/

http://www.scmfocus.com/scmhistory/2011/10/how-mps-changed-through-time/

http://www.scmfocus.com/supplychainsimulation/2011/10/25/a-sensitivity-analysis-approach-for-supply-chain-optimization/

http://www.scmfocus.com/supplychainsimulation/2011/11/08/the-shadow-price/

http://www.scmfocus.com/sapplanning/2010/03/27/how-sap-dp-should-not-be-used-for-consensus-based-forecasting/

Chapter 9

http://www.scmfocus.com/demandplanning/2010/02/managing-the-politics-of-forecasting-bias/

Chapter 10

http://www.scmfocus.com/demandplanning/2010/07/zero-demand-periods-and-forecast-error-measurement/

http://www.scmfocus.com/demandplanning/2010/07/prototype-environment-and-background/

http://www.scmfocus.com/supplychainsimulation/

Chapter 11

http://www.scmfocus.com/demandplanning/2010/09/the-problem-using-dp-for-lifecycle-planning/

http://www.scmfocus.com/sapplanning/2011/03/21/understanding-apo-add-ins/

http://www.scmfocus.com/supplychaininnovation/2010/08/the-benefit-of-blended-solutions-based-upon-component-based-software/

Chapter 12

http://www.scmfocus.com/fourthpartylogistics/

http://www.scmfocus.com/demandplanning/2010/07/crostons-vs-smoothie-methods/

http://www.scmfocus.com/demandplanning/2010/06/forecastable-non-forecastable-formula/

Chapter 13

http://www.scmfocus.com/demandplanning/2010/02/incorrect-forecasting-article-by-cio-on-nike/

http://www.scmfocus.com/demandplanning/2011/09/what-if-you-paid-nothing-for-sap-software-how-saps-tco-compares-for-demand-planning/

http://www.edwardtufte.com/bboard/q-and-a-fetch-msg?msg_id=0001yB&topic_id=1

Chapter 14

http://www.scmfocus.com/demandplanning/2012/03/outsourced-forecasting/

http://www.scmfocus.com/demandplanning/2012/03/why-not-all-attribute-and-rolap-solutions-are-equal/

http://www.scmfocus.com/demandplanning/2012/02/how-much-can-your-forecasting-accuracy-be-improved/

References

Anbarci, Nejat and Jungmin Lee. *Economic Bias of Weather Forecasting: A Spatial Modeling Approach.* Deakin University, 2008.

Armstrong, J. Scott. "Forecasting by Extrapolation: Conclusions of 25 Years of Research." *Interfaces*, 14(Nov-Dec). University of Pennsylvania, 1984. http://www.forecastingprinciples.com/paperpdf/Forecasting%20by%20Extrapolation.pdf.

Armstrong, J. Scott. *Principles of Forecasting: A Handbook for Researchers and Practitioners.* Springer, 2001.

Armstrong, J. Scott. *Selecting Forecasting Methods.* University of Pennsylvania, 2001. http://repository.upenn.edu/cgi/viewcontent.cgi?article=1181&context=marketing_papers.

Bayus, Barry L., and William P. Putsis Jr. "Product Proliferation: An Empirical Analysis of Product Line Determinants and Market Outcomes." *Marketing Science.* November 2, 1999. http://public.kenan-flagler.unc.edu/faculty/bayusb/webpage/papers/bayus%26putsis(ms).pdf.

Blockbuster Inc. Company History. "The Funding Universe." http://www.fundinguniverse.com/company-histories/Blockbuster-Inc-Company-History.html.

Cecere, Lora. *Let's Face It, We Have Not Done a Good Job on CPFR or VMI.* Last modified October 14, 2010. http://www.supplychainshaman.com/new-technologies/lets-face-it-we-have-not-done-a-good-job-on-cpfr-of-vmi/.

Choosing Best Fit. ParkerSoft. http://www.ezforecaster.com/ChoosingBestFit.htm.

Collaborative Planning Forecasting and Replenishment. Wikipedia. Last modified March 7, 2012. http://en.wikipedia.org/wiki/Collaborative_planning,_forecasting,_and_replenishment.

Cornacchia, Eugenio, and Joseph Shamir. "Mastering Lumpy Demand." *ToolsGroup.* February 2012.

Cowles, Alfred. "Can Stock Market Forecasters Forecast?" *Econometrica*, 1(3), July 1933, pp. 309–324.

Dot com Bubble. Wikipedia. Last modified February 4, 2012. http://en.wikipedia.org/wiki/Dot-com_bubble.

Dubler, Carl and Colin Wilcox. *Just What Are Cubes Anyway? (A Painless Introduction to OLAP Technology).* Microsoft Corporation, April 2002. http://msdn.microsoft.com/en-us/library/aa140038(v=office.10).aspx.

Fildes, Robert and Paul Goodwin. *Optimism Bias and Differential Information use in Supply Chain Forecasting.* Grant provided by SAS & The International Institute of Forecasters. August 2011. http://forecasters.org/pdfs/SAS-IIFpaper_PGoodwinRFildes.pdf.

Few, Stephen. *Now You See It: Simple Visualization Techniques for Quantitative Analysis.* Analytics Press, 2009.

Ford, Ian. "E-Procurement – Electronic Data Integration Comes of Age." *Finance Director Europe.* October 30, 2007. http://www.the-financedirector.com/features/feature1420/#adEnd.

"Friend or Foe?: The Close Partnership Between SAP and Microsoft Headed for Trouble." *The Economist.* October 18, 2001. http://www.economist.com/node/822247.

Gilliland, Michael. *The Business Forecasting Deal: Exposing Myths, Eliminating Bad Practices, Providing Practical Solutions.* Wiley and SAS Business Series, 2010.

Gilleland, Michael. "Forecast Value Added Analysis: Step-by-Step." SAS Whitepaper. http://www.sas.com/resources/whitepaper/wp_6216.pdf.

Gilleland, Michael. "The Lean Approach to Business Forecasting, Eliminating waste and inefficiency from the forecasting process." SAS Whitepaper.

Grischuk, Walt. *Supply Chain Brutalization: Handbook for Contract Manufacturing.* Book Surge Publishing, 2009.

Hierarchical database model. Wikipedia. Last modified February 24, 2012. http://en.wikipedia.org/wiki/Hierarchical_database_model.

Herrin, Richard. "Managing Products Via Demand Variability and Business Importance." *Journal of Business Forecasting.* Spring 2007.

Hopp, Wallace J. and Mark J Spearman. *Factory Physics.* Waveland Press, 2008.

Inferential Statistics. Wikipedia. Last modified March 11 2012. http://en.wikipedia.org/wiki/Inferential_statistics.

"In Memory OLAP." *BIBW Directory.* http://www.bi-dw.info/in-memory-olap.htm.

Kroger Edi website. http://edi.kroger.com/homepage_edi.htm.

List of Cognitive Biases. Wikipedia. Last modified March 12, 2012. http://en.wikipedia.org/wiki/List_of_cognitive_biases.

Mass, Clifford F., Jeffrey Baars, Garrett Wedam, Eric Grimit and Richard Stee. *Removal of Systematic Model Bias on a Model Grid.* University of Washington, 2007.

Master Production Schedule. Wikipedia. Last modified February 22, 2012. http://en.wikipedia.org/wiki/Master_Production_Schedule.

Meta Analysis. Wikipedia. Last modified March 11, 2012. http://en.wikipedia.org/wiki/Meta-analysis.

Netflix. Wikipedia. Last modified March 9, 2012. http://en.wikipedia.org/wiki/Netflix.

Plott, Charles R. "Markets as Information Gathering Tools." *Southern Economics Journal.* 2000.

Prediction Market. Wikipedia. Last modified February 28, 2012. http://en.wikipedia.org/wiki/Prediction_market.

Product Lifecycle Management. Wikipedia. Last modified February 1, 2012. http://en.wikipedia.org/wiki/Product_lifecycle_management.

Product Proliferation. Wikipedia. Last modified August 11, 2011. http://en.wikipedia.org/wiki/Product_proliferation.

Reilly, David P. "How to Select a Dedicated Forecasting Software." *Journal of Business Forecasting.* 2007.

Safety Stock. Wikipedia. Last modified February 1, 2012. http://en.wikipedia.org/wiki/Safety_stock.

Schuster, Edward W., Chatchai Unahabhokha and Stuart J. Allen. "Master Production Schedule Stability Under Conditions of Finite Capacity." MIT. Date undeclared.

Scherbina, Anna. *Analyst Disagreement, Forecast Bias and Stock Returns*. Harvard University, 2004.

Schweber, Bill. "Product proliferation is driving me crazy—and we do it, too." *EE Times*, December 7, 2011. http://www.eetimes.com/electronics-blogs/planet-analog-designline-blog/4231183/Product-proliferation-is-driving-me-crazy-and-we-do-it--too-.

Sheriden, William A. *The Fortune Sellers*. John Wiley & Sons, 1998.

Snapp, Shaun. *Inventory Optimization and Multi-Echelon Planning Software*. SCM Focus Press, 2012.

Snapp, Shaun. *Bill of Materials in Excel, Planning, ERP and BMMS/PLM Software*. SCM Focus Press, 2012.

Snapp, Shaun. *Supply Planning with MRP/DRP and APS Software*. SCM Focus Press, 2012.

Star Schema. Wikipedia. Last modified February 16, 2012. http://en.wikipedia.org/wiki/Star_schema.

Sun, Jinping, ed and Thomas D. Lynch, ed. *Government Budget Forecasting: Theory and Practice*. Auerbach Publications, 2008.

"Supermarket Overview." *FMI*, 2010. http://www.fmi.org/facts_figs/?fuseaction=superfact.

Tanne, Janice. "Clinical Trials Funded by Profit Making Organizations Tend to Find Positive Results." PubMed Central, 2006. http://www.ncbi.nlm.nih.gov/pmc/articles/PMC1463954/.

Taleb, Nassim Nicholas. *The Black Swan: The Impact of the Highly Improbable*. Random House, 2007.

Armstrong, J. Scott, ed, Jim Hoover and Leonard J. Tashman. "Diffusion of Forecasting Principles Through Software." *Principles of Forecasting*. Kluwer Academic Publishers. Boston, 2001.

Toome, Lars. "Quotes by Joseph J. Cassano." http://lars.toomre.com/quotes/author/Joseph%20J.%20Cassano.

Trepte, Kai and Rajaram Narayanaswamy. "Forecasting Consumer Products Using Predictive Markets." MIT, 2009.

Thaler, Richard H. "The Overconfidence Problem in Forecasting." The New York Times. August 21 2012. http://www.nytimes.com/2010/08/22/business/economy/22view.html?_r=2&scp=1&sq=overconfidence&st=cse.

Utley, Craig. "Designing the Star Schema Database." *CIO Briefings*. http://www.ciobriefings.com/Publications/WhitePapers/DesigningtheStarSchemaDatabase/tabid/101/Default.aspx.

VanAuken, James. "OLAP Explained." http://jvanauken.com/olap_explained.htm.

Williams, John. "Government Economic Reports: Things You've Suspected But Were Afraid to Ask!" *Shadow Government Statistics*. October 1 2004. http://www.shadowstats.com/article/consumer_price_index.

Wolfers, Justin and Eric Zitzewitz. "Prediction Markets in Theory and Practice." November 2005. http://www.dartmouth.edu/~ericz/palgrave.pdf.

Answering the Sales Forecasting Challenge for Manufacturers, Right90 http://www.right90.com/whitepapers/answering_the_sales_forecasti...ge_for_manufacturersFINALPRINT.pdf.

Demand Works Smoothie Help, Version 5.3, Demand Works, 2010.

Elements of JDA Demand Building a Strong Forecast, Volume 1 Student Guide Version 7.7, JDA Educational Services, September 2011.

Removing Risk from your Sales Forecast, Right90 http://www.right90.com/whitepapers/removing_risk_from_your_sales_forecastFINALPRINT.pdf

Right90 Sales Forecast Capture, Driving an Actionable Sales Forecast, Right90 https://docs.google.com/viewer?url=http://www.right90.com/pdf/Right90-Sales-Forecast-Capture.pdf&pli=1

7 Secrets of Sales Forecasting, Right90 http://www.right90.com/whitepapers/7_secrets_of_sales_forecastingFINALPRINT.pdf

Index

adaptive smoothing, 234
Advanced Planning and Scheduling (APS) forecast, 15, 146
aggregations, forecasting, 59–60, 69, 72, 111, 113, 133
Agile, 177
AIG Financial Products, 124
AMR Research, 213–4
analytics, forecasting software and, 78, 90
APO Lifecycle Assistant, 178
application-based forecast collaboration, 144–5
Arena Solutions, 112, 144
Armstrong, J. Scott, 17–18, 188, 199
assemble-to-order environments, 10
attribute sequences, 61–2. *See also* hierarchy.
attributes-based forecasting
    attribute groupings and, 71–2
    background information about, 55
    case study of, 73–6
    causal models and, 39, 42
    data management with, 84–6
    defined, 59
    forecast disaggregation and, 70–1
    forecasting by customer in, 67, 69, 72
    forecasting by service level agreements in, 69, 73
    implementation of, 221–2
    importance of, 59–60, 71–2
    limited use of, 59
    multi-attribute forecasting and, 69–70, 75
    S&OP process and, 129
    software for, 221–2
    static hierarchies and, 56–8, 60–1, 72, 220–1
    top-down forecasts in, 59–60, 68–71, 75–6, 85
    virtual hierarchies and, 59–65, 72
auto-optimized parameters, 34–5, 52

baselining, naïve forecasts and, 172–5, 219
best-fit procedure
    choice of mathematical forecasting method and, 24
    forecast parameters and, 34–5, 52, 234

misuse of, 220
software functionality, 14, 43–7, 52–3, 74–6
stable, unstable demand histories and, 190
bias, forecast
cognitive bias and, 154
consensus based forecasting and, 121–3, 125–8
defined, 149–50
detection capability and, 224
financial services industry and, 150–4
forecast bias adjustment workflow and, 157–8
forecast error vs., 149–50
forecasting applications and, 156–62, 224
incentives and, 150–4, 161, 212
marketing forecast and, 125
removal of, 157–61
sales forecast and, 121, 125–8, 152
supply chain planning and, 156
tendency to overlook, 223–4
UK Department of Transportation and, 154–5
See also under consulting companies.
bill of material management systems (BMS), 177
Blockbuster Video, 196–7
built-to-order environments, 9–10

Cassano, Joseph J., 124
categories, forecasting, 12–14
causal forecasting techniques, 11–12, 28, 35–43, 51
causation, correlations vs., 38–9
Cecere, Lora, 146–7
characteristic value combinations (CVCs), 83–4
Chase, Charles, 125
cognitive bias, 154
collaboration, applications enabling, 111–13
collaborative forecasting
application based, 144–5
category of demand planning application, 10–12
Collaborative Planning Forecasting and Replenishment (CPFR) vs., 146–7
consensus based forecasting vs., 141–2, 145, 147
differentiation from other forecasting techniques, 11–12
EDI-based, 142–3, 147–8
effectiveness of, 139–41, 147–8
forecast accuracy and, 145
inputs into forecast and, 145
non-EDI based, 142–3, 147
SaaS and, 143–4, 147
software for, 139, 142–5
Collaborative Planning Forecasting and Replenishment (CPFR), 13, 146–7
complexity of method
forecastabiltiy and, 188, 197–200, 205
improvement of forecast and, 17–18, 35, 41, 50–1, 72–3, 119–20, 173, 188, 197–200
lumpy demand and, 197–200
statistical forecasting and, 18, 23, 50–1
consensus based forecasting (CBF)
background on, 103
basic concept of, 12
bias and, 121–3, 128–9
category of demand planning application, 10–12
collaborative forecasting vs., 141–2, 145, 147
Consensus Point and, 107–13, 144
current views of, 117–21
differentiation from other forecasting methods, 11–13, 107
disaggregation and, 111, 113
false opposition to statistical forecasting, 213–4
Inkling Markets and, 114–17
misconceptions about, 117–21
origins of, 104
prediction markets and, 104–7, 113
S&OP and, 11–12, 123, 129–34, 136

SaaS and, 111–13
sales forecast and, 117, 123–8, 139
software applications for, 134–7, 209
statistical forecasting systems used for, 134–6, 220, 222
trend toward, 134–5
Consensus Point, 107–13, 144, 159–60, 238
constraint evaluation, S&OP and, 131–3, 137
consulting firms
biases of, 3–4, 91–2, 140, 134–5, 212, 214–5, 219–20
collaboration projects and, 145, 148
reliability of, 137, 210–12
Croston's method, 197–200, 205
cubes, 79–81
customers, forecasting by, 67, 69, 72
Consumer Price Index (CPI), 41
correlation, causation vs., 38–9
cost uplifts, correction of bias and, 154

data layer
background information about, 77
data inputs into system and, 84–6
historical adjustment and, 86–90
MOLAP and, 78–82, 84, 90
OLAP and, 78, 82–3
OLTP and, 78
ROLAP and, 78–86
software competency with, 221
technology to create relationships in, 77–8. *See also specific technologies, e.g.,* MOLAP.
Delphi Method, 104. *See also* consensus based forecasting.
demand-planning, supply-planning relationship, 9–11, 15
demand shaping, intermittency and, 191–3
Demand Works Smoothie, 44–5, 48, 60–72, 75–6, 85, 88–90, 95, 98–100, 133–4, 174, 205, 227–9, 237
dependent demand products, forecastability analysis and, 205–6
descriptive statistics, 24–5, 51

disaggregation, forecast, 59, 70–1, 111, 113, 249
Distribution Requirements Planning (DRP), 15, 237
dot com stock bubble, 153–4

E2Open, 144
econometric forecasting. *See* causal forecasting techniques.
Einstein, Albert, 31
electronic data interchange (EDI), collaborative forecasting and, 142–3, 147
Enterprise Resource Planning (ERP) system, 10, 15, 78, 146–7, 177, 211
Excel, 5, 49, 71, 85–6, 198, 212
exponential smoothing
complexity of method and, 199
forecasting model, method, 12–13, 29–35, 50
lumpy demand forecasting and, 205
EZForecaster, 43

Facebook, forecast collaboration and, 144
finance departments, relation to operations, 192
financial forecasting, 37
Food Marketing Institute, 195
forecast accuracy
aggregation of error and, 166–7
attributes-based forecasts and, 59–60, 69, 75
collaborative forecasting and, 12
complex methods and, 17–18, 35, 41, 50–1, 72–3, 119–20, 173, 188, 197–200
consensus based forecasting and, 117, 119–20
forecast input and, 12, 103, 119–29, 137, 145, 159–60, 225
forecastabilty and, 224. *See also* unforecastability.
historical adjustment and, 89, 94
sales forecasts and, 123–8
statistical forecasting and, 117, 119–20

See also forecast error.
forecast error
    best fit-functionality and, 14
    contextual factors in measurement of, 165–72, 175–6
    demand planning and, 163–4
    duration of error measurement and, 171–2
    forecast bias vs., 149–50
    lead time demand error at product location and, 171–2, 176
    measurement methods for, 163–5, 175
    product location and, 169–70
    product type and, 167–8
    system-generated, 169, 223
    See also forecast accuracy.
forecast locks, 231–2
forecast parameter optimization, 34–5, 52–3
forecast value added (FVA) analysis, 164
forecastability. *See* unforecastible products.
ForecastWatch, 168
Fu, Wayne, 198

Gartner, Inc., 125, 212
Gilliland, Michael, 122–3, 164–5, 173, 187, 189, 191, 199
Grischuck, Walt, 140

hierarchies
    static, 56–8, 60–1, 72, 220–1
    virtual, 58–65, 72, 221
historical adjustment
    applications and, 88–90
    defined, 86
    inflexibility in, 82
    reasons for, 87–8
historical removal, 93–9
Hollywood Stock Exchange, 104–6

i2 Technologies, 53, 80–1
IBM, 215 n.23
implementation, barriers to effective, 219–21, 226

incentives
    forecast bias and, 150–4, 157–8, 161, 212
    software review and, 212–3
inferential statistics, statistical forecasting and, 24–5, 51
Inkling Markets, 114–17, 160, 239
intermittent demand. *See* lumpy demand.
intersections of data elements, 78–9
inventory optimization and multi-echelon planning (MEIO) software, 69, 135
IT departments
    attribute forecasting file and, 56
    data management and, 81–3, 85–6, 91
    selection of forecast system and, 49–50

JDA DM, 14, 33, 47, 87, 97, 100–1, 180, 202–3, 229, 231, 234, 238

Kroger Co., 142

lead times
    lead time demand and, 171–2, 176
    relation of forecasting to, 9–10
leading indicator forecasting. *See* causal forecasting techniques.
Lewandowski algorithm, 233–5
lifecycle planning
    background information about, 177–8
    copying demand history and, 180–2
    Demand Works Smoothie for, 182–5
    JDA DM for, 180
    SAP DP for, 178
    ToolsGroup for, 179
location adjustments, 89
lumpy demand, 190–200, 202–4, 224

manually adjustable parameters, 34–5
marketing forecasts, unreliability of, 125. *See also* sales forecast.
master production schedule, 129–30
Materials Resource Planning (MRP), 15, 237
mathematics
    application's leveraging of, 49–50

See also statistics.
Mean Absolute Deviation (MAD), 163–4
Mean Absolute Percentage Error (MAPE), 163–4
method, forecasting, 12–14
model, forecasting, 12–14
moving averages, 14, 22, 24, 29–30, 203–4
multi-attribute forecasting, 69–70, 75
Multi-Dimensional Online Analytical Processing (MOLAP), 78–82, 84, 90

naïve forecast, baselining and, 172–5, 219
Netflix, handling of lumpy demand by, 196–7
Nike, consensus methods and, 213–4
Nordstrom, Kristen, 179

Online Analytical Processing (OLAP), 78, 82–3
online retailing, 196–7
Online Transaction Processing (OLTP), 78
operational forecast, 123, 126, 129. *See also* sales and operations planning.
operations departments, forecasting, 192, 224
Oracle, 143, 147
organizational sales structures, static hierarchies and, 57
outlier removal, 99–102
outsourcing forecasting, 73, 220, 225
over-fitting, 199

past forecasts, storing, 227–9
Peyton (Kroger Co.) distribution centers, 142
phase-in, phase-out profiles, SAP DP's, 178, 185
PowerPivot, Excel's, 86
prediction intervals, 26–7
prediction markets, CBF and, 104–7, 113
probability theory, statistics and, 25–7
product database segmentation, 137–8
Product Lifecycle Management (PLM). *See* lifecycle planning.
product proliferation, forecastability and, 194–6, 207
prototype environments, 74–5

RAND Institute, 104
realignment
    external realignment tables and, 82–4, 88, 91, 221
    static hierarchies and, 57
record keeping, bias removal and, 23
regression forecasting. *See* causal forecasting techniques.
Relational Online Analytical Processing (ROLAP), 78–86
relational databases, 77–80
reorder points, unforecastable products and, 206–7, 225
reporting requirements, 57
Right90, 123, 127, 136, 157–8, 160, 166–7, 238
Root Mean Squared Error (RMSE), 163–4

safety stock formula, forecast error and, 172
sales and marketing departments
    intermittent demand and, 191–3, 207, 224
sales and operations planning (S&OP)
    collaborative forecasting and, 143–4, 147
    consensus-based forecasting and, 11–12, 123, 129–34, 136
    constraint evaluation in, 131–3, 137
    demand-side, 133–4
    finance and, 129, 137
    master production schedule and, 129–30
    operations in, 129
    sales input into, 125–6
    software applications for, 130–1
    statistical forecasting and, 225
    subcategory of consensus-based forecasting, 11–12
sales forecast
    bias and, 121, 125–8, 152
    consensus forecasting and, 117, 123–8, 136
    product database segmentation and, 137–8

SAP, 143, 147, 177–8, 237
   APO F&R, 146
   APO SNP, 169–70
   BW, 78, 81, 215 n.23
   DP, 31–4, 40, 44, 73–6, 78, 80–1
   SNC, 139, 144
scalability, data layer's, 84
Scherbina, Anna, 151–3
SCM Focus, 3–4, 6
sensitivity analysis, 131–3, 137
service level agreements, forecasting by, 69, 73
Servigistics, 198
shadow prices, 132–3, 137
ShadowStats, 41
Siemens, 177
simple arithmetic, forecasting methods, 13, 29–30
simulation, forecast, 175, 233–5
social media, forecast collaboration and, 144, 147
software as a service (SaaS)
   application based collaboration and, 144
   Consensus Point and, 111–13
   electronic trading and, 143–4
software selection
   effective, 214–7, 221–2
   future trends and, 225
   reasons for poor, 209–12, 216, 219
   unbiased information about, 212–3
   user communities and, 49–50, 53
speculative markets, CBF and, 104–6
star schemas, 78–81
static hierarchies, attributes-based forecasting and, 56–8, 60–1, 72, 220–1
statistical forecasting
   adoption issues with, 49–50
   attributes-based forecasting. See *separate entry*.
   causal forecasting techniques and, 11–12, 28, 35–43, 51
   case study of software systems, 52–3
   category of demand planning application, 10–12
   complexity of method and, 18, 23, 50–1
   consensus based forecasting and, 117–21, 134–6, 213–4, 220, 222
   data layer relationships and, 77–91
   early history of, 17–18
   ease of use of applications and, 52
   historical removal in, 93–9, 102
   incorrect use of, 134–6, 210–11, 220, 222
   inferential statistics and, 24–5
   manual adjustment to forecast and, 47–8
   outlier removal in, 99–102
   product data base segmentation and, 137–8
   relationship to other forecasting methods, 11, 13, 28
   SaaS and, 225
   standard in market, 15–16
   statistics and, 21–7
   time series forecasting techniques and, 11–12, 28–30, 51. *See also* simple arithmetic *and* exponential smoothing.
   unforecastability and, 187–90, 203–8, 224
statistics
   descriptive, 24–5, 51
   inferential, 24–5, 51
   statistical forecasting and, 24–7
   macroeconomic statistics and, 41–2
   probability theory and, 25–7
Steelwedge, 130, 215 n.23
supersession, 179, 185
supplier collaboration applications, 139

textbook industry, lumpy demand in, 190–1
third-party logistics, 192–3
time series forecasting techniques
   exponential smoothing methods and, 29–35
   methods within, 13, 29
   relation to other forecasting techniques, 11–12, 51

simple arithmetic methods and, 12–13, 29–30
ToolsGroup, 19–20, 179, 193–4, 238
Tonetti, Bill, 70, 90, 204–5
top-down forecasting, 59–60, 68–71, 75–6, 85
total cost of ownership (TC) analysis, software selection and, 216
Trader Joe's, handling of lumpy demand by, 194–6, 224
Twitter, 144

UK Department of Transportation, bias correction efforts of, 154–5
unforecastable products
    complex forecasting methods and, 188, 197–200, 205, 207
    dependent demand products and, 205–6
    discernable patterns and, 46, 187–90, 201, 203, 208, 224
    examples of, 200–2
    indentifying, 204–5
    lumpy demand and, 190–200, 202–4, 224
    supply planning with, 206–7
usability, software, 215
user interfaces
    best-fit procedure and, 46–7
    bias and, 158–9, 162
    cubes in, 79
    early forecasting methods and, 18
    effective, 18–20
    forecast collaboration and, 144–5, 147
    lifecycle planning and, 179–80

virtual hierarchies
    adjusting with Smoothie, 61–5
    attributes-based forecasting and, 58–60, 72, 221

weather forecasting, relative accuracy of, 168
Whole Foods, 195

XML, 141, 143, 147

zero demand periods, 164

CPSIA information can be obtained at www.ICGtesting.com
Printed in the USA
BVOW09s2128220916

462774BV00015B/45/P

9 780983 715528